J1/16
X4
L11/15

Yogurt Culture

Yogurt Culture

A Global Look at How to
Make, Bake, Sip, and Chill the World's
Creamiest, Healthiest Food

CHERYL STERNMAN RULE

PHOTOGRAPHY BY ELLEN SILVERMAN

A RUX MARTIN BOOK
Houghton Mifflin Harcourt
Boston / New York / 2015

For information about permission to reproduce selections from this book,
write to Permissions, Houghton Mifflin Harcourt Publishing Company,
215 Park Avenue South, New York, New York 10003.

www.hmhco.com

Library of Congress Cataloging-in-Publication Data
Rule, Cheryl Sternman.
  Yogurt culture: a global look at how to make, bake, sip, and chill the
world's creamiest, healthiest food / Cheryl Sternman Rule;
photography by Ellen Silverman.
    pages cm
  "A Rux Martin Book."
  ISBN 978-0-544-25232-5 (paper over board) —
  ISBN 978-0-544-25171-7 (ebook)
1. Cooking (Yogurt) I. Title.
  TX759.5.Y63.R85 2015
  641.6'71476—dc23
                              2014039690

Book design by Rita Sowins / Sowins Design
Food styling by Christine Albano
Prop styling by Marina Malchin

Printed in China
c&c 10 9 8 7 6 5 4 3 2 1

To Andrew and Alex

"Sweeten and salt your food yourself."

—Michael Pollan, rule #34,
Food Rules: An Eater's Manual

---

*"Although its popularity in Europe and
America is fairly recent, yogurt is an ancient food
and probably the sole major
contribution of the nomadic peoples to the
gastronomic resources of the world."*

—Ayla Algar, Classical Turkish Cooking:
Traditional Turkish Food for the American Kitchen

Contents

Introduction

WE DIDN'T HAVE MUCH. WE HAD A COUCH MY HUSBAND, COLIN, MADE BY FOLDING A MATTRESS IN HALF AND TYING A FEW LOGS TO IT WITH YELLOW NYLON ROPE. We had a pink, cushy toilet seat my mother-in-law, in a gesture equally well-intentioned and ludicrous, shipped to us in Africa from her home in Dallas. And we had a small kerosene stove, big enough for a single pot, yet small enough to be nudged under that couch if we ever needed more legroom.

Such was our Peace Corps life in Eritrea, the tiny nation where Colin and I spent two years teaching English as newlyweds in the mid-1990s. During our initial months on-site, we experienced many firsts: our first (and last) locust swarm, our first puppy, and our first time bathing in buckets the size of a large pancake.

Over time, we began to hand-make those creature comforts we missed from home. Not just the couch, which served its purpose well until, one day, it collapsed in a spectacular heap, but the foodstuffs that reminded us of our modern American lives. Colin fashioned a reflector oven out of an old cardboard box, some foil, and a few coats of black paint. We bought a second pot—nothing fancy, just the one type of thin aluminum pot sold in every shop in town—and he spray-painted that black, too. He made a basic yeast dough, laid it in the pot, set it in the sun, and hours later—lo and behold—we had bread. It wasn't artisanal. It didn't have fancy Asiago cheese or a crackly crust, but it was bread, and he had made it in a pot, in a box, in the sun.

It wasn't long after that that we made our first yogurt. Yogurt, *rug'o* in the local language, was a staple in every tea shop; served with bread and a spicy tomato sauce, it was the star ingredient in a piquant, creamy dish called *fata* (see page 190). So it wasn't tough for us to procure some yogurt to use as a starter.

Our early yogurt-making efforts were disappointing; it took a few tries before we got it right. (The reflector oven concentrated the heat way too much, for starters.) But that black pot, with its black lid and a nice, big towel, created a fine incubator of ideal temperature when set in a sunny spot out on the ledge in front of our house.

After that, we made yogurt all the time. Sweetened with sugar or with honey or served plain as a coolant to the spicy Eritrean stews we were just

A tart, creamy ingredient, beautifully pure in its own right.

learning to make ourselves, we always had a batch working, ready to go. And we promised ourselves, and each other, that when our Peace Corps service ended, we'd continue making yogurt forever.

We didn't, of course. Not for fifteen years.

But I've started again. And now I can't stop.

A VERSATILE SUPERSTAR

Yogurt isn't new. Not even a little. In fact, it has been around since Neolithic times, when the people of Central Asia discovered, most likely by happy accident, that fermenting milk made life easier by increasing fresh milk's longevity.[1] Most trace this discovery to nomads who transported milk in goatskin sacks, which served as warm incubators in which the fermentation process first occurred.

Sure, in the past few years, a near maniacal Greek yogurt craze has swept the United States, reigniting the industry, but this is not a modern food. It's ancient, historical, widespread, mythical,[2] healthful, versatile, and—perhaps above all—delicious. No longer is yogurt a fuddy-duddy, hippie-dippy half-solid relegated to 1970s commune culture; it's an economic superstar, a craveable commodity whose newly chic appeal has won over celebrities, power lifters, professionals, parents, kids, and shoppers of all stripes and all backgrounds. This sky-high interest has forever changed the look of the dairy aisle.

Yogurt has legs now; it's standing up tall and marching far, further than the breakfast table, further than the lunchbox, further than the gym bag. But it has further to go still, and that's where this book comes in. In the pages that follow, I strip yogurt of its premixed accessories and bring it back to what it used to be: a tart, creamy ingredient, beautifully pure in its own right, one that can be paired not just with fruit but with meat, not just with sugar but with salt, not just alone but in combination with hearty grains, crunchy vegetables, protein-rich legumes, intense chocolate, fresh-squeezed juices, endless herbs, and exotic spices whose provenance spans the globe.

Herein, I offer you a look back, a look ahead, and a look across world cultures, all with the goal of broadening your understanding of what yogurt is at its most naked and how you can dress it up and customize it at home, in your kitchen. You'll learn to take advantage of the hidden potential that plain yogurt—the kind you make yourself or the blank-canvas kind you'll find in larger tubs in any grocery store—has to offer and start to wean your-self from the little fruity containers that have but a single use. (Eat, toss.)

Let's begin at the beginning.

A GLOBAL YOGURT CULTURE

Yogurt's precise temporal and geographic origins remain hazy, but sources agree that cultured milk products have been around for thousands of years. In the warm climates of Central Asia and the Middle East, thermophilic (heat-loving) bacteria in the environment would ferment the natural sugar (lactose) in the standing milk of domestic mammals, chiefly cows, camels, and goats, but also sheep, buffalo, yaks, and more. This fermentation process metabo-lizes milk's lactose and produces lactic acid as an end product. In so doing, it coagulates the milk's proteins, drops its pH, sours its taste, preserves its longevity, and increases its digestibility.

Early documentary evidence points to nomadic medieval Turks as espe-cially early yogurt eaters, and in fact, the etymology of the word yogurt itself harkens back to the Turkish language. Fast-forward to the sixteenth century, when yogurt spread to France. Legend has it that when the French monarch Francis I fell ill with intestinal distress, an Ottoman sultan named Suleiman the Magnificent dispatched a physician to cure the king with yogurt. Apparently, it worked.[3]

Despite its presence in French lore and its widespread propagation and consumption as a dietary staple in countless home kitchens throughout Turkey, Greece, Syria, and the Near East as a whole, yogurt didn't really catch on in Western Europe as a consumer food until the early 1900s. In 1907 the Russian-born scientist Élie Metchnikoff, who was working in Paris, discovered that rural Bulgarians enjoyed unusually long life expectancies. He credited their longevity to avid yogurt consumption and put forth the

Ah, Greek yogurt. Two magic words that lit a fuse.

exciting theory that yogurt's bacterial cultures could combat the natural effects of aging.

Yogurt took on fresh life at this point. Newly valued as a health tonic, the ancient food, not yet produced at scale or marketed in any way in Europe, received a major boost. Then, in 1917 or 1918, Greek-born Isaac Carasso, who'd learned the art of yogurt making in Switzerland, immigrated to Barcelona to reconnect with his family's Spanish roots. While there, he encountered children who suffered from digestive problems due to poor diet and the unhygienic conditions endemic during the rough economic years of World War I. Motivated, he saw an opportunity to make yogurt commercially, in part to help combat these scourges, but also (presumably) to make some money as a businessman. In 1919, he founded Danone, a company he christened after his son Daniel.[4] (Danone is the Spanish diminutive of the name Daniel.) To read a more complete account of Danone and its later American incarnation, Dannon, see page 48.

To provide a more intimate snapshot of how yogurt is consumed around the world, I've interviewed yogurt-lovers from vastly different backgrounds. You'll learn from home cooks and culinary pros with roots in Afghanistan (page 168), Eritrea (page 243), Greece (page 150), India (page 121), Iran (page 136), Israel (page 233), Lebanon (page 125), Mongolia (page 316), Pakistan (page 229), Serbia (page 300), and Turkey (page 281).

I hope these small windows into other cultures will bridge the still-wide gap between how myopically many of us view yogurt—presweetened in disposable, single-serving cups, bottles, pouches, or tubes—and the versatility with which plain yogurt is enjoyed globally in countless incarnations and preparations, both savory and sweet, across every meal. Many of my sources were generous enough to share a nation-specific recipe or two as well, so you'll enjoy an embarrassment of culinary riches, both mine and theirs, throughout these pages.

YOGURT TODAY—A DAIRY-AISLE COUP

We glanced at the past; now let's look to the present and the future. What does the yogurt market look like here in the United States? And is what you've noticed in your local dairy aisle—that yogurt occupies a greater proportion of shelf space than ever before—borne out by the numbers?

On July 17, 2012, the blog of *Fortune Magazine/CNN Money* reported that "Yogurt's growth has outpaced the rest of the U.S. food industry."[5] The April 2013 issue of *Dairy Foods* includes a graph showing that yogurt production in 2012 topped 4.4 billion pounds.[6]

So let's break it down. At the time of this writing, according to the market research firm Mintel: Yogurt sales have grown for five consecutive years from 2009 to 2013; in 2013, sales topped $7 billion; by 2018, sales are anticipated to top $9 billion; and yogurt sales are driven primarily by "exceedingly strong demand for Greek yogurt varieties."[7]

Ah, Greek yogurt. Two magic words that lit a fuse.

In 2005, when Turkish-born businessman Hamdi Ulukaya took out a loan to buy a 90-year-old Kraft Foods factory in New Berlin, New York, he took the first step toward upending an industry dominated to that point by corporate giants Dannon and Yoplait (now part of General Mills). Greek yogurt wasn't unheard of when Ulukaya entered the game, but the primary player at the time—Athens-based Fage (*FA*-yeh), which had started importing its yogurt from Greece—had failed to transform the industry the way Ulukaya

came to do at breathtaking speed. Ulukaya, who'd spent a few years selling feta through his company Euphrates, branded his new Greek yogurt business after the Turkish word for shepherd (*çoban*), calling it Chobani.[8] As further evidence of Chobani's impact on the economy, Ulukaya was invited to ring the closing bell of the NASDAQ in January 2014.[9]

Soon Greek yogurt was red-hot. It wasn't long before both larger players with more infrastructure and name recognition, and smaller, independent upstarts, caught wind of the public's rabid interest in higher-protein yogurts with an ultracreamy mouthfeel and an appealing health profile. The number of producers swelled, and sales boomed. Mintel's report shows that for the year ending May 19, 2013, Dannon's Oikos brand of Greek yogurt led the market in terms of sales, enjoying a single-year increase of 164.7%.

The media, for its part, loves covering the "yogurt wars" (as more than one major news source dubbed it),[10] which creates great buzz when things go well and new product lines launch but stings hard when companies falter, as Chobani did when it issued a large recall in September 2013.

Yogurt appears almost daily in food news. Whole Foods Market created a firestorm in December 2013 when it announced it would no longer carry Chobani "to make room for more product choices not readily in the market," according to a 2013 tweet on the company's Twitter account. The 2014 Super Bowl featured ads for both Chobani and Dannon's Oikos brand. And celebrities—from Bobby Flay (Fage) to Michael Symon, John Stamos, and Reba McEntire (various Dannon subbrands) to Hugh Acheson (Liberté)—have partnered with major brands, all of which keeps yogurt in the spotlight.

What drives yogurt manufacturers' sales and marketing? How do they come up with their flavors? How do their factories actually work to make yogurt day in and day out? What makes them tick, makes them special, makes them distinct from their competitors? In 2013 I visited the New York headquarters of Dannon (page 48), the Vermont home of Commonwealth

Dairy (page 22), and the California hub of Straus Family Creamery (page 84). These first-hand accounts, as well as recaps of my interviews with representatives of Smári Organics (page 79), goat yogurt maker Redwood Hill Farm (page 30), and New York–based Blue Hill Yogurt (which makes vegetable-flavored yogurts; page 66), provide insight into the sheer diversity of players driving demand and innovation in the yogurt category. Individually and collectively, they're all contributing to today's yogurt zeitgeist.

And that's just fresh yogurt. What about the frozen stuff? As the refrigerated yogurt market thrives, frozen yogurt keeps pace beside it, with shops popping up at breakneck speed. (Sales increased from $279 million in 2011 to $486 million in 2013.)[11] From self-service kiosks on college campuses to proliferating frozen yogurt chains offering endless toppings—think Fruity Pebbles, sour gummi worms, and "cheesecake bites"—fresh and frozen yogurt have both blossomed and veered off in sometimes outlandish directions.

I'm not just talking about hypersweetened yogurt tubes in head-scratching flavors like melonberry and cotton candy (produced by the pizza giant Chuck E. Cheese's), but the debut of a frozen yogurt chain called Cups that immediately drew comparisons to Hooters for what the Huffington Post called its "boobs-as-ambiance business model";[12] the launch of products like Post's Honey Bunches of Oats Greek Honey Crunch cereal with an ingredients list that includes Greek yogurt powder and "Greek yogurt style coated granola" (whatever that is);[13] frozen yogurt treats for dogs (made with vegan carob chips and bourbon vanilla extract);[14] and organic freeze-dried fruit and yogurt drops for babies.[15]

For all its popularity, yogurt risks jumping the shark (if it hasn't already). In straying so far from its roots, something crucial may be lost forever. I do support product innovation, but I also fear that the wholesome essence of this ancient and remarkably simple food may soon vanish under an avalanche of coatings, candies, powders, and pellets.

WHAT IS YOGURT, ANYWAY?

At heart, yogurt is milk that has been inoculated with bacterial strains and left to culture at warm temperatures until it thickens. Of course, things are somewhat more complex, so let's get technical for just a bit.

The live bacterial cultures that create yogurt—specifically *Streptococcus thermophilus* and *Lactobacillus delbrueckii bulgaricus*—are thermophilic, meaning they propagate in a warm environment. That's why you can't simply stir a spoonful of yogurt into milk cold from the fridge, wait a few hours, and voilà: yogurt. Certain temperature protocols must first be met. (Keep in mind that the protocols vary slightly for commercial yogurt factories versus home yogurt making. I'll be addressing home yogurt making below, but the broader concepts apply in both realms.) A complete homemade yogurt recipe appears on page 320, but here's the basic science.

FIRST, THE MILK IS BROUGHT TO 180°F. This heating process kills any harmful—and potentially competing—microorganisms that may already be present in your milk, thereby providing a blank slate in which new cultures can grow. (This is also why experts advise against making yogurt from raw milk.) Heating the milk also denatures the whey proteins and allows them

Yo!

A 6-ounce serving of yogurt generally supplies between 5 and 10 grams of protein. Greek yogurt typically provides between 10 and 20 grams of protein, or more. Many yogurts also contain vitamin D, which helps the body absorb calcium, and lactic acid, which improves the body's ability to absorb minerals and digest calcium. Studies suggest that the body is better able to absorb calcium from yogurt than from unfermented milk.

Generic Yogurts and the Rise of Copackers THE STORY OF COMMONWEALTH DAIRY

You've probably never heard of Vermont's Brattleboro-based Commonwealth Dairy, one of this country's newest large-scale yogurt makers. That's because its name doesn't appear on the vast majority of its packaging. Instead the company produces private-label yogurt under the Green Mountain Creamery name and also acts as what's known as a copacker, meaning it produces yogurt for third parties and packages it under those stores' in-house labels.

A contractual agreement between the copacker and the stores generally prevents the publicizing of the relationship. This opacity may leave customers with the impression that the private labels are produced by the grocery chain itself and/or are exclusive to that store when neither may be true.

Ben Johnson and Tom Moffitt cofounded Commonwealth back in 2011 after working together in the corporate office of Ahold, the parent of the Northeast-based Stop & Shop supermarket chain.

Johnson was hired first, and Moffitt was hired as Johnson's boss soon thereafter. "That lasted about two weeks," Johnson said, laughing. The two soon worked side by side.

While employed in Ahold's private-label division, Johnson says he and Moffitt started researching using their private-label experience to start their own business. Johnson says he realized that the three private-label yogurt manufacturers in the region had become complacent about quality and customer service and suffered from a lack of product innovation. This sparked an idea. "We said, Jeez, if we could provide a high-quality product and give great customer service, we knew we could do a lot."

Johnson and Moffitt had never made yogurt, so they knew they'd need a partner not just for investment but to help with technical know-how. They formed a strategic partnership with a German company in the European market, Ehrmann AG.

I asked Johnson about the difference between the yogurts they make in Brattleboro and the yogurt that its partner Ehrmann AG makes in Europe. Is the customer base the same? Is the product? In short, no. The Germans were shocked by the sugars common in the U.S. market, he said, and sugar substitutes don't work in the European market. "The overall sweetness is completely different."

What about fat?

"In Europe, they offer a lot of 3½ percent fat and even higher. They don't have a lot of nonfat products."

I spent the next hour touring the plant, suited up in a hairnet, sanitized foot coverings, and a lab coat, typical gear for anyone entering a food-production facility. I viewed the 6,500-gallon milk tanker, on which a man stood holding the biggest ladle I've ever seen. His job was to scoop milk samples into a bucket and run them down to a microbiology lab to check the somatic cell count and bacteria levels, which have to fall within a certain range. Once the lab signs off, the milk gets dispersed to different silos for separation, homogenization, and pasteurization. There's a room with a "blend table" where the starches and sugars are added. A room with a fermentation tank, where the yogurt is cultured and left to ferment for 6 hours at 100°F, much as I do at home on a much, much smaller scale. A reverse-osmosis machine takes water out of the whey to help with disposal. The unfilled cups get sprayed with hydrogen peroxide, fruit is added, and then the yogurt is pumped on top. An ultraviolet light provides another layer of sanitation, and then the lid goes on. This filling machine pumps yogurt into ninety 2-pound cups every minute. Finally, all of the cups go through an X-ray machine before they hit the pallet. (Any foreign material will set the X-ray off.)

In 2011 Commonwealth Dairy pulled in $17 million. While they predicted they'll employ 40 to 50 people within a five-year span, at the time of my visit in 2013, Johnson said, they already had 100 people on staff. And by the end of that year, they broke over $70 million in sales.

The company has since expanded to a second facility in Casa Grande, Arizona. "Our goal is to double that this year with the new Arizona plant on board," he said.

to absorb water, ensuring a more stable end product. There are different schools of thought regarding how long the milk should stay at this temperature before cooling, but it's really a matter of preference. "Holding" the milk before cooling tends to improve gelation (the gelling process), creating a thicker and firmer texture.

SECOND, THE MILK IS COOLED DOWN TO ABOUT 115°F (108°F in factories). This is the temperature range at which your starter cultures, once introduced, will thrive. You can cool milk by pulling your saucepan from the heat and waiting, or you can plunge it into an ice bath. If the milk cools too far, it must be rewarmed.

THIRD, THE MILK IS INOCULATED WITH A STARTER CULTURE. You can use either a powdered (generally freeze-dried) yogurt culture containing live bacteria, or—easier and more practical—a small portion of yogurt from a prior home-made batch or store-bought container. The starter should be fresh—used within a few days of opening, in other words—and must have "live, active" cultures in order to propagate, so look for these words on store-bought cups.

FOURTH, FERMENTATION BEGINS. By maintaining a temperature close to 110°F throughout incubation, the cultures you've introduced begin to convert lactose into lactic acid, thereby lowering the pH of the milk and causing it to gel, or thicken, and to take on the sour tang characteristic of plain yogurt. This process takes several hours. Once the pH dips below 4.6 (evidenced by the thick consistency and tangy flavor), transfer the yogurt to the refrigerator. Chill for several hours before eating.

Now you have yogurt.

HEALTH AND PROBIOTICS

Yogurt is packed with a wide range of nutrients. Not just calcium, which shouldn't surprise you. And not just protein, of which Greek yogurt is an especially rich source. But yogurt also contains B vitamins, vitamin D, potassium, phosphorus, magnesium, and zinc.

What really sets yogurt apart from other foods, though, is one word: probiotics. In *Microbiology and Technology of Fermented Foods*, Robert W. Hutkins defines probiotics as "organisms that confer a health benefit to the host." He further explains that two especially common probiotics, *Lactobacillus acidophilus* and *Bifidobacterium*, are among those most often added to yogurt to supplement the cultures needed for fermentation. So long as they're "live" and "active," these bacterial strains may help support immune function; inhibit and control the growth of problematic yeasts and flora, especially in women; improve digestion and the general well-being of those with intestinal disorders, inflammatory diseases, and abdominal discomfort; and even possibly improve mood.[16]

Research is ongoing.

Some scientists, like Justin L. Sonnenburg, assistant professor of microbiology and immunology at the Stanford University School of Medicine, say

Yogurt is packed with a wide range of nutrients.

that research into probiotics and other so-called "functional foods" occupies a gray area that has led to confusion for consumers. Yes, he says, some concrete data have shown that probiotics can help treat certain forms of viral intestinal distress, but many of the other data are less clear-cut. "There are very few probiotic bacteria that have been studied really in depth by multiple labs with reproducible findings concerning human health," he told me. He nevertheless sees a legitimate evolutionary argument for eating fermented foods like yogurt. "The state of our mucosal immune system is constantly being fine-tuned by exposure to bacteria—things like fermented foods, any dirt we may eat, and probiotics." This fine-tuning may help our immune system fight invaders or prevent it from spiraling out of control in the form of allergies or autoimmune diseases. So while eating yogurt isn't a lock against future illness, exposure to diverse microbes is a generally wise and health-promoting dietary strategy.

In fact, more and more research is beginning to emerge connecting overall gut health to the body's ability to ward off disease. Michael Pollan has written extensively about what he calls the microbiome,[17] the trillions of microbial organisms that reside in the human body whose health influences our own. Both he and Sonnenburg have advanced theories that the more diverse the array of *good* bacteria in our guts, the better.

Don't be misled into thinking that the yogurts with the largest number of bacterial strains listed on their labels are necessarily the "best." Each probiotic has a different function, some have been studied more widely than others, and more is not always "better." When I interviewed Joseph F. Frank, PhD, a professor of food science and technology at the University of Georgia, he told me: "You have to consume a sufficient number of probiotics for them to have an effect, and you have to consume them on a daily basis. Otherwise, they don't maintain themselves in your gut." Furthermore, he added: "The probiotic bugs need good food to grow on in your gut or they don't stick around."

So where does one find this "good food" to which he refers? That's where *prebiotics* come in. Dr. Frank says prebiotics—found in foods like artichokes, beans, leeks, asparagus, onions, and more—serve as food for the probiotic organisms. Eating a diet rich in fruits, vegetables, and dietary fiber is a good way to ensure you're creating a naturally prebiotic-rich environment in which the probiotics you consume will thrive.

My take? Enjoy yogurt primarily for its taste, versatility, and nutrients, not as a response to marketing claims that it will cure the sniffles or prevent medical problems.

SHOPPING FOR YOGURT

Now that you know what yogurt is, how can you know you're getting the real thing when shopping at the store? In the United States, the Food and Drug Administration (FDA) uses something called the Code of Federal Regulations (CFR) to determine which food products are legally permitted to carry a particular name. In the case of yogurt, the CFR provides a two-page description of the acceptable bacterial strains, the range of milk fat, and the list of optional ingredients (flavorings, colorants, and stabilizers) that may be present for a product to be labeled "yogurt."[18] If a manufacturer deviates from this standard, the word yogurt cannot appear without qualification on the label. Examples include "cultured dairy blends" or cultured nondairy products that look like yogurt and may be sold next to yogurt—and may, in fact, contain the same live, active bacterial cultures as yogurt—but that do not meet the overall yogurt criteria. Because these products are not currently governed by the CFR, they're not standardized or regulated in the same way. If you want yogurt, look for the word on the label.

HOW TO READ A YOGURT LABEL

In addition to making sure the yogurt has live, active bacterial cultures, read the ingredients list carefully. Some manufacturers use thickeners, stabilizers, and other ingredients to optimize the flavor, texture, mouthfeel, and shelf life of their products. These may or may not bother you, but it's good to know what they're called so you can be as informed as possible.

FLAVOR: Yogurt can be enhanced not only with real fruit and fruit juices but also with different sugars and sweeteners, such as plain sugar, fructose (fruit sugar), dextrose (a form of glucose), sucralose (like Splenda), acesulfame potassium or Ace-K, aspartame, sodium citrate (made from the fruit acid called citric acid), cane juice, and the always vague and thoroughly nondescript "natural flavors" and "artificial flavors," among others.

TEXTURES: Yogurt can be thickened, stabilized, and/or emulsified with pectin, gelatin (which may be derived from meat bones or cattle hide) or kosher gelatin (which may be derived from fish bones), cornstarch or modified cornstarch, tapioca starch, modified food starch, carrageenan, and gums like locust bean gum and guar gum, among others.

COLORANTS: Yogurt's appearance can be changed by spices like turmeric (a common rhizome), extracts like annatto (derived from the seeds of achiote trees), food dyes like carmine (derived from ground insects), and artificial (and controversial) dyes like red 40, yellow 5, and blue 1 (which are synthesized from petroleum).[19]

PRESERVATIVES can enhance yogurt's shelf life, inhibit mold growth, and maintain freshness and may include potassium sorbate and natamycin (an antifungal), among others.

Of course, not every manufacturer uses all, or even any, of these additives, but if they do, they must be labeled. Furthermore, not all of these ingredients are "bad," however broadly you choose to define that term. Some are naturally derived, and all have been approved for use by the FDA. It comes down to this: You have the authority to decide what you want in your yogurt. Reading labels is the best way for you to exercise this authority wisely.

My philosophy? I often choose to make yogurt from scratch and add any supplemental ingredients myself, at home. When I do buy commercial yogurt, I go organic and always buy plain yogurt made without additives, colorants, or stabilizers.

MOO, NEIGH, BAA, OR . . . WHAT SOUND DOES SOY MAKE?

Different livestock, and their attendant milks, dominate in different regions of the world, so yogurts made from these milks vary accordingly. In her comprehensive book, *Milk: The Surprising Story of Milk Through the Ages*, Anne Mendelson refers to sheep, goats, and cows as "the big three" milk-providing domesticated animals. This is not to say that other mammals don't also give milk that makes great yogurt. They do. In Mongolia and Tibet, for example, yak milk predominates. In India, buffalo milk is common. In *The Complete Yogurt Cookbook*, Karen Cross Whyte writes that reindeer and mare milk are used to make yogurt in Lapland (Finland). She adds, "Ass's milk produces a fine curd and is easily digested by infants." Perhaps it's time to get a donkey.

In the United States, of course, the vast majority of yogurt is made from cow's milk. In *Milk*, Mendelson posits: "The comparative blandness of cow's-milk products emerged as the way many people thought dairy foods *ought* to taste." I have developed all of my recipes using cow's milk yogurt, save for the Goat Cheese Cheesecake on page 259, for purely practical reasons: Sourcing both cow's milk and cow's milk yogurt is easier than finding other varieties.

That doesn't mean goat's milk and sheep's milk yogurt aren't worth eating. Quite the contrary. I've enjoyed both kinds at home and abroad.

To learn more about goat's milk yogurt and its properties, I spoke by phone with Jennifer Bice, owner and CEO of Redwood Hill Farm in Sebastopol, California. I asked her to explain the major differences between goat's and cow's milk yogurt. She noted that the butterfat particles in goat's milk are smaller and more delicate than those in cow's milk. Correspondingly, goat's milk yogurt has a softer, more pourable consistency. In addition, many people find goat's milk yogurt easier to digest because its lactose has a different composition from that of cow's milk. Finally, the milk protein, called casein, differs as well, she said. Goat's milk casein more closely resembles that of human milk and is therefore less likely to be allergenic than

Gender and Yogurt

DO WE REALLY NEED YOGURT FOR MEN?

For decades, yogurt companies seemed to market their products to women in subtle and not-so-subtle ways: from the iconic "get a Dannon Body" rollerskater of the late 1970s (and a short-lived, hot-pink packaged yogurt called Essensis marketed in Europe specifically as a beauty food to women) to Yoplait's ubiquitous, and eventually controversial, pink lids for breast cancer research[20] to Nestlé's Sveltesse, a European brand of yogurt and related dairy products whose very name carries a built-in feminine suffix.

And then something changed. Though within a year it had rebranded itself as a yogurt for athletes, Powerful Yogurt was launched in early 2013 for men. With an unapologetically brash, hypermasculine campaign to differentiate itself from decades of feminized yogurt competition, everything from the size to the color scheme to the logo was designed with the heretofore neglected male yogurt consumer in mind.

Powerful's macho black and red Greek yogurt containers featured a bull's head and horns. Its container held a manly 8 ounces versus the industry standard of 6 ounces at the time (a standard that soon dropped: Chobani, Yoplait Greek, and Dannon Oikos now weigh in at 5.3 ounces per single-serve cup).

The company's tagline ("Find your inner abs") put a male twist on decades of advertising featuring women's flat bellies; Powerful's ads showcased shirtless male torsos instead. In the summer of 2013, Danone (Dannon's European parent) launched Danone Men in black packaging. Is this progress?

The genderization of food strikes me as a silly but inescapable part of product marketing, one that won't disappear anytime soon.

cow's milk casein. Some traditionally "milk-allergic" people can thus tolerate goat's milk without incident.

Furthermore, goats are less conducive to factory farming and are therefore less likely to be raised under those crowded and controversial conditions. She adds that there is no parallel in goat farming to the artificial growth hormone rBGH used in some cows. It should be noted that goat's milk costs about twice as much as cow's milk. Consequently, goat's milk yogurts tend to cost more as well.

For vegans, there are even yogurt products without any dairy whatsoever.

Yogurt made from sheep's milk exclusively, or sheep's and goat's milk combined, is common throughout Greece and Turkey. When I visited the home of the noted Greek cooking authority Aglaia Kremezi and her husband, Costas Moraitis (see page 150), they served a trio of yogurts—one cow's milk, one goat's milk, and one sheep's milk—so we could enjoy a comparative tasting. At 6.6 percent fat, the sheep's milk yogurt was by far the richest and most luxurious of the lot, with a deeper, tangier profile that contrasted beautifully with the fruit "spoon sweets" they served alongside. (Two spoon sweets recipes appear on pages 290 and 291.) "The Greeks like sheep's milk yogurt," Costas said, passing the little clay pot of yogurt back my way. Though the goat's and cow's milk yogurt were both good, the sheep's milk yogurt was extraspecial.

For vegans, there are even yogurt products without any dairy whatsoever. Those made from soy, tree nuts, rice, and coconut milk are becoming increasingly popular and easy to find. *Specialty Food Magazine* notes that Turtle Mountain, a maker of almond- and coconut-based yogurts under the So Delicious brand name, enjoyed a 46 percent sales increase between 2009 and 2011 to $5.3 million.[21] WholeSoy, a San Francisco–based company, recently hit the big time after a setback in 2013 forced the company to halt production; Whole Foods Market announced in January 2014 that it would award WholeSoy a $400,000 loan and within a few months, the brand was back on the market in a newly constructed, all-dairy-free production facility.

"Cultured blends" generally contain live cultures (often the same kind found in actual yogurt), but in general they have a different sweetness level, taste profile, and, occasionally, texture from dairy yogurt, and they have not been tested for success in the recipes in this book.

A BRIEF NOTE ON LACTOSE INTOLERANCE

According to the National Institutes of Health, between 30 million and 50 million U.S. adults are lactose intolerant, meaning they lack sufficient lactase (an enzyme) to digest the sugars (lactose) in milk.[22] As mentioned earlier, yogurt's fermentation process converts a good part of the milk's lactose into lactic acid, thereby reducing the amount of lactose in yogurt. As a result, many people who suffer from lactose intolerance find that they can tolerate yogurt well, especially Greek yogurt, since when the whey is drained out, a good part of the lactose is lost as well. In fact, Greek yogurt can be a terrific way for the lactose intolerant to get calcium. (If you're lactose intolerant, be aware that some dishes in this book contain dairy products in addition to yogurt, so read the recipes carefully.)

ORGANICS, GMOS, AND GRASS-FED DAIRY

Yogurt, like milk, may be conventional or organic. If you make your own yogurt with conventional milk and a conventional starter, you'll produce conventional yogurt. If you start with organic milk and an organic starter, your yogurt will be organic. Similarly, if you want your yogurt to be free of rBST and GMOs, look for these indicators on the milk and yogurt labels, where in many cases it is included as a selling point (where applicable) even when not required by law. (Some states—at the time of this writing, Maine, Vermont, and Connecticut—have passed laws requiring GMO labeling, though the laws have not yet taken effect. Legislation in this area is evolving.)

Organic dairy recently enjoyed a boost in popularity after an eighteen-month research study concluded that organic dairy production produces a better and more healthful ratio of helpful to harmful fatty acids in milk. This benefit can be traced to the natural grasses and pastured diet that cows on organic dairy farms graze on, making grass-fed milk an especially appealing option for those who can afford it.

LET'S TALK ABOUT FAT

Because of my personal views and evolving research in this area, I choose to make yogurt from whole milk or buy whole-milk yogurt at the store. I find it superior in taste, texture, mouthfeel, and culinary versatility.

From a health standpoint, the fat in milk and yogurt helps increase feelings of satiety, or fullness, which means you need less of it to feel satisfied and stave off cravings. Some recent articles, like a September 2013 *JAMA Pediatrics* article by David S. Ludwig, MD, PhD, and Walter C. Willett, MD, DrPhD, both renowned physicians and researchers at Harvard Medical School, underscore this point, suggesting that recommendations to consume reduced-fat dairy instead of full-fat dairy to promote weight loss and curb

*My goal is simple: To encourage
you to play with plain yogurt.*

obesity may be misguided, especially when carbohydrates are consumed in place of fat. Reduced-fat dairy, therefore, isn't solving the problems many consumers think it solves. It may, in fact, lead to overeating and unhealthy food swaps. I agree with the Greek cookbook author Aglaia Kremezi, who notes, "It's extremely strange that Americans want to eat all this bacon and all this butter, and then they don't want to eat 3.5 percent fat yogurt."

YOGURT—OR CANDY?

On the yogurt section of its website, Maple Hill Creamery of Stuyvesant, New York, sports a boldly lettered banner with several phrases: "100% GRASS-FED," "REAL FOOD, MADE WITH LOVE," "NO CORN, NO GRAIN JUST GRASS," and "THIS IS NOT CANDY."[23]

This is not candy? Why on earth would a yogurt maker have to be explicit that its product is not candy? Because candy and yogurt have become so firmly connected in the marketplace that a company that doesn't further this trend with its yogurt feels compelled to call it out boldly, in all caps.

Sugar, in all its forms, is everywhere in U.S. yogurt. Not just in the toppings in frozen yogurt shops and the stir-ins in those little plastic kids' yogurt cups (I'm looking at you, YoCrunch), but even in some of the most innocent-sounding fruit-flavored yogurts. Case in point: BuzzFeed's January 13, 2014, rundown, "16 Supposedly Healthy Foods with More Sugar than a Snickers Bar," included entries for yogurt products from Chobani, Stonyfield, and Starbucks.

In a 2013 opinion piece in the *San Francisco Chronicle*, UCSF pediatric endocrinologist Robert H. Lustig, author of *Fat Chance: Beating the Odds Against Sugar, Processed Food, Obesity, and Disease*, writes: "The Nutrition Labeling and Education Act of 1990 requires the disclosure of total sugars on the nutrition facts label for processed food. That includes the strawberries in your strawberry ice cream, the lactose in the milk (neither of which is a problem), *and* the added sugar. Yet how much of that sugar is lactose, and how much is added sugar? The label doesn't say, but you can figure it out." Lustig then turns his attention to yogurt:

"Consider a 6-ounce carton of pomegranate yogurt, which has 19 grams of sugar. A plain yogurt has 7 grams of sugar, all lactose. Thus, each pomegranate yogurt has 12 grams of added sugar, the same as a bowl of Cap'n Crunch. . . . Not so healthy after all."[24]

Keep in mind when reading labels that some of the "sugar" in your 6-ounce yogurt is (natural, unproblematic) lactose rather than added sugar. Now pick up your favorite brand of sweetened yogurt. How much sugar does it have? 21 grams? 23 grams? 26 grams? In most cases, you can get this number way down by sweetening plain yogurt yourself, topping it with fresh fruit (or a few scant spoonfuls of homemade fruit puree), or by going completely rogue and discovering all the savory flavors that pair beautifully with plain, tart yogurt.

To be clear: I am not antisugar. I regularly sweeten my yogurt, drizzling it with local honey or floating a glossy pool of real maple syrup on top. I bake with yogurt and sugar together, and add modest amounts of sugar to many (but not all) of my frozen yogurt bases and fruit purees.

But I believe you should choose your sweeteners mindfully and use them sparingly. Add them yourself, using as much as you need to get a flavor you love—and then stop. Taste as you go, and enjoy every spoonful. When you take charge of the sugar bowl, the honey jar, the maple syrup bottle, you'll likely use far less sweetener than you'll find in many of the mass-produced products designed to please the average, sweet-loving American palate. (Some companies, like Dannon, have reduced their sugar content proactively,[25] but you still need to read labels carefully.) When you flavor yogurt yourself (see pages 41 to 72) or make chilled desserts (page 283) or make frozen yogurts (page 303), you're better off when you're fully in charge of the amount of sweetener.

SO YOU WANT TO MAKE YOUR OWN YOGURT

Fantastic! Turn to Make beginning on page 318, where I offer recipes for making both traditional (loose-style) and strained (Greek-style) yogurt, from both cow's and goat's milk. I also show you how to make labneh, that smooth and thick yogurt cheese common throughout the Middle East.

That said, if you've become enamored with a particular yogurt brand available near you and don't want to dive deep into yogurt making, we can still be friends. *Every single recipe in this book will work with either homemade or commercially sourced plain yogurt.* The choice to buy or make is yours.

My goal is simple: to encourage you to play with plain yogurt. To embellish it, sure, but also to appreciate what it brings to the table, namely flavor, creaminess, nutrition, and a global sense of possibility.

Shall we begin?

The choice to buy or make is yours.

Flavor

Flavor

The spices, flavorings, and mix-ins in this chapter are designed to be served with plain, unsweetened yogurt and customized—at serving time—to suit your tastes. By uncoupling the fruit flavorings from the yogurt, you can stir in as little or as much as you like. You can even layer multiple flavors together, swirling them to create a brand-new flavor profile.

Why expend the effort to make your own flavorings when there are so many readily available, preflavored yogurts on the market?

» So you can control the sweetness of your food. It's easy to add additional sugar, honey, maple syrup, or agave nectar to taste at the table if you like.

» Keeping the flavorings separate from the yogurt gives you more flexibility. Each of the fruit compote recipes here is terrific served over ice cream, slathered on buttered toast, or spooned atop a giant stack of pancakes whenever yogurt isn't on the docket.

» Guided by market research and driven by profit motive, yogurt companies generally sell only those flavors guaranteed to please the masses. But you are not similarly constrained. You can experiment.

» And if you love vanilla, maple, or lemon yogurt and want to use these as the base for the concoctions in this chapter, by all means, go ahead, though I'd encourage you to pair the fruit flavors with plain yogurt first to open your mind to the beautiful contrast of sweet and tart.

The Recipes

Strawberry-Rhubarb Compote

¼ cup sugar

Zest of 1 small lime

⅛ to ¼ teaspoon ground cinnamon

6 ounces rhubarb, sliced ¼ inch thick (1½ cups)

8 ounces strawberries, hulled and quartered (about 2 cups)

Plain Greek yogurt, sliced strawberries, and fresh lime zest, for serving

Yo!

I don't oversugar my rhubarb, so this amount suits me perfectly. But if you prefer a sweeter profile, especially against the tartness of the yogurt, toss in a few extra teaspoons of sugar.

MAKES 1 GENEROUS CUP COMPOTE

Rhubarb's bizarre. It's a sour vegetable, but when allowed to moonlight as a fruit, kissed with sugar and heat and paired with strawberries, magic happens. I've added a squeeze of bright lime and the barest hint of cinnamon as subtle enhancements. You'll have enough compote here for several servings. If you'd like to double the recipe, use a larger baking dish and up the cook time by a few minutes.

PREP. In a small bowl, stir the sugar, lime zest, and cinnamon until thoroughly combined. In a 2-quart rectangular (preferably glass) baking dish, combine the rhubarb and strawberries. Sprinkle with the cinnamon-lime sugar and stir well. Let stand for 30 minutes, uncovered and at room temperature, stirring occasionally.

After 15 to 20 minutes, preheat the oven to 425°F, with a rack in the center position. Line a baking sheet with foil.

Set the baking dish on the baking sheet (in case the compote bubbles over). Roast, uncovered, for 30 minutes, stirring once halfway through, until the juices bubble vigorously and the rhubarb is completely tender. Whisk to dissolve any chunky fruit. Cool completely. (It will thicken further as it cools.)

SERVE. For each serving, create alternating layers of compote, yogurt, and sliced strawberries in a small jar, glass, or bowl. Top with lime zest. Or simply stir a bit of compote into the yogurt (to taste). Top with the sliced berries and zest.

STORE. Scrape into a lidded glass jar or other covered container and refrigerate for up to 2 weeks.

Roasted Blueberry Compote

2½ cups fresh blueberries

2 to 2½ tablespoons sugar

½ teaspoon fresh lemon juice

Plain yogurt, for serving

Optional add-ins: toasted pecans, crispy rice cereal, dried blueberries, tangerine segments, banana chunks, diced kiwi

Yo!

Spoon any extra over waffles, pancakes, or French toast.

MAKES 1½ CUPS COMPOTE

My college admissions essay was all about the small quirks that set me apart from other teenagers, including, somewhat presciently, my mad love for blueberry yogurt. Choose fat, juicy berries here, as they'll shrink down considerably in the oven and you'll want a nice, drippy, scoopable mound at the end for your yogurt. Taste your berries before beginning, opting for the greater amount of sugar if they're on the tarter side.

PREP. Preheat the oven to 350°F, with a rack in the center position. Line a baking sheet with parchment.

ROAST. Tumble 2 cups of the blueberries onto the parchment and sprinkle evenly with the sugar. (A good bit of the sugar may fall onto the paper; carry on.) Roast for 18 to 20 minutes, until the skins burst and thick, purple juice pools on the parchment. Carefully lift the long edges of the parchment toward the center and tip the berries and their juices into a medium bowl. (If you wait too long, the juices will harden.) Stir in the remaining ½ cup fresh berries and the lemon juice. Let cool. (To speed cooling, stir over an ice bath.)

SERVE. For each serving, swirl as much of the blueberry compote as you like through yogurt. If desired, top with one or more of the suggested add-ins.

STORE. Refrigerate any extra compote, covered, for up to 2 weeks, giving a stir every now and again.

A Pioneer in Connecting Health to Yogurt
THE STORY OF DANNON

As teenagers, my brother Mark and I were daily Dannon eaters in 1986, the year Dannon moved into its White Plains, New York, headquarters ten miles from our childhood home. Once I decided to write a yogurt book, I felt a nostalgic pull to learn more about the brand.

In 1908, a Russian scientist named Élie Metchnikoff of the Pasteur Institute in Paris won the Nobel Prize in Medicine. His research focused on cellular immunity and the pathology of inflammation. He later studied the intestinal benefits of lactic fermentation, and it was these findings that inspired Isaac Carasso to found the Danone company in Barcelona in 1919. (Danone is the diminutive form of Danon, the Catalan nickname of Carasso's young son Daniel.) Carasso introduced yogurt as a treatment for children who were suffering from intestinal disorders, so Danone yogurt and health were closely tied from the outset. Carasso became the first person to commercialize the mass manufacture of yogurt, a product that until that point had only been produced on a small scale or in individual homes.

A decade later, Isaac's son Daniel, now grown, introduced the company's yogurt into the French market. In the 1940s, at the height of World War II, Daniel and his wife emigrated to the United States and purchased a small yogurt factory in the Bronx. They Americanized the spelling of the company's name stateside from Danone to Dannon.

By the 1950s, Daniel began marketing his yogurt to doctors, urging them to try it "on a select group of patients" and touting its "natural, physiologic approach" to a wide array of medical problems, everything from gastrointestinal upset to colitis to "the abdominal distress of pregnancy." In 1955 Dannon introduced low-fat yogurt in the United States but not overseas. Early low-fat flavors included orange, coffee, vanilla, strawberry, banana, pineapple, and prune whip.

Fast-forward fifty-one years to 2006, when Dannon introduced Activia, its yogurt marketed to promote digestive regularity. Net sales topped $100 million in its first year on the market.

Michael Neuwirth, Dannon's current public relations director, said simply: "We're a food company, but we're a health company first."

Even today, the company is focused on spreading the word about yogurt's health benefits. Health Affairs Director Miguel Freitas joined Dannon's U.S. arm to help launch Activia and disseminate this messaging. Born in Portugal, he worked for Danone in Europe while getting his PhD on lactobacillus and has also studied the probiotic's impact on preventing rotavirus in children. He's now charged with educating and influencing health care providers and teaching them about probiotics here in the United States.

Freitas talked to me about yogurt's other nutritional benefits, too: its ability to enhance metabolic profile and improve weight and cardiovascular health. He said that most people with lactose intolerance can safely consume yogurt, that dairy is a complete protein, and that the calcium, vitamin D, and potassium found in yogurt is lacking in many of our diets.

Though we in the United States no longer consume yogurt as a medicinal food, our current love affair with probiotics, gut health, and our "microbiome" can in some ways be traced back to Élie Metchnikoff, the very man whose research inspired Isaac Carasso to begin manufacturing yogurt at scale. Pioneers like them still influence us in ways large and small, whether we pick up a carton of Dannon or some other brand, and eat it because it tastes great or makes us feel a little healthier.

Cherry-Raspberry Stir-In

1⅓ cups fresh raspberries (one
5- to 6-ounce basket)

1 cup fresh cherries (about
5 ounces), stemmed, pitted, and
chopped

1 tablespoon sugar

1 teaspoon raspberry vinegar or
pomegranate molasses (see Yo!)

Plain yogurt, for serving

MAKES 1¾ CUPS COMPOTE

A single teaspoon of sweet-tart raspberry vinegar or pomegranate
molasses jolts this ruby-red stir-in to life.

MAKE. In a medium bowl, toss the raspberries, cherries, sugar, and
vinegar (or pomegranate molasses). Set aside for 10 minutes at room
temperature so the juices exude.

SERVE. Layer with yogurt, spooning plenty of juicy fruit on top.

STORE. Pack leftover fruit into a jar and refrigerate for up to
1 week.

Yo!

Cherries tend to oxidize and brown once cut. For this
reason, I prefer dark red cherries here to golden/blush
varieties to minimize obvious signs of discoloration. Pack-
ing the fruit into the smallest jar that will accommodate it
and giving the jar an occasional shake will best preserve its
vivid color.

Raspberry vinegar is a combination of vinegar, raspberry
juice, and raspberry puree. Find it in the oil and vinegar
aisle of larger supermarkets.

Pomegranate molasses is a sweet, tart, and syrupy pomegranate juice reduction. Find it in Middle Eastern markets
or online at Kalustyans.com.

Kumquat-Date Compote

¾ cup orange juice

12 kumquats, halved and seeded (extract the seeds with the tip of a small knife), plus 12 kumquats, sliced and seeded, for serving

½ vanilla bean, split lengthwise

4 Medjool dates, pitted and diced (see Yo!)

2 cups plain Greek yogurt, for serving

12 almonds, toasted (see Yo!) and chopped, for serving

Yo!

Large, soft, and honey-sweet, Medjool dates contain a central pit. To remove, slice the date in half and pluck it out. You'll find these dates in the produce section.

Toast almonds in a preheated 350°F oven for 5 to 7 minutes, shaking the baking sheet halfway through.

Don't discard the vanilla bean until the compote is gone.

MAKES 1 CUP COMPOTE; SERVES 4

Kumquats, with their sweet, edible skins and tart juice, mellow in a quick-simmered compote thick with Medjool dates and vanilla-spiked orange juice. Pairing the compote with cool, creamy yogurt, toasted nuts, and a few raw, sliced kumquats achieves an ideal balance that's neither too timid nor too stark. Each spoonful's a seduction, a come-hither yin-yang.

MAKE THE COMPOTE. In your smallest saucepan, combine the orange juice, halved kumquats, and seeds scraped from the vanilla bean (toss in the spent vanilla pod, too). Bring to a hard simmer. Reduce the heat to as low as possible and let bubble gently for 5 to 10 minutes, stirring or swirling the pot a few times, until the kumquats are tender but not mushy. Remove from the heat. Stir in the dates. Cool completely. Scrape the compote (and the vanilla bean) into a glass jar or lidded container. Refrigerate until cold and thick, several hours or overnight.

SERVE. For each serving, scoop ¼ cup compote into an 8-ounce jar, glass, or bowl. Top with ½ cup yogurt. Sprinkle with the sliced kumquats and the almonds.

STORE. Refrigerate the compote, covered, for up to 1 week.

Burnt Sugar–Apricot Halves

3 tablespoons turbinado sugar (see Yo!) or granulated sugar

¾ teaspoon ground ginger

2 pounds very ripe apricots, halved and pitted

Fresh lemon juice, just a touch (optional)

Plain Greek yogurt, for serving

Yo!

Turbinado sugar is a coarse-crystalled, raw brown sugar that retains a molasses flavor.

Once the leftover apricots are refrigerated, the sugar topping will liquefy and bathe the apricots in syrup. You can stir a bit of this syrup into your yogurt, if desired, or simply lift out the apricots with a slotted spoon. You can also puree the apricots, creating a smooth, velvety sauce.

MAKES 3½ PACKED CUPS COLLAPSED FRUIT

You'll want the ripest fruit possible to make these quick-broiled apricots with dark, sugar-crusted edges. Enjoy for dessert or for a special breakfast.

PREP THE TOPPING. In a small bowl, stir together the sugar and ginger.

BROIL THE APRICOTS. Line a baking sheet with parchment or foil. Set the apricot halves cut sides up in a single layer. You should be able to fit them all. Divide the ginger-sugar evenly among the hollows and tops of all the apricots. Set a broiler rack 5 inches from the heat source. Broil the apricots for 4 to 5 minutes, watching carefully (flip on the oven light). The sugar should melt, then bubble, then begin to burn along the edges. I like there to be some black spots, but pull the apricots out of the broiler a bit earlier if this bothers you. Cool for a few minutes and then serve warm, or squeeze on a touch of lemon juice (to inhibit browning), pack into a quart-size jar, cover, and refrigerate until cold before serving (see Yo!).

SERVE. Spoon the yogurt into serving bowls. Top with the collapsed apricots.

STORE. Refrigerate, covered, for up to 1 week.

VARIATION

For an especially pretty variation, top the apricots with fresh raspberries, a spoonful of Strawberry-Rhubarb Compote (page 45), or a handful of toasted, chopped pistachios. If serving for dessert, dust with a few crushed gingersnaps.

Plum-Allspice Compote

1½ pounds red- or purple-fleshed plums (about 6 medium), pitted, cut into rough ¾-inch pieces (3½ cups chopped), plus (optional) additional diced plums, for serving

2 tablespoons sugar, plus (optional) additional sugar, for serving

½ to ¾ teaspoon ground allspice

1 tablespoon orange juice

Plain yogurt, for serving

MAKES 2 CUPS COMPOTE

Plum fans, rejoice! With a bit of heat and time, plums cook into a gorgeous yogurt stir-in. The longer the puree sits in the refrigerator, the thicker and glossier it becomes, so give it plenty of time to gel. I like the soft back note of ½ teaspoon allspice here so the plum flavor stays center stage, but go ahead and use the larger amount for a more pronounced allspice flavor.

PREP THE PLUMS. Set aside 1 cup of the plums. Toss the remaining 2½ cups plums in a large bowl with the sugar, allspice, and orange juice. Give a good stir. Let macerate at room temperature for 30 minutes to 1 hour for the plums to release their juices.

PUREE AND REDUCE. Transfer the macerated plums to a blender or food processor, scraping in every last bit of sugary juice. Puree until smooth. (Some bits of peel may remain visible; carry on.) Pour into a small saucepan along with the reserved 1 cup plums. Set over medium-high heat and bring to a steady bubble, stirring. Cook at a hard simmer, moderating the heat between medium and medium-high (use caution as the puree may pop a bit as it cooks), until the mixture reduces to 2 cups, stirring almost constantly (sweeping the sides and bottom), about 10 minutes. Remove from the heat.

COOL AND REFRIGERATE. To speed cooling, make an ice bath by filling a large bowl with ice cubes and water. Set a slightly smaller bowl sturdily on top. Scrape the plum puree into the top bowl. Stir frequently until the puree reaches room temperature. Transfer to a covered glass container or jar and refrigerate until cold and thick, ideally for at least 2 hours. (The puree will continue to gel as it chills.)

SERVE. Taste the compote with a bit of yogurt. Lightly sweeten the remaining yogurt to taste, only if desired. Serve a few generous spoonfuls of compote with the yogurt, topping with diced, fresh plums if so inspired.

STORE. Refrigerate, covered, for up to 1 week.

Yo!

Two of my favorite dark-fleshed plums are Santa Rosa and Elephant Heart. If you're not sure whether the flesh inside your plums will be golden or red, ask your produce vendor.

Cranberry-Pomegranate Compote

1 cup pomegranate juice or blueberry-pomegranate juice

1½ cups fresh or frozen (not thawed) cranberries

⅓ cup sugar

4 whole allspice berries (optional)

¼ teaspoon pure vanilla extract

½ cup plain yogurt per serving

2 tablespoons fresh pomegranate seeds per serving

Yo!

When fresh pomegranate seeds are unavailable, substitute raspberries, blueberries, purple grapes, or any other deep-colored fruit.

MAKES 1 TO 1½ CUPS COMPOTE; SERVES 8

Cranberries, sadly, are often relegated to the last two months of the calendar year. Since they freeze so well, stock up on them before Thanksgiving when they're both plentiful and priced to move. Once you freeze your haul, pull out the cranberries you need to make this intense, sweet-tart compote all year long.

***

MAKE THE COMPOTE. In a small, heavy saucepan, combine the juice, cranberries, sugar, and allspice berries, if using. Set over medium heat and cook, stirring, for 3 to 4 minutes, until the sugar dissolves. Keeping the heat constant, let the mixture simmer until it bubbles vigorously, foams, and all the cranberries pop, 10 to 15 minutes more. Stir frequently and make sure the compote doesn't boil over. You'll know it's ready when you drag a silicone spatula across the bottom of the pot and it creates a "wake" that stays put for a second or two. Remove from the heat. Stir in the vanilla. Cool completely. The compote will thicken as it cools. Pluck out and discard the allspice berries.

SERVE. For each serving, stir 2 tablespoons of the compote into ½ cup yogurt. Garnish with the pomegranate seeds. For a layered look, alternate the yogurt, compote, and seeds in a small glass or jar. Stir before eating.

STORE. Refrigerate, covered, for up to 2 weeks.

Rosy Apple-Grape Sauce

2 pounds mixed red, green, and golden apples (about 5 good-size apples)

3 Medjool dates, pitted and coarsely chopped (see Yo!, page 51)

1 juicy orange, such as Valencia

2 cinnamon sticks or ¾ teaspoon ground cinnamon

Pinch of kosher salt

½ cup purple grapes, such as Concord (about 14 grapes)

1 tablespoon (or more, to taste) muscovado sugar (see Yo!) or dark brown sugar

Plain yogurt and chopped toasted pecans or Ultimate Granola (page 92), for serving

MAKES 2½ CUPS SAUCE

Sweetened lightly with dates and just a hint of muscovado sugar, this homespun applesauce-with-a-twist gets a color jolt toward the end of cooking from deep purple Concord grapes. You can pass the sauce through a food mill for complete textural submission, but I like the extra character the skins provide. Spoon any leftovers over your morning oatmeal.

PREP AND COOK. If desired, peel some or all of the apples. I like to leave on the red peels for added color and remove the green or yellow peels, but it's completely up to you. Core the apples and chop into rough ¾-inch pieces. Place in a medium saucepan (enameled cast-iron is great, if you have it) with the dates, the juice of half the orange, the cinnamon, and salt. Cover and cook over medium-low heat for 20 minutes, stirring occasionally to prevent sticking.

MEANWHILE, SEED THE GRAPES. Halve the grapes. If using Concords, pluck out the seeds with the tip of a paring knife. If using a different (and seedless) variety, move on.

SIMMER AND FINISH THE SAUCE. Reduce the heat to low and continue to cook, covered, stirring every now and again. After 15 more minutes, toss in the grapes and 1 tablespoon of the muscovado or dark brown sugar. Cook, stirring gently, for 5 minutes. The apples should be completely tender, though some may still retain some shape. Discard the cinnamon sticks. Gently press on the fruit with a potato masher. The grape skins will bleed a beautiful rosy color into the sauce and the skins will slough off. Taste, adding additional sugar and a few quick squeezes from the remaining orange half, if desired.

SERVE. Serve dollops of sauce warm or cold with the plain yogurt and toasted pecans or granola.

STORE. Refrigerate, covered, for up to 1 week.

> ### Yo!
>
> If you'd like to forgo the dates, substitute 2 tablespoons muscovado or dark brown sugar in their place early in the recipe (as well as where it's called for at the end).
>
> Moist and sticky due to its high molasses content, muscavado sugar, which is unrefined, has a deeper, more full-bodied sweetness than ordinary brown sugar, which is refined.

Chamomile-Poached Quince

1 pound quince (see Yo!)

1½ cups apple juice

⅓ cup sugar

1 chamomile tea bag

Juice of ½ lemon

¼ cup dried cherries

½ cup plain whole-milk or low-fat Greek yogurt per serving

MAKES ABOUT 3 CUPS POACHED QUINCE

Nothing prepares you for the first whiff of quince, a bumpy, yellow fruit whose scent is the stuff of dreams: heady, sweet, exotic, and singular. It's the kind of fruit you want physically near you to inhale several times a day. I poach thin slices in apple juice bolstered with soothing chamomile. The tea heightens the fruit's floral notes and the juice brings forth its appley essence. Chilled in its own liquid, quince makes a unique and very special stir-in for Greek yogurt.

PREP. Use a vegetable peeler to rid the quince of its yellow rind. Cut the fruit in half like an apple, then cut into very thin (¼-inch) slices, ignoring the core and seeds for the moment. Once sliced, go back and use your knife to carve out and discard the core and seeds, which won't soften at all during cooking. Place the sliced quince in a medium saucepan.

POACH. Add the apple juice, sugar, tea bag, lemon juice, and dried cherries to the saucepan and place over medium-high heat. Bring to a simmer, stirring a few times to dissolve the sugar. Cover, reduce the heat to low, and simmer gently, stirring now and again so the fruit cooks evenly, until the quince is very tender and pierces easily with a fork, 35 to 45 minutes.

REDUCE. Using a slotted spoon, remove the quince and cherries to a bowl or glass jar with a capacity of at least 3 cups. Discard the tea bag. Over medium heat, reduce the poaching liquid to ⅔ cup, 5 to 15 minutes longer. Pour the liquid over the quince and cool. Cover and refrigerate.

SERVE. For each serving, whisk ½ cup Greek yogurt in a bowl until smooth and light. Spoon some of the quince and cherries over the yogurt and drizzle generously with some of the poaching liquid.

STORE. As long as the quince stays submerged in the poaching liquid, it will keep in the refrigerator for up to 2 weeks.

Yo!

Look for quince at farmers' markets, Middle Eastern shops, and Asian grocery stores. There is no substitute.

Use caution when slicing quince. Its hardness and irregular shape encourage knife slips, so minimize distractions and work carefully.

Fresh Oranges with Cinnamon-Toast Croutons

3 navel, Cara Cara, or blood oranges

2 teaspoons sugar

⅛ teaspoon ground cinnamon

2 slices whole-grain bread

Soft unsalted butter

3 cups plain Greek yogurt

4 tablespoons orange marmalade

Yo!

Supreming is a French technique for freeing orange segments from their membranes one by one. It's a bit messy, but with a little practice, you'll get the hang of it.

SERVES 4

Yogurt can be slapdash or dressed up for company. This flavor combination is a case in point. Made quickly, with a haphazard chop of the fruit, it's a 5-minute weekday affair. To make it more upscale, take your time supreming the orange and composing the elements in a pretty bowl. Be forewarned: Orange marmalade is quite bitter, as it contains plenty of peel. If bitter notes aren't your thing, substitute a milder jam.

SUPREME OR CHOP THE ORANGES. Slice the top and bottom ends off one orange, exposing the flesh. Perch on a flat end. Holding a large knife at an angle, sweep down the sides of the orange, hugging the fruit, to remove the peel and all the white pith. To supreme, working over a bowl, slide a paring knife between each membrane, releasing the orange segments into the bowl. Squeeze the remaining juice into the bowl. (A citrus reamer is helpful here.) Repeat with the remaining oranges. Alternatively, coarsely chop the peeled oranges.

MAKE THE CROUTONS. In a small bowl, stir the sugar and cinnamon together. Toast the bread, butter it, and sprinkle liberally with the cinnamon-sugar. Cut the toast into small cubes.

SERVE. Divide the yogurt among four serving bowls. Stir a few teaspoons of the orange juice into each bowl to flavor the yogurt. Top each serving with 1 tablespoon marmalade, a smattering of the orange segments, and a handful of the cinnamon-sugar croutons. Drizzle with additional orange juice, if desired, and serve immediately.

Triple Almond-Raisin Stir-In

1 tablespoon golden raisins

½ teaspoon pure almond extract

½ cup plain Greek yogurt, preferably whole-milk

3 amaretti cookies

1 tablespoon toasted slivered almonds (see Yo!)

Yo!

Amaretti are crunchy Italian macaroons sold in the cookie aisle of the grocery store. They've got a subtle sweetness and a sophisticated, bitter almond flavor.

To toast the small quantity of almonds used here, heat them in a dry skillet over medium heat, stirring frequently, for about 2 minutes, or until speckled. Cool on a cutting board.

SERVES 1

Why settle for a single hit of almond when you can double or even triple your pleasure? Tart yogurt here underpins a three-part almond stir-in, with almond extract, amaretti cookies, and toasted slivered almonds, all lending their unique, nutty flavor notes. I like the interplay of bitter and tart here, but if you need more sweetness than the amaretti and raisins provide, go ahead and stir a touch of sugar or honey into your yogurt before beginning.

MAKE. In a small bowl, sprinkle the raisins with ¼ teaspoon of the almond extract. Let stand for 5 minutes to absorb. Add the remaining ¼ teaspoon almond extract to the yogurt, stirring for a good 20 seconds to loosen. Combine the amaretti cookies and almonds in a small zip-top bag. Bash with a rolling pin, meat mallet, or the curved back of an ice cream scoop until crushed.

SERVE. Spoon the raisins over the yogurt and top with the crushed amaretti-almond mixture.

VARIATION

When fresh cherries and apricots are in season, slice them up and toss them over the amaretti-almond topping. Both fruits complement almond flavors beautifully.

Honey-Nutmeg Fleur de Sel Yogurt

½ cup Greek yogurt, preferably whole-milk

Really good honey

1 whole nutmeg (you'll just grate a bit) or a scant pinch of ground nutmeg

Fleur de sel

SERVES 1

The most exciting flavor combinations offer bold contrast rather than a single dominant note. Pairing the clean acidity of yogurt with the sweetness of pure honey and the crunch of fleur de sel takes just seconds, but the effect—so simple, so sublime—both delights and surprises.

MAKE. Scoop the yogurt into a small bowl. Stir vigorously to loosen and lighten. Drizzle generously with honey. Swipe the whole nutmeg against your grater a few times, releasing a small shower of fluffy shreds. Finish with a pinch of crunchy fleur de sel.

Yo!

With recipes as straightforward as this one, treat yourself to the best, creamiest yogurt you can find, whether that means making yours at home with whole milk or buying a premium brand for a special splurge. Same goes for the honey, which I urge you to buy from a local vendor, if at all possible. The least processed, the better.

When you buy whole nutmeg instead of preground, you get maximum nutmeg bang for your buck.

Vegetable Yogurt IS THE MARKET READY?

Move over, strawberry. Parsnip's here!

Brothers David and Dan Barber spent childhood summers on their grandmother Ann Marlowe Straus's farm in the Berkshires. Straus leased the land, called Blue Hill Farm, to dairy farmers, who used the property mostly to raise Angus for beef. In the late 1970s and 1980s, the dairy belt got crushed, the farm went fallow, and the land was left unutilized.

After 1999, when David and Dan opened Blue Hill—the first of their two widely lauded, highly successful fine dining restaurants in New York State (the second is Blue Hill at Stone Barns)—the brothers brought the farm back to life. "It's been operating as a dairy for twelve years now," David said. They looked into making cheese, but yogurt seemed the more attractive option. David hopes to get the savory yogurts into the hands not only of the two restaurants' established fan base—well-heeled, elite diners—but also into those of mass-market yogurt lovers.

The yogurts contain 30 percent vegetable puree from family farms in the Hudson Valley. Because of the Barbers' commitment both to making yogurt affordable and to promoting sustainable agriculture, pricing is tricky. A 6-ounce container costs $3, far less than a dinner at the restaurant but still not cheap compared to the average non-Greek yogurt on the market.

At the time of this writing, Blue Hill Yogurt comes in six all-vegetable flavors: carrot, tomato, beet, parsnip, sweet potato, and butternut squash. The milk is all grass-fed, with a portion coming from Blue Hill Farm itself and the rest from dairy farms with which the family works. Flavors have evolved after much trial and error and are influenced not only by what tastes best, but by which hues are most visually appealing. David noted that they can be mixed into tacos, soups, and salads.

"I just want to make sure that we're positioning ourselves to be thought-leaders in this new category," David said. "I think there's a place for yogurt in more meals than breakfast."

Coffee Yogurt

1 cup strong brewed coffee

½ cup milk, preferably 2% or whole

2 teaspoons instant espresso powder (see Yo!)

½ cup sugar

¼ teaspoon pure vanilla extract

½ cup plain Greek yogurt per serving

Yo!

Instant espresso powder and espresso beans you grind finely at home are not interchangeable, so avoid the latter in this recipe. Two brands of instant to look for in the baking or coffee aisles are Ferrara and Medaglia d'Oro.

You may want to prepare this in bulk instead of one serving at a time. Whisk ½ cup of the homemade coffee concentrate into 2 cups plain Greek yogurt.

MAKES ABOUT 1⅔ CUPS COFFEE CONCENTRATE

It's not easy to find coffee yogurt on store shelves. According to yogurt giant Dannon, it's a "love-it-or-hate-it" flavor—but those who love it are die-hard fans. So here's my version, made with a homemade coffee concentrate intense with brewed coffee and instant espresso powder.

MAKE THE COFFEE CONCENTRATE. In a small saucepan, combine the coffee, milk, espresso powder, and sugar. Set over medium-high heat and whisk until the sugar completely dissolves. Bring just to a simmer, then remove from the heat, add the vanilla, and cool completely. Transfer to a lidded jar, scraping in any sugar or solids clinging to the pot. Refrigerate until needed.

SERVE. Shake the jar with the coffee concentrate well before using. For each serving, combine ½ cup Greek yogurt with 2 tablespoons coffee concentrate in a small bowl. Stir well until completely smooth.

STORE. The coffee concentrate on its own may be refrigerated for 7 days, depending on the freshness of the milk. If making the yogurt in bulk (see Yo!), it will keep, covered and refrigerated, for up to 1 week.

Tomato, Avocado, and Cucumber Salad

1 cup plain yogurt

½ avocado, diced

½ cup diced unpeeled English cucumber

1 thick slice tomato, diced

2 teaspoons extra-virgin olive oil

Finishing salt, such as Maldon

Substantial sprinkling of minced fresh herbs or microgreens of your choice

SERVES 1 OR 2

If you've never traveled to a country where savory yogurt rules, you may be surprised by how much you love the simple and healthful marriage of diced salad ingredients with plain yogurt drizzled with olive oil. The clean flavors shine at breakfast, lunch, or anytime you need an energy boost. And yes, you can swap in any fresh, seasonal, raw vegetables you like.

MAKE. With the back of a spoon, spread the yogurt in a wide, shallow bowl. Sprinkle in the avocado, cucumber, and tomato. Drizzle with the oil. Season with salt and garnish generously with the herbs or microgreens.

Yo!

I opt for whole-milk Greek yogurt here and encourage you to do so as well.

Fennel, Pear, and Carrot Slaw

½ lemon

1 small hard pear, such as Bosc, unpeeled but cored

1 medium carrot, peeled

1 small or ½ medium fennel bulb, fronds minced and reserved for garnish

½ cup plain Greek yogurt per serving

Kosher salt and freshly ground pepper

1 handful minced dried cranberries or dried cherries, or whole dried barberries (see Yo!)

Extra-virgin olive oil

SERVES 6

On its own, this hand-cut slaw makes a refreshing salad. Atop Greek yogurt, it becomes an unusual savory breakfast or postworkout snack. I serve it in pasta bowls so I can spread out the yogurt and get a scoop with every bite.

PREP. Squeeze the lemon half into a medium serving bowl. Slice the pear and carrot into matchsticks. Add to the bowl and toss with tongs so the pear doesn't brown. Core the fennel and slice the bulb into matchsticks. Add to the bowl, tossing well. (The slaw may be made up to 2 days ahead. Refrigerate, covered.)

SERVE. For each serving, stir ½ cup yogurt in a shallow, wide bowl (like a pasta bowl) with a pinch each of salt and pepper until light. Mound a tepee of slaw (about 1 cup) on top. Sprinkle with some of the dried fruit, drizzle with olive oil, and garnish with a pinch of reserved fennel fronds.

Yo!

Barberries look like tiny dried cranberries but have a tarter, sourer flavor. They're common in Persian and other Middle Eastern cuisines. Find them in Middle Eastern markets. They are available from Amazon.com, Nuts.com, and Indianfoodsco.com.

Wake

Wake

Throughout the world, yogurt has a prominent seat at the breakfast table. Early risers the world over agree that yogurt makes a sensible start to the day whether in the labneh (yogurt cheese) of the Middle East (page 329), the drinkable yogurts in Serbia (page 300), or the thick Mediterranean yogurts so common in Greece and Turkey.

Here I offer recipes for incorporating yogurt into classic American breakfast fare—waffles, French toast, and pancakes, not to mention scones, crepes, and the best granola you have ever tried—but push the bounds a little wider, too. I add yogurt to eggs, and even to a flatbread smothered with grapes and tomatoes.

Whether sweet or savory, in-your-face or subtle, yogurt lends a nearly endless versatility to the day's first meal.

The Recipes

Flat Omelet with Yogurt, Hot Sauce, and Herbs

¼ cup plain low-fat or whole-milk yogurt

1 to 2 tablespoons milk or water

6 large eggs

Kosher salt and freshly ground pepper

1 tablespoon unsalted butter

Hot sauce

Tender minced fresh herbs, such as parsley, chives, dill, tarragon, or chervil

Yo!

Taste different varieties of hot sauce to find one you really love.

For even more heat, fold in a bit of minced fresh serrano or jalapeño chile.

SERVES 2 TO 4

Like traditionally folded omelets, flat omelets set up in minutes. The best way to ensure both sides are cooked is to invert the omelet onto a large plate and then slide it back into the skillet for a few seconds. This takes a bit of practice, but isn't difficult. Once the omelet's cooked, slap on your favorite hot sauce and some yogurt, and you're done.

PREP. In a medium bowl, whisk the yogurt with 1 tablespoon milk or water. Lift the whisk; it should drip easily. If it clings, whisk in a second tablespoon of liquid. Set aside at room temperature for 10 minutes to lose its chill.

MAKE THE OMELET. Whisk the eggs with a generous pinch each of salt and pepper. Heat the butter in a medium nonstick skillet (9- to 10-inch) over medium-high heat until foamy and then brush it over the surface and up the sides of the skillet with a silicone pastry brush. Add the eggs. With your nondominant hand, shake the skillet back and forth. With your dominant hand, sweep the sides of the skillet with a silicone spatula, allowing the liquid eggs to flow underneath and set up. Continue shaking and sweeping until the bottom is set, 3 to 5 minutes. Protecting your hands, place a large plate over the skillet and invert the omelet. Slide it back into the skillet cooked side up. Cook until the bottom is set, 30 seconds to 1 minute longer.

SERVE. Drizzle the omelet with the yogurt, waving the whisk back and forth over the eggs to make stripes. Shake over some hot sauce, sprinkle with the herbs, and serve straight from the skillet.

Folded Omelet for One with Lox, Shallot, and Yogurt

Kosher salt and freshly ground pepper

2 tablespoons plain Greek yogurt, at room temperature

2 large eggs

2 to 3 teaspoons extra-virgin olive oil (depending on how nonstick your skillet is)

1 to 2 shallots, thinly sliced (about ½ cup)

¼ cup minced smoked salmon (lox)

A few snipped fresh chives, for garnish

SERVES 1

Everything I know about lox, eggs, and onions comes from my mother, who often ordered this breakfast during my New York youth. After swiping bites off her plate for years, I finally began requesting it myself, wooed by the interplay of salty lox and dots of rich cream cheese. Now I make it at home whenever I have scraps of lox on hand. Yogurt is just as luxurious as cream cheese, more so even, because it oozes throughout the omelet, kissing every single bite.

SEASON THE YOGURT AND EGGS. In a small bowl, whisk a generous pinch each of salt and pepper into the yogurt. In a separate small bowl, do the same with the eggs, whisking well.

COOK THE SHALLOT. In a small nonstick skillet, heat the oil over medium heat and, using a silicone pastry brush, brush it up the sides of the skillet. Add the shallot and a generous pinch each of salt and pepper. Cook, stirring, for 2 to 3 minutes, until it starts to sizzle, then reduce the heat to low and cook more slowly until it softens and turns translucent but not brown, 8 to 10 minutes longer.

MAKE THE OMELET. Pour in the eggs and crank up the heat to medium-high. With your nondominant hand, shake the skillet vigorously back and forth. With your dominant hand, circle the perimeter of the eggs with a silicone spatula. As the eggs set, tilt the skillet and lift the set eggs so the liquid eggs flow underneath. After about a

Folded Omelet *(continued)*

Yo!

This French omelet-making method works best when your skillet has a truly nonstick surface, or better yet, if you have a nonstick omelet pan.

minute, the bottom will be set. Flip the omelet (just go for it with a confident flick of the wrist, or use a larger spatula, or put a plate over the skillet and invert, then slide the omelet back in), and cook for 15 to 30 seconds longer. Remove from the heat.

ADD THE LOX AND YOGURT. Scatter the minced lox evenly over the omelet. Spoon the yogurt on the lox.

SERVE. Fold the omelet in half, slide onto a plate, sprinkle with the chives, and eat immediately.

Icelandic Skyr in the United States
SMÁRI YOGURT

Icelander Smári Ásmundsson's journey to becoming a skyr producer began with a case of the Icelandic-style strained yogurt that his mother would carry in her suitcase every time she came to visit him. A former photographer, he turned his attention to food, spurred on by his new role as a father. "I became interested in improving our diet," he said. "I was discouraged by the conventional foods that were here in the United States."

"Skyr is a huge part of Icelandic culture," Ásmundsson said. "When I was growing up, it was the fast food of my youth. It's very healthy and satisfying."

As he began to research the yogurt market, Ásmundsson discovered that an old family friend in Iceland was a well-regarded skyr master. "So I studied with him and started making it for my boy at home."

Though Smári Organics, headquartered in Petaluma, California, now sells Pure (its version of plain), strawberry, vanilla, and blueberry, the skyr of Asmundsson's youth was always unflavored. "We'd eat the pure one and put a little milk on it to thin it out, or after dinner we'd eat it with cream and brown sugar." He'd also top it with muesli, blueberries, or crowberries (small, dark berries also found in Alaska).

Most Icelandic skyr is naturally nonfat because the whey was traditionally strained off to be used for meat preservation and the cream was skimmed from the top and churned into butter. This is how Smári Organics makes its skyr today. Made from nonfat milk from a Wisconsin co-op, Smári has 20 grams of protein per serving.

Some other manufacturers follow this process, but they add milk fat back in. "We would never," Ásmundsson said. Our goal is to make yogurt as healthy and tasty as possible. It has to be healthy enough so I feel good about giving my son a cup or two a day, and it has to be tasty enough that he will want to eat a cup or two a day."

As a parent myself, I can't question that logic.

Tenderest Cardamom Pancakes

3 cups all-purpose flour

2 teaspoons baking powder

1 teaspoon baking soda

1 teaspoon ground cardamom

¼ teaspoon kosher salt

1½ cups plain yogurt (not Greek) or whey (see page 331)

1½ cups milk, preferably whole or 2%

4 large eggs

4 tablespoons (½ stick) unsalted butter, melted and cooled slightly, plus additional butter for the griddle

Maple syrup and/or additional yogurt, for serving (optional)

MAKES 30 TO 40 PANCAKES

Yogurt transforms a simple whisk-up batter into the lightest, fluffiest, tenderest, and most magical pancakes imaginable. Any extra batter keeps nicely in a covered jar in the fridge for 2 or 3 days.

MIX THE BATTER. In a large bowl, whisk together the flour, baking powder, baking soda, cardamom, and salt. In a medium bowl, whisk the yogurt and milk until smooth. Then whisk in the eggs, followed by the butter. Scrape the wet ingredients into the dry. Switch to a large silicone spatula and combine thoroughly, sweeping the sides and bottom of the bowl; do not overmix. The batter will be a bit lumpy but should have no powdery pockets. Set aside to rest for 5 to 10 minutes.

COOK AND SERVE. Heat a cast-iron griddle or skillet over medium-high heat. When a drop of water on the griddle sizzles and evaporates, coat the griddle with butter. Dragging your spoon or scoop in a round (this creates thinner pancakes), distribute about 3 tablespoons batter per pancake onto the griddle. Cook for 1 to 2 minutes per side, until deep golden. Work in batches, slicking the griddle with more butter as you go. Serve with maple syrup and additional yogurt, if desired.

Yo!

If you make pancakes with any regularity, invest in a cast-iron griddle or skillet. Nonstick pans won't come anywhere close to helping you reach true pancake nirvana.

Yogurt Crepes with Assorted Fillings

4 tablespoons (½ stick) unsalted butter, melted and slightly cooled, plus a few tablespoons additional melted butter for the skillet

1 cup all-purpose flour

1 cup plain yogurt (not Greek)

4 large eggs

About ⅔ cup whey (see page 331) or water

¼ teaspoon kosher salt

Fillings and/or accompaniments of your choice (see sidebar)

Yo!

The laws of nature almost guarantee that the first crepe will be a dud. Have heart if yours falls apart and make sure your skillet is hot enough.

MAKES 9 OR 10 CREPES

Yogurt crepes are just as lacy, versatile, and special as traditional ones, but with a pleasant tang. Plus, this batter whisks up fast—no blender required. I've listed some of my favorite sweet and savory crepe pairings here, but don't feel boxed in. Use what you love and what you have on hand. If you've got any leftover whey from straining your own yogurt, go ahead and use it here.

MAKE THE BATTER. In a large bowl, whisk the butter, flour, yogurt, eggs, whey or water, and salt until smooth. Let rest for 10 minutes. The batter should have some body but should drip easily from the whisk.

MAKE THE CREPES. Heat a 10-inch nonstick skillet over medium-high heat until a drop of water on the skillet sizzles and evaporates. Using a silicone pastry brush, brush the bottom and sides of the skillet generously with melted butter. Tilt the skillet forward, then pour ⅓ cup batter close to the lip of the skillet. Quickly swirl so the batter coats the bottom. (If the batter is too thick to swirl and coat easily, whisk 1 to 2 tablespoons water into the remaining batter.) Cook until the underside of the crepe is lacy and nicely browned and the edges look dry, 1 to 2 minutes. Flip and cook for 1 to 2 minutes longer. Invert onto a plate. Brush a bit more butter onto the skillet and repeat with the remaining batter, brushing the skillet with more melted butter between batches. Stack the crepes on the plate. Serve with the accompaniments of your choice.

The Fillings

» Fresh lemon juice and coarse sugar

» Fresh fruit and Greek yogurt

» Butter and maple syrup

» Bananas and Nutella

» Roasted Blueberry Compote (page 46)

» Strawberry-Rhubarb Compote (page 45)

» Burnt Sugar–Apricot Halves (page 53)

» Fried eggs and ham

» Spinach, apples, and Gruyère

» Any frozen yogurt (see Lick, page 303), for dessert crepes

From one country to another, one region to another, milk varies in flavor. This makes sense, since the grasses animals graze upon vary in their composition, which is intimately tied to the environment, the geography, the seasons, the weather, and the soil. This is terroir, that elusive concept that a region's foods reflect both the tangible and intangible qualities of the earth. Local variability in food is something to be sought, valued, and preserved.

However, when a handful of huge, industrial dairies and factory farms monopolize the market, feed their cows grain, and produce milk on enormous scale, terroir is lost. Terroir is also lost when milk is ultrapasteurized, that process of heating it to superhigh temperatures to extend its shelf life. Uniformity rushes in; terroir seeps out. It's one or the other.

So to discover an operation like Straus Family Creamery in Marshall, located in Marin County, California, is a joy. "The whole reason we exist is to give small family farmers a reason to survive," said Albert Straus on my visit in the fall of 2013. The Straus Creamery works hand in hand with a select group of small local farms that supply their organic milk. This allows them to support their producers, and it also allows them to control the Creamery's products from farm to bottle. The quality and flavor in all their dairy comes from the unique grasses growing on the coastal plains of Tomales Bay.

Albert's parents, Bill and Ellen Straus, were European Jews who escaped the Continent and moved to the United States. In 1941 they began farming in California with twenty-three cows they named after friends and family. Ellen was actively involved in environmental advocacy throughout her life, working tirelessly to protect as much local land as possible through the creation of the Marin Agricultural Land Trust, which she cofounded.

Albert Straus occupies an unusual position in the industry: He's both a dairy farmer and a processor, and because he wears both hats, he's spent much of his career pioneering ways for producers and processors to work together toward common goals. When his father fell ill, Straus took over the dairy and made the risky decision to convert it to 100 percent organic, the first of its kind in the western United States. The creamery soon followed, since the dairy needed a place to sell its organic milk. Thus Straus Family Creamery was born, becoming the first certified-organic creamery in the nation, producing both pourable "European-style" and thick Greek yogurt. Its distribution is regional, with sales channels concentrated in California and the western United States.

The whole-milk Greek yogurt sells better than its nonfat counterpart. But why, I asked, since everyone says people want nonfat yogurt? Straus laughed. "Because people say and do different things."

The European-style yogurt that Straus produces is thinner than other yogurts. It's "vat-set," meaning the inoculated milk ferments in large stainless-steel vats overnight, and once the pH drops, it is pumped into a filler to fill the cups. ("Cup-set" yogurt is more common in the industry. In that process, the inoculated milk ferments in the actual cups—generally plastic—that consumers purchase, rather than in large tanks. Straus prefers his vat-set method, because "you're not volatilizing plastics" by filling them with hot liquid. He also doesn't have to worry about off flavors from the plastic since stainless steel is inert.)

Straus yogurt is tarter than most since it's pulled from processing at a lower pH than that of many of its competitors. "It's a flavor profile that I like," Straus said. It's the flavor of the land, and if you close your eyes, you can almost smell the grass.

Harvest Waffles

3 cups all-purpose flour

1 tablespoon pumpkin pie spice

2 teaspoons baking powder

1 teaspoon baking soda

¼ teaspoon kosher salt

1 cup pumpkin puree (canned pure pumpkin is fine)

1 cup plain seltzer

1 cup plain yogurt (not Greek), preferably low-fat or whole-milk

4 large eggs, lightly beaten

4 tablespoons (½ stick) unsalted butter, melted and slightly cooled, plus additional melted butter for the waffle iron

1 medium unpeeled red apple, grated on the small holes of a box grater (it will be pulpy)

3 tablespoons dark brown sugar

Soft butter and maple syrup, or creamy maple syrup (see Yo!), for serving

MAKES 6 TO 10 BELGIAN-STYLE WAFFLES, DEPENDING ON THE SIZE OF YOUR WAFFLE IRON

With whispers of pumpkin, apple, and fall spices, these crisp-on-the-outside, light-on-the-inside waffles are made for cool autumn week-ends. Go old-school by topping them with soft butter and plenty of maple syrup, or see Yo! for a creamier alternative. Extra batter stores well, covered and refrigerated, and may be thinned with a bit of milk to make pancakes the next day.

MIX THE BATTER. Into a large bowl, sift the flour, pumpkin pie spice, baking powder, baking soda, and salt. In another large bowl, whisk the pumpkin, seltzer, yogurt, eggs, melted butter, apple, and brown sugar until smooth. Pour the wet ingredients into the dry. Using a whisk at first and then switching to a silicone spatula, blend until all powdery bits are incorporated. Do not overmix. Set aside to rest for about 10 minutes while you preheat the waffle iron.

COOK AND SERVE. Brush melted butter on the top and bottom plates of the hot waffle iron. Ladle in the batter according to the manufac-turer's directions (¾ cup to 1 cup, most likely) and cook through. I recommend serving these as they come out of the iron. Repeat with the remaining batter. Serve hot, with soft butter and maple syrup, or with the creamy yogurt maple syrup.

(continued)

Yo!

The secret to a perfectly textured waffle lies in generously brushing the hot waffle iron with melted butter. Cooking spray prevents sticking, but it doesn't deliver the same textural benefits. Use a silicone brush.

For a creamy take on maple syrup: Slowly whisk ¼ cup warm maple syrup into ½ cup plain yogurt until very smooth and the color of café au lait. (The mixture will look separated at first, but keep whisking and it'll smooth right out.) This will yield ¾ cup.

Overnight Challah French Toast

1 loaf challah

2 tablespoons soft unsalted butter, plus 1 tablespoon cold unsalted butter

1 cup plain yogurt (not Greek)

2 large eggs

1 tablespoon honey

2 teaspoons pure vanilla extract

Zest of 1 large orange, plus (optional) additional zest for garnish

Confectioners' sugar and/or additional honey, for serving (optional)

Yo!

There's no reason to remove the crust from your challah. The custard will soak into the bread fully and soften everything (crusts included) overnight.

SERVES 4 TO 6

Prep this breakfast the night before and come morning, slide it in the oven while you sip your morning brew. In 30 minutes, you'll have a rich, filling breakfast for family or friends.

PREP THE BREAD. Cut the challah into ¾-inch slices. Do a test run to see how many pieces will fit into your baking dish in a single layer without overlapping. I recommend a broilerproof 13-by-10-inch or 14-by-10-inch baking dish with 2-inch sides, or thereabouts. Using half the soft butter, butter one side of each bread slice and lay into the dish, buttered side down. Now tear as many of the remaining slices as you'll need to fill in any corners, crevices, or spaces between the existing slices. Spread the rest of the soft butter on one side of each of those pieces. Fit them in, also buttered side down. (Reserve the tablespoon of cold butter for baking.)

MAKE THE CUSTARD. In a large bowl, whisk together the yogurt, eggs, honey, vanilla, and zest. Pour over the challah, smoothing with an offset spatula to coat evenly. Lift up a few pieces to let the custard flow underneath. Cover and refrigerate overnight.

BAKE. In the morning, preheat the oven to 350°F with a rack in the upper third.

Dot the challah all over with the remaining 1 tablespoon butter. Bake, uncovered, for about 30 minutes, or until the custard is set and the challah is nearly firm to the touch. Flip on the broiler and broil for 2 minutes, watching carefully, until the top is golden brown and speckled.

SERVE. Garnish the French toast with more orange zest, if using, and sift with confectioners' sugar and/or drizzle with honey, if desired.

Green Apple Scones with Cider Glaze

½ cup (solid) coconut oil (see Yo!)

2⅓ cups all-purpose flour

¼ cup dark brown sugar

2 teaspoons baking powder

½ teaspoon baking soda

¼ teaspoon ground cinnamon

½ teaspoon kosher salt

¾ cup plus 2 tablespoons plain Greek yogurt

1 large egg

½ teaspoon pure vanilla extract

½ large tart green apple (such as Granny Smith), unpeeled, cored and cut into ¼-inch dice (about 1 cup)

1 cup confectioners' sugar

1 to 2 tablespoons apple cider or apple juice, mixed with a pinch each of ground cinnamon, cloves, and nutmeg

MAKES 8 SCONES

I met Coco Morante, a young professional opera singer who also knows her way around the kitchen, in a weekly food writing group. (Her website is titled It was Just Right.) When she offered to contribute a yogurt-based scone to this collection, I was thrilled, especially when she allowed me to tinker ever so slightly with her offering. What follows is my cider-glazed green apple twist on her original pastry. (See the Variation for Coco's version.)

CHILL THE FAT. After measuring, chill the coconut oil for 15 to 30 minutes.

PREP. Preheat the oven to 400°F, with racks in the upper and lower thirds. Line two baking sheets with parchment.

MAKE THE DOUGH. In a large bowl, whisk together the flour, brown sugar, baking powder, baking soda, cinnamon, and salt. Cut in the chilled coconut oil with a pastry blender or a fork until all the chunks are floury and the size of large peas. In a small bowl, whisk the yogurt, egg, and vanilla until smooth, then scrape this over the flour-fat mixture. Stir slowly with a wooden spoon until moist clumps form. (The mixture will start out dry, but be patient.) With a floury hand, start squeezing the clumps together until you get a single kneadable mass. Knead the mixture in the bowl 3 to 5 times, sprinkle in the apple, then knead about 5 more times until you have a cohesive dough. Do not overwork.

Yo!

Coconut oil is a subtly flavored, shelf-stable saturated fat lauded for its heart-healthy fatty-acid profile. Find it in glass jars near the other oils in major supermarkets and natural foods stores.

While I love the subtle flavor here from the coconut oil, you may substitute 8 tablespoons (1 stick) of cold unsalted butter—cut into cubes—instead.

BAKE. Turn the dough onto a floured board and pat into a 7-inch circle, 1¼ inches thick. Cut the dough into 8 wedges and transfer 4 to each baking sheet. (If the scones feel warm to the touch, pop the sheets in the freezer for about 10 minutes.) Bake for 18 to 22 minutes, until the scones are firm and the undersides are golden brown. Cool on a rack.

MAKE THE GLAZE. Sift the confectioners' sugar into a medium bowl. Whisk in 1 tablespoon of the cider or juice. Slowly add the second tablespoon as needed to produce a thick glaze. Drizzle the glaze over the scones and serve.

VARIATION

To stick with Coco's original flavors, replace the apple with diced Bosc pear. For the glaze, steep 2 bags of black tea in 1 cup boiling water for 5 minutes. Mix 1 cup confectioners' sugar with ½ teaspoon each ground cardamom and cinnamon, ¼ teaspoon each cloves and ginger, and ⅛ teaspoon nutmeg, then whisk in 2 tablespoons of the tea.

Ultimate Granola

3 cups old-fashioned rolled oats

1 cup flaxseed meal (see Yo!)

½ cup hemp seeds

½ cup chopped pecans

½ cup chopped almonds

½ cup chopped walnuts

½ cup raw unsalted pepitas (pumpkin seeds)

½ cup unsweetened shredded coconut

1½ teaspoons ground cinnamon

1 tablespoon kosher salt

⅔ cup dark brown sugar

⅓ cup coconut oil (see Yo!, page 91)

⅓ cup honey

⅓ cup water

2 teaspoons pure vanilla extract

MAKES ABOUT 10 CUPS GRANOLA

A yogurt cookbook merits the best granola recipe possible, one exploding with crunch, flavor, and personality. This version came about the way many well-loved recipes do: It was passed on to me by a friend, Denise Madruga, who'd spent years tinkering with a recipe from an old issue of *Bon Appétit* magazine. I tooled around with Madruga's version, massaging the flavor profile, tweaking the cook time and temperature, and trying to get the texture to meet my platonic ideal of crispness, crunchiness, and toasty goodness. I also leave out the traditional dried fruits, preferring to toss them on top when serving.

PREP. Preheat the oven to 275°F, with a rack in the center position. Line a large, heavy baking sheet with parchment. (If your baking sheet is smaller than 18 by 12 inches, use two.)

MAKE. In a large bowl, combine the oats, flaxseed meal, hemp seeds, pecans, almonds, walnuts, pepitas, coconut, cinnamon, and salt. Sprinkle the brown sugar on top, breaking up any clumps with your hands. Toss thoroughly.

If the coconut oil is solid, microwave the amount you'll need until melted, about 1 minute. (Or melt it over low heat in a small saucepan.) Whisk the honey, water, and vanilla into the coconut oil.

Pour the wet ingredients over the dry, scraping in every last clingy drop, and stir for a solid minute so all the oats, nuts, and seeds are evenly moistened and coated. Transfer to the baking sheet, smooth into a thick, even layer, and slide into the oven. Bake for 65 to 75 minutes total, stirring carefully every 20 to 25 minutes (set a timer, as

stirring is vital), lifting the edges toward the center and then smoothing out the layer each time you stir. The granola should be good and brown. Turn off the oven but leave the granola in with the door closed for 10 minutes longer.

COOL. Let the granola cool completely on the baking sheet. (The granola will become crisp and crunchy as it cools.) Transfer to a lidded airtight container.

STORE. Store at room temperature for up to 10 days.

Yo!

You'll find flaxseed meal and hemp seeds—rich with protein, fiber, and good fats—in natural foods stores. After locating them, head to the bulk bins to stock up on all the remaining dry ingredients. Buying in bulk will help keep costs down and ensure you get exactly the quantities you need. If you can't find hemp seeds, skip them in favor of chia seeds, sesame seeds, or even unsalted sunflower seeds. Don't drive all over creation to find them.

September Breakfast (Sweet-and-Sour Flatbread)

1 cup seedless red grapes, such as Red Flame

1¼ cups multicolored cherry or grape tomatoes, halved

2 tablespoons extra-virgin olive oil

1 teaspoon syrupy balsamic vinegar, or a bit more, to taste

½ cup walnuts, toasted (see Yo!) and coarsely chopped

Kosher salt (optional)

4 to 8 tablespoons labneh, homemade (page 329) or store-bought (see Yo!)

4 whole-wheat flatbreads or pitas, toasted

Freshly ground pepper

Yo!

Toast the walnuts in a preheated 350°F oven for 8 to 10 minutes, until fragrant and lightly colored.

SERVES 4

In northern California, prime tomato and grape seasons collide in early September. Cherry tomato plants go haywire and grapes spill from market tables in riotous hues. I love pairing these two foods together for a sweet-and-sour morning bite, letting their juices run for an hour or so before spooning them over flatbread smeared with labneh (yogurt cheese). This is knife-and-fork food (because it's messy) but not the least bit formal.

PREP. Preheat the oven to 300°F, with a rack in the center position. Line a baking sheet with parchment.

ROAST. Tumble the grapes onto the prepared baking sheet. Roast for 65 to 75 minutes, until the grapes look sunken and shriveled with a few darkish spots. (You'll have about ½ cup postroasting.) Cool completely. Use immediately, or pack into a covered container with any juices from the baking sheet and refrigerate until needed.

MACERATE. In a medium bowl, combine the roasted grapes, tomatoes, oil, and vinegar. Toss well. Let stand for 1 hour at room temperature so that everything becomes very juicy. Stir in the walnuts and a pinch or two of salt, if desired.

(continued)

SERVE. Spread the labneh over the toasted flatbreads, using 1 to 2 tablespoons per serving. Spoon the grape-tomato mixture over each flatbread. Finish with a generous grinding of black pepper.

Yo!

Roasting the grapes concentrates their sweetness, but the resulting flavor is deep and complex, not at all sugary.

For maximum convenience, roast the grapes at least 1 day ahead. Refrigerated, covered, they will keep for several days. Since you're taking the time to roast them, consider doubling their quantity and pairing the extras with cheese, olives, and prosciutto for a predinner bite.

If you're not making your own (see page 329), look for plastic containers of labneh in the refrigerated case at Middle Eastern markets.

Dip, Dress, Drizzle, Spread

Dip, Dress, Drizzle, Spread

Dips are inherently social. They're shareable, casual, and generally simple to make, all of which add to their enduring and worldwide appeal.

The dips, spreads, and dressings in this chapter span the distance from a California-centric avocado ranch to the infinitely customizable Indian raita to a bevy of spreads using labneh, that smooth and salty yogurt cheese enjoyed throughout the Middle East. Greek tzatziki swallows a head of garlic, and spinach goes Turkish, all in the service of soothing your hunger before or during a meal.

Unless otherwise noted, most of the recipes benefit from a few hours in the refrigerator. This chills them nicely, of course, but time also deepens, infuses, and melds flavors, making them more impactful. If a bit of whey floats on top during this rest period, just stir it gently back in before serving.

The Recipes

Sun-Dried Tomato and Feta Dip

1½ cups plain Greek yogurt, preferably whole-milk

¼ cup (1 ounce) drained oil-packed sun-dried tomatoes

¼ cup (1 ounce) crumbled feta

1 garlic clove, coarsely chopped

½ or 1 anchovy fillet (from a tin), coarsely chopped

1 teaspoon fresh lemon juice

½ teaspoon freshly ground pepper

¼ teaspoon dried or ½ teaspoon chopped fresh oregano, plus (optional) fresh oregano leaves, for garnish

Crudités, chilled, for serving

MAKES 2 CUPS DIP

This dip may look like Russian dressing, but it's got a bit more body and far greater depth of flavor. Break out your favorite crudités and a few more upscale dippers (try blanched and iced asparagus spears, endive leaves, and jicama sticks), grab some friends, and sweep through the dip till there's nothing left. The small amount of anchovy may sound like something you can skip, but don't. Refrigerate for at least 2 hours so the flavors can blend.

MAKE. Combine all the ingredients, except the fresh oregano garnish (if using) and the crudités, in a food processor. Process until completely smooth. Scrape into a bowl, cover, and refrigerate for at least 2 hours and up to 1 day.

SERVE. Garnish with a few leaves of fresh oregano, if desired, and serve with the crudités.

Turkish-Style Spinach Dip

1 5- or 6-ounce bag baby spinach (3 to 4 cups, packed)

1 cup plain low-fat or whole-milk yogurt, preferably Greek

Kosher salt and freshly ground pepper

1 or 2 garlic cloves, to taste

⅛ teaspoon dried mint

Squeeze of fresh lemon juice

Extra-virgin olive oil, for drizzling

Warm flatbreads or Yogurt-Plumped Lamb Kebabs (page 208), for serving

MAKES 1⅓ CUPS DIP

The most popular yogurt dip in Turkey may be *cacik*, a cooling mix of yogurt, grated cucumbers, and garlic, essentially Turkey's version of Greek tzatziki (see page 108). Versions of this dip are also widely consumed in Iran and the Balkans. Swap spinach in for the cucumber, sauté some onions, and you've got *yoğurtlu ispanak*, a thicker, greener dip with an otherwise similar flavor profile. In my streamlined version, I've opted for baby spinach and omitted the onions.

WILT THE SPINACH. Rinse the spinach in a colander but do not dry. Heat a large skillet over medium-high heat. Add the spinach and toss with tongs until wilted and the liquid evaporates, 2 to 3 minutes. Transfer to a triple thickness of paper towels and let cool completely. Squeeze out any moisture, then finely chop.

MAKE THE DIP. Whisk the yogurt in a medium bowl with a generous pinch each of salt and pepper until light. Grate in the garlic. Add the spinach and mint and stir well. Cover and refrigerate for at least 2 hours so the flavors can develop.

SERVE. Transfer the dip to a serving bowl and make a slight indentation in the dip with the back of a spoon. Squeeze the lemon over the dip, drizzle with olive oil, and season lightly with salt. Serve with warm flatbreads or the kebabs.

Smoky Eggplant-Tahini Dip

3 to 3½ pounds globe eggplant (3 or 4), pricked in spots

1½ teaspoons kosher salt

3 garlic cloves

½ cup plain whole-milk Greek yogurt

2 tablespoons tahini

¼ teaspoon ground white pepper or freshly ground black

Sumac (optional; see Yo!), ½ lemon, and extra-virgin olive oil, for serving

Warm pita or other flatbreads and crudités, for serving

MAKES 2½ CUPS DIP

While visiting Tel Aviv, I toured the kitchen at Dallal, a charming restaurant where I cracked the code of something that had mystified me for years: how Middle Eastern restaurants impart such strong, smoky, intoxicating flavors to eggplant. The cooks charred eggplants directly over the grates of an indoor grill. Eureka! Blackening eggplants infuses their flesh with notes of deep, intense smoke, an effect not achievable with other cooking methods. My yogurt-based twist on baba ghanouj incorporates this technique. Chill for a few hours before serving, if time allows, so the flavors can fully develop.

PREP THE GRILL. Heat an outdoor grill to 500°F.

BLACKEN THE EGGPLANT. Lay the whole eggplants on the hot grates. Close the lid and grill until the skins have charred, blackened, and become brittle and the flesh yields easily when pricked, 40 to 45 minutes, turning every 10 minutes to evenly blacken all sides. Alternatively, you can broil the eggplants (see Variation).

MAKE THE GARLIC PASTE. Meanwhile, on a cutting board, spoon the salt over the garlic cloves. Mince the garlic and salt together, then, using the flat side of your knife, slide and press the mixture against the board repeatedly until you have a smoothish paste. Stir the garlic paste into the yogurt. Cover and chill until needed.

DRAIN THE EGGPLANT. When the eggplants are ready, halve them lengthwise. Scrape the flesh into a strainer set over the sink or a bowl. Discard the skins. Let drain until the flesh is completely cool. Puree. You should have 2 cups.

FINISH, CHILL, AND SERVE. Stir the eggplant puree, tahini, and pepper into the garlicky yogurt. Cover and refrigerate for a few hours, if you can. (If not, serve right away.) Spread the dip in a shallow bowl, sprinkle lightly with sumac (if using), squeeze with the juice of the lemon half, and drizzle with olive oil. Serve with warm pita and crudités.

VARIATION

Broil the pricked, whole eggplants on a foil-lined baking sheet 9 inches from the heat source until charred and collapsed, 40 to 50 minutes total, turning every 7 to 10 minutes. Proceed as directed. If going this route, make sure your oven's impeccably clean or it will smoke.

Blood Orange, Kalamata, and Red Onion Dip

¾ cup plain whole-milk Greek yogurt or labneh, homemade (page 329) or store-bought (see Yo!, page 97)

Kosher salt

1 blood orange (or Valencia, Cara Cara, or navel orange if blood oranges are unavailable)

¼ cup pitted kalamata olives, drained and minced

1 tablespoon minced red onion

2 teaspoons extra-virgin olive oil

Freshly ground pepper

⅛ teaspoon sumac (optional; see Yo!, page 105)

Toasted whole-wheat pita triangles, for serving

SERVES 2

This is one of my favorite ways to eat yogurt. Heaped with bright and juicy blood oranges, briny olives, and flecks of sharp red onion, it's a luxuriously simple interplay of flavors, textures, and colors with very few ingredients.

PREP THE YOGURT AND ORANGE. If using yogurt, season it with a good pinch of salt. (Don't salt the labneh.) Scrape the yogurt into a shallow bowl and smooth it with the back of a spoon to create a wide indentation. Using a sharp knife, cut away the peel and white pith from the orange and dice the flesh.

SEASON AND SERVE. Scatter the orange pieces over the yogurt. Sprinkle the olives and onion on top. Drizzle with the oil in a thin stream. Season lightly with salt and more aggressively with pepper. Dust with the sumac, if using. Serve immediately with the toasted pita triangles.

Yo!

The orange will weep juice into the dip over time, so plan to make this just before serving.

Avocado Ranch Dressing

1 cup plain low-fat or whole-milk yogurt (not Greek)

½ cup mayonnaise

2 tablespoons water

1 tablespoon minced fresh chives or scallion greens

2½ teaspoons white wine vinegar

1 teaspoon granulated onion or onion powder

½ teaspoon each kosher salt and freshly ground pepper

1 garlic clove

½ small ripe avocado

Yo!

Older garlic cloves have a central green shoot, which is bitter. Cut it out and discard.

MAKES 2 CUPS DRESSING

At some point, I stopped buying salad dressing. It wasn't a moral choice, but over time I found myself whisking up vinaigrettes and blending dressings so regularly that I no longer reached for bottled versions at all. Now I like to experiment—with different vinegars, flavored oils, fresh herbs, and spices plucked from my jumbled mess of a spice drawer. Here's my version of a mild, creamy ranch. Drizzle it over simple lettuce leaves or more complex (and colorful) vegetablecentric salads.

MIX THE YOGURT. In a medium bowl, whisk together the yogurt, mayonnaise, water, chives or scallion, vinegar, granulated onion or onion powder, salt, and pepper. Using a Microplane, grate the garlic clove directly into the bowl. (Otherwise, mince it.)

ADD THE AVOCADO. If you have an immersion blender, add the avocado and blend the dressing until smooth. If you don't have an immersion blender, whisk the dressing, then mash the avocado thoroughly with a fork and whisk it vigorously into the dressing to combine. Transfer to a covered jar and refrigerate for at least a few hours or up to 3 days, covered. (The flavors intensify over time.) Shake before using.

Stella's Tzatziki

1½ English cucumbers, the whole cucumber peeled, the half cucumber unpeeled

2½ teaspoons kosher salt

1 medium head garlic (about 2 ounces), peeled

2 teaspoons white vinegar

2 tablespoons extra-virgin olive oil, plus additional for drizzling

4 cups plain whole-milk Greek yogurt (see Yo!)

½ teaspoon ground white pepper

Warm pita, for serving

Yo!

You may use sheep's milk or cow's milk yogurt in this dip. (Leonetti likes both.)

Give yourself plenty of time for the cucumber to drain and for the dip to chill. The flavors really pop after a few hours.

MAKES 5 CUPS DIP

On the Greek island of Paros, Stella Leonetti's Restaurant Rafeletti serves an intense, creamy tzatziki flavored with a head of garlic. This may be the best tzatziki you'll ever have.

PREP THE CUCUMBER. Using the large holes of a box grater or the medium shredding disk in a food processor, grate all the cucumbers. Toss with 1½ teaspoons of the salt, transfer to a fine-mesh strainer set over a deep bowl, and let stand for 1 hour to drain. Spoon the cucumber into a nut milk bag (a mesh bag generally used for making almond milk; see Sources), cheesecloth, or large swath (and double thickness) of paper towels and squeeze dry.

MAKE THE GARLIC PASTE. Put the garlic cloves in a food processor. Add the remaining 1 teaspoon salt and the vinegar. Turn the machine on, stream the 2 tablespoons oil in through the feed tube, and let the machine run until it pushes all the garlic to the sides. Stop the machine, scrape down the sides, push the garlic toward the center, and process again. You'll need to do this five or six times, as the blade will keep pushing the garlic toward the perimeter of the machine before it has a chance to fully puree. Eventually, the garlic will turn into a wet, mushy, emulsified paste. You should have about ⅓ cup. Transfer to a bowl and cover until ready to use.

COMBINE AND CHILL. Add the cucumber and garlic paste to a large bowl. Stir in the yogurt and white pepper. Combine thoroughly, sweeping the sides and the bottom of the bowl so the garlic paste gets evenly incorporated. Cover tightly and refrigerate for at least 2 hours.

SERVE. Drizzle with more olive oil, and pass warm pita alongside.

Greek Yogurt with Lemon Vinaigrette

2 cups plain Greek yogurt, preferably whole-milk

¼ cup extra-virgin olive oil

2 tablespoons fresh lemon juice

Kosher salt and freshly ground pepper

1 tablespoon pine nuts, lightly toasted in a dry skillet

¼ teaspoon *za'atar*, or a few leaves fresh parsley, chopped

Warm whole-wheat pita triangles, for serving

Yo!

Za'atar is a type of wild thyme often mixed with sumac (a brick-red, sour spice; see page 105), salt, and sesame seeds. Look for it in Middle Eastern markets.

MAKES 2¼ CUPS DIP

A bold pool of lemon vinaigrette adds a sunny hue to a bowl of yogurt, creating a dip with two colors, two textures, and two flavors. I ate a version of it in the morning at a small Israeli inn called Pausa.

MAKE. In a large bowl, beat the yogurt until light and smooth. Scrape it into a shallow, wide serving bowl and smooth with the back of a spoon to create a wide indentation. In a small bowl or liquid measuring cup, whisk the oil and lemon juice until emulsified; season well with salt and pepper. Pour the vinaigrette over the yogurt so it floods the indentation. Sprinkle with the pine nuts and *za'atar* or parsley. Taste, adding a bit more salt, if desired. Serve with warm pita.

Beet Raita with Cumin and Mustard Seeds

1 pound beets (about 5 medium)

2 tablespoons vegetable or grapeseed oil

2 tablespoons water

¾ teaspoon cumin seeds

½ teaspoon black mustard seeds (see Yo!)

4 or 5 fresh curry leaves (see Yo!; optional)

1¼ cups plain low-fat or whole-milk yogurt (not Greek)

½ teaspoon kosher salt

SERVES 4

Cheerful beets bleed their vibrant color into this gorgeous, nearly hot pink raita, a modern spin on a classic Indian side dish. My friend Shefaly Ravula, who generously provided this recipe, adds an additional garnish of crushed peanuts and edible flowers, though I prefer the beautiful simplicity of the seasoned finishing oil (known in India as *tarka* or *tadka*) on its own.

PREP. Preheat the oven to 375°F. Line the bottom of a glass or ceramic baking dish with a sheet of parchment, if desired (to facilitate cleanup).

PREP AND ROAST THE BEETS. Lop off the leafy beet tops, leaving a ½-inch stem attached to the bulbs. (Reserve the leaves for another purpose or discard.) Scrub the beets. Set them in the baking dish and rub with 1 tablespoon of the oil. Splash the water into the dish and cover tightly with foil. Roast for about 1 hour, or longer, until a skewer comes out easily (see Yo!). Cool. Scrape gently with a paring knife to peel, then cut into small dice. (Makes about 2 cups. Use 1 cup here and refrigerate the remaining beets for another use.)

TOAST THE CUMIN. In a small, dry skillet, toast ½ teaspoon of the cumin seeds for 1 to 2 minutes, until fragrant and one shade darker, shaking the skillet so they don't burn. Transfer to a spice grinder or a mortar and pestle and grind into a powder. Set aside. (Note: If using a spice grinder, you'll have an easier time pulverizing a greater quantity of seeds. Consider toasting and grinding 1 to 2 tablespoons at a time and using the extra for a different recipe. It'll keep well in a small, sealed spice jar.)

MAKE THE SEASONED OIL. To the same skillet over medium heat, add the remaining 1 tablespoon oil. Drop in a few mustard seeds. When they begin to pop audibly, add the remaining mustard seeds, the remaining ¼ teaspoon whole (untoasted) cumin seeds, and the curry leaves. Stand back, as they will sputter. (Keep a lid handy to protect against splatters, if needed.) After a few seconds, remove from the heat and transfer to a small dish to stop the cooking.

FINISH THE RAITA. In a medium bowl, whisk the yogurt with the reserved ground cumin and the salt until loose. The consistency should be pourable. Gently stir in the 1 cup diced beets. Scrape in the seasoned oil, making sure to transfer all the seeds from the dish to the raita. (Use all the seasoned oil or leave some behind, if desired.) Serve immediately or refrigerate until ready to eat.

Yo!

Though you'll have more than you need for this recipe, I encourage you to roast a full bunch of beets (generally 1 pound) at a time. They take an hour whether you roast 2 or 12, and once they're cooked, you can enjoy them on salads throughout the week. To test if your beets are thoroughly roasted, poke a thin skewer directly through the foil into each beet. If it withdraws with no resistance, the beets are done. Beets can vary wildly in size, even within a bunch, so you may need more roasting time.

You'll find black mustard seeds at Indian grocers and natural foods stores.

Fresh curry leaves, sold plastic wrapped in Indian markets, resemble small, pliable bay leaves. When sizzled in oil, they add crisp texture, heady aroma, and a unique, exotic flavor to South and Southeast Asian dishes. Despite their name, they are unrelated to the dried, bright yellow Indian spice mix commonly sold as "curry" in American grocery stores. If you can't find them, simply leave them out. (There's no substitute.)

Pomegranate Raita

1 cup plain yogurt (if using Greek, whisk with 3 tablespoons water)

⅓ cup pomegranate seeds

⅓ cup diced tomato

⅓ cup peeled, diced English cucumber

¼ teaspoon kosher salt, or more to taste

A few whole fresh cilantro leaves, for garnish

Cooked rice, naan, or your favorite curry, for serving

MAKES ABOUT 2 CUPS RAITA

Here's a fruity but mild raita that's extraordinarily easy to throw together. It pairs beautifully with any Indian food, like the Chicken Curry with Almond Cream (page 205). Remember to salt it well to bring forth its maximum flavor. Chittu Nagarajan, from Chennai (formerly Madras), who taught me this recipe, says, "We eat this with rice, with naan, with rotis, with anything!"

MAKE. Whisk the yogurt vigorously in a small bowl to loosen. Fold in the pomegranate seeds, tomato, cucumber, and salt. Sprinkle with the cilantro leaves. Serve immediately with rice, naan, or your favorite curry.

VARIATION

To turn this raita from soothing and gentle to zingy and flavor-forward, stir in a bit of freshly grated ginger and/or minced green chile (with or without seeds).

An Everyday Staple

Shefaly Ravula, an Indian-American cooking teacher based in Austin, Texas, explains that while many Americans view raita as a condiment—something to dip, just barely, the corners of their naan into, or to drizzle lightly over their main courses—Indians do not. "You're meant to eat a good amount of it," she says. "People here don't realize how much of it you're supposed to eat. It's a side dish. You're supposed to spoon it into your mouth." She adds that cooling yogurt dishes like raita are more of a staple feature of afternoon meals than of those eaten in the evening.

Shefaly loves developing creative raitas with fresh produce, like beets, finely diced carrots, or chopped nectarines. These yogurt-based sides accompany nearly every Indian curry.

Labneh Spheres Preserved in Olive Oil

1 cup labneh, homemade (page 329) or store-bought (see Yo!, page 97)

Olive oil

Crackers and/or toasted flatbreads, for serving

MAKES ABOUT 16 TABLESPOON-SIZE SPHERES

All across the Middle East, you'll find these small, creamy bites of labneh (yogurt cheese) in most homes, since they're a popular way to extend labneh's shelf life. I enjoyed them in Israel as part of a spread before the meal when my hostess appeared with a repurposed glass jar and fished out the spheres one by one from their pool of fruity, green oil. Plan ahead, as you need to drain the little spheres overnight to rid them of their moisture.

MAKE THE LABNEH SPHERES. Set a rack over a baking sheet. Line the rack with a single layer of paper towels.

Using a tablespoon-size scoop (or a melon baller and a spoon), dole out mounds of labneh onto the rack. Don't worry too much about making perfect spheres at this point. Rough mounds are fine.

REFRIGERATE THE LABNEH. Cover the labneh with another single layer of paper towels and refrigerate for 24 hours, changing the paper towels both on top of and underneath the labneh two or three times if you think of it. The whey from the labneh will drain away, leaving the mounds a bit drier and firmer.

STORE IN OIL. The next day, remove the mounds and massage them lightly between your palms to make them more spherical. Transfer to a jar and top off with olive oil, making sure the spheres are completely submerged, as the oil acts as a preservative. Refrigerate until ready to serve, up to several weeks. (If the oil solidifies, fish out the spheres you plan to eat and leave them at room temperature. The oil will liquefy.)

Toppings

¼ to ½ teaspoon of any or all of the following

» *Za'atar* (see Yo!, page 111)

» Saffron threads

» Sumac (see Yo!, page 105)

» Dried or minced fresh mint

» Minced fresh herbs (tarragon, parsley, thyme, oregano, and/or chives are all nice)

» Crushed organic rose petals

» Other pulverized toasted seeds, herbs, or ground toasted nuts that suit your fancy (get creative!)

SERVE. Serve with crackers or flatbreads, on a platter with or without toothpicks.

VARIATION: FANCY-STYLE LABNEH SPHERES

Using a small spoon, remove each labneh sphere from the jar and blot off the excess oil, if necessary. Set on a platter. Dust each sphere lightly with a different topping from the accompanying list, using a small strainer for the sumac to sift out any clumps. Drizzle with olive oil, if desired, and serve with crackers and/or toasted flatbreads.

Labneh with Tomatoes, Pesto, and Tapenade

FOR THE ROASTED TOMATOES

2 cups cherry tomatoes, halved

1 tablespoon extra-virgin olive oil

Kosher salt and freshly ground pepper

FOR THE PISTACHIO PESTO

1 garlic clove, smashed

¼ cup unsalted pistachios

½ cup (packed) fresh basil leaves, coarsely chopped

¼ teaspoon kosher salt

3 tablespoons extra-virgin olive oil

(continued)

SERVES UP TO 12, FEWER IF YOU SERVE THE SPREADS IN STAGES

My inspiration for this recipe comes from a dip I enjoyed at the boisterous Jerusalem restaurant Machneyuda. There, Chef Uri Navon serves several colorful spreads in a single bowl, and the result, which resembles a painter's palette, is both playful and renegade. I start with a base of creamy labneh, then top it with generous mounds of roasted tomatoes, pistachio pesto, and kalamata tapenade. Make each component separately (you can prepare them all ahead) and use as much as you like of each element.

You'll want to compose only as much of this dip as you plan to serve at once. Store the remaining components separately in the fridge, and use fresh labneh for subsequent batches. The smaller amount of labneh will serve 4 to 6, the large amount 10 to 12.

ROAST THE TOMATOES. Preheat the oven to 325°F. Line a baking sheet with parchment.

Lay the tomatoes cut side up on the sheet and drizzle with the oil. Sprinkle lightly with salt and pepper. Roast until collapsed, 30 to 40 minutes. Cool. (Makes 1 generous cup.)

MAKE THE PESTO. In a mini food processor, pulse the garlic, pistachios, basil, and salt until finely chopped. Add the oil a bit at a time, processing in bursts, until the pesto is emulsified. (Makes ⅓ cup. A little goes a long way.)

(continued)

FOR THE TAPENADE

1 cup pitted kalamata olives, rinsed

1 tablespoon drained capers

¼ teaspoon anchovy paste (optional)

Extra-virgin olive oil, for drizzling (optional)

Squeeze of fresh lemon juice

FOR SERVING

¾ to 1½ cups labneh, homemade (page 329) or store-bought (see Yo!, page 97)

Warm, toasted pita wedges (see Yo!)

MAKE THE TAPENADE. In a mini food processor, pulse the olives, capers, and anchovy paste, if using, until paste-like. Drizzle in a touch of oil, only if desired. Season with lemon juice to taste. (Makes ¾ cup.)

SERVE. Spread the labneh in a shallow serving bowl, using the back of a spoon to make a wide indentation in the center. Dollop with distinct, heaping scoops of the roasted tomatoes, pesto, and tapenade. Serve with warm pita wedges.

Yo!

Because you're making smaller portions of each element than you normally might, I highly recommend using a mini food processor. It's the perfect size for the pesto and tapenade.

To make toasted pita wedges: Cut whole-wheat pitas into wedges. Drizzle lightly with olive oil and sprinkle with salt and pepper, or *za'atar.* Bake in a preheated 400°F oven until crisp, about 10 minutes. Make more than you need, as these disappear fast.

"We live for yogurt," said Chittu Nagarajan, a high-tech entrepreneur who lives in Chennai (formerly Madras), the capital of Tamil Nadu in South India. Nagarajan grew up eating yogurt (which is often referred to as "curds" in South India, or dahi) every day, and still does today.

One reason for yogurt's widespread appeal in South India is the heat not just of the climate but of the food: Fresh and dried chiles feature prominently. Dairy products are better coolants than water; plus water is more likely to be served after an Indian meal than with it. "Give us rice and curds, some salt and pickle, and we South Indians are happy," she said. Many meals also include curd rice, a yogurt-rice mixture, and raita—a yogurt side dish with fruits or vegetables (see page 112 and page 114).

Curd rice was also a fixture in the South Indian home of Pankaj Uttarwar, the Quality Assurance and Resource and Development Director of Straus Family Creamery in Marin County, California. "My mom used to give me curd rice before I'd go to exams," he said. "It's part of the Indian culture to consume yogurt when you're going to an important meeting or you're going through some decision-making process." The reason, he guesses, is a widespread belief that the probiotics in yogurt create enzymes that promote calm and "a stable mental condition." When he reads the new studies concerning relationships among probiotics, gut health, and overall health as part of his work at Straus, Uttarwar understands these long-held traditions in a new light: "Now," he said, laughing, "I know why my mom was forcing us to eat yogurt and curd rice."

Labneh Shmear with Scallion, Dill, and Chive

1 cup labneh, homemade (page 329) or store-bought (see Yo!, page 97)

2 fat scallions, roots trimmed, white and green parts minced, plus additional minced scallions for garnish

2 tablespoons minced shallot

1 tablespoon minced fresh chives, plus additional minced chives for garnish

2 teaspoons (packed) minced fresh dill, plus additional minced dill for garnish

1 small garlic clove, grated

⅛ teaspoon freshly ground pepper

Kosher salt

2 teaspoons extra-virgin olive oil, for garnish

Crackers, bagels, and/or toasted flatbreads, for serving

MAKES 1¼ CUPS SPREAD

Dairy and oniony flavors are a time-tested marriage, whether in sour cream and onion potato chips or the scallion and chive cream cheese at your corner bagel shop. This shmear gets pretty green colors and sharp flavors from various members of the allium family: chives, scallions, shallots, and garlic. Together they cut through the mellow richness of the labneh, but the spread still tastes supremely comforting.

MAKE. In a medium bowl, stir together the labneh, scallions, shallot, chives, dill, garlic, and pepper. Taste. I generally add ½ teaspoon salt to wake up the flavors, but as different labnehs have different salt profiles, you may need less or more. Cover and let stand at room temperature for 30 minutes so the flavors can meld. For best results, refrigerate for a few hours, then return to room temperature for 30 minutes to remove the chill.

SERVE. Drizzle with the oil and sprinkle with minced scallions, chives, and dill. Serve with crackers, bagels, and/or toasted flatbreads.

Labneh Shmear with Garden Vegetables

1 cup labneh, homemade (page 329) or store-bought (see Yo!, page 97)

⅓ cup minced peeled carrot

¼ cup diced red bell pepper

¼ cup diced seeded unpeeled cucumber

2 tablespoons minced red onion

A generous fistful of fresh Italian parsley leaves, minced

Scant ½ teaspoon tomato paste

⅛ teaspoon granulated onion or onion powder

Kosher salt and freshly ground pepper

Bagels, crackers, and/or toasted flatbreads, for serving

MAKES ABOUT 1¼ CUPS SPREAD

A fine dice of crunchy raw vegetables adds texture to this labneh, pretty with flecks of bright orange, red, and green. Vary the vegetables here according to what's in season, and cut them as small as you comfortably can with a knife. (Avoid the temptation to use a food processor, as it causes the vegetables to leach too much liquid.)

MAKE. In a medium bowl, stir together the labneh, carrot, bell pepper, cucumber, red onion, parsley, tomato paste, granulated onion or onion powder, and salt and pepper to taste. (I generally use ¼ teaspoon salt and ⅛ teaspoon pepper, but as different labnehs have different salt profiles, you may need less or more.) Cover and let stand at room temperature for 30 minutes so the flavors can meld.

SERVE. For best results, refrigerate for a few hours, then return to room temperature for 30 minutes to remove the chill before serving with bagels, crackers, and/or toasted flatbreads.

Yo!

For a peppery bite, add a minced radish.

Labneh Shmear with Smoked Salmon and Lemon

1 cup labneh, homemade (page 329) or store-bought (see Yo!, page 97)

4 ounces smoked salmon, minced

2 tablespoons minced red onion

1 teaspoon (packed) lemon zest, plus (optional) additional lemon zest for serving

¼ teaspoon fresh lemon juice

⅛ teaspoon freshly ground pepper

A thin drizzle of extra-virgin olive oil, and/or minced fresh dill, for garnish

Crackers, bagels, and/or toasted flatbreads, for serving

MAKES ABOUT 1⅓ CUPS SPREAD

Bagels smothered with cream cheese and draped with smoked salmon were a Sunday-morning fixture of my youth, one I continue to enjoy on annual visits to my family's home in suburban New York. The salmon platter always features fresh lemon wedges and red onion slivers and is accompanied by a tall pepper mill. I've featured those ingredients in this simple spread with labneh in the starring role.

MAKE. In a medium bowl, stir together the labneh, salmon, onion, lemon zest, lemon juice, and pepper. Cover and let stand at room temperature for 30 minutes so the flavors can meld. For best results, refrigerate for a few hours, then let stand at room temperature for 30 minutes to remove the chill.

SERVE. Garnish with additional lemon zest (if desired), a drizzle of oil, and/or dill, and serve with crackers, bagels, and/or toasted flatbreads.

Yo!

Some seafood counters sell smoked salmon scraps for less money than whole slices. Feel free to use those here.

Salty-Smooth, Creamy-Rich

"To me, yogurt is not sweet."

So says Maureen Abood of Harbor Springs, Michigan, author of *Rose Water & Orange Blossoms: Fresh and Classic Recipes from My Lebanese Kitchen* (2015).

Lightly salted and drained of its whey, yogurt plays a central role on the Lebanese table in the form of rich, thick, and supercreamy labneh. Paired with pita and *za'atar*—that wild thyme–based spice mix common throughout the Middle East—labneh is a breakfast staple.

It's also an integral fixture in *maza*, the small dishes that celebrate bounty. "I really enjoy the fullness of the Lebanese plate," Abood said, sounding almost rhapsodic. "You eat all the flavors together—dips such as hummus, baba ghanouj, labneh—they're all part of this experience." In fact, these dips are meant to be melded and enjoyed as an ensemble, with labneh a crucial player.

Abood makes yogurt (*laban*) every week, a tradition she picked up from her mother, Maryalice, and her grandmother Sarah. She enjoys both the ritual and the results. Store-bought yogurt, she said, "just doesn't taste the same." On special occasions, she employs a trick she learned from her Aunt Hilda: She makes the yogurt, then strains out the whey and adds a touch of cream in its place, using a mixer to incorporate the cream so that the yogurt is perfectly smooth.

The Lebanese love their yogurt, whether salt speckled or cream mounted, in the early hours or when the dinner bell tolls. It's a food integral to their rich, varied, colorful, and flavor-forward diet.

Sip

Few beverages quell hunger and thirst simultaneously like those made with yogurt.

Fruit smoothies, with nothing more than yogurt, fruit, and some kind of liquid to get the blender moving, have been wildly popular in Western cultures for decades; they've also been extremely straightforward.

Now, though, you'll find smoothies packed with leafy greens, oil-rich seeds and nuts, fresh herbs, and exotic spices alongside those with more familiar ingredients like berries and bananas.

If you look further afield, crossing the globe over to Turkey, Iran, and much of South Asia, you'll enjoy yogurt drinks that skate on the side of savory instead of sweet. Whether in Turkish *ayran*, Persian *doogh*, or Indian *chaas*, salt, not sugar, reigns supreme, flavoring yogurt to beat the heat with nary a berry, sugar cube, or honey drizzle in sight.

The pages that follow offer quick and simple recipes for both familiar and less familiar quaffable yogurts. Pull out the blender, grab a straw, and indulge in a classic or try something new. All you need is thirst and a sense of adventure.

The Recipes

Classic Cherry-Banana Smoothie

1 cup frozen pitted cherries

1 fresh or frozen banana, sliced

1 tablespoon seeds (chia, hemp, or ground flaxseed)

⅓ cup plain yogurt

½ cup cold apple juice or other juice (for a sweeter smoothie) or milk (for a less-sweet smoothie)

Yo!

During cherry season, stem, pit, and freeze as many as you can. In the winter months, frozen cherries can be tough to find, and you'll pay dearly for them when you do.

SERVES 2 (8 OUNCES EACH)

Sometimes the simplest recipes are those most worth sharing. Think of this one as a jumping-off point for fruit smoothies in general. Swap in 1 cup of frozen fruit chunks or berries and ½ cup of any fruit juice or dairy or nondairy milk for the fruit and liquid to create endless variations. While fruit smoothies can be made from almost any fruit, cherries and bananas work especially well in balancing yogurt's acidity, erasing the need for added sweeteners.

Combine all the ingredients in a blender and blend until thick and smooth. Serve immediately.

Deep Purple Smoothie

½ cup cold pomegranate juice

1 fresh or frozen banana, cut into chunks

1 cup frozen blueberries

½ cup plain yogurt

½ cup (packed) stemmed kale leaves (I use baby)

1 tablespoon hemp seeds or ground flaxseed

2 teaspoons almond butter (optional)

SERVES 2 (8 OUNCES EACH)

Along with great fruit flavor and stunning, royal color, this smoothie delivers a solid punch of antioxidants to power you for hours. You won't taste the kale.

Combine all the ingredients in a blender and blend until thick and smooth. Serve immediately.

My Green Smoothie

1 cup fresh or frozen pineapple chunks

1 cup seedless grapes

1 cup (packed) baby spinach

3 1-inch-thick slices unpeeled English cucumber

⅓ cup plain yogurt

Scant 1-inch chunk peeled fresh ginger, coarsely chopped

½ cup ice-cold water

A few ice cubes

SERVES 3 (8 OUNCES EACH)

This green smoothie derives its natural sweetness from pineapple and grapes. If you're feeling intrepid, do as the juice bars do and add a shot of wheatgrass juice (available at natural foods stores). Ginger gives it an energizing lift and a lightly spicy mojo.

Combine all the ingredients in a large, ice-crushing blender and blend until thick and smooth. Serve immediately.

Pineapple Lassi *(pictured on page 130)*

1½ cups plain whole-milk yogurt

1¼ cups coarsely chopped peeled fresh or frozen pineapple

3 to 4 tablespoons sugar, or to taste

Pinch of ground cardamom

2 ice cubes

Ice-cold water (optional)

Scant pinch of saffron threads, for garnish (optional)

SERVES 3 OR 4 (6 TO 8 OUNCES EACH)

A pineapple lassi is just the thing when you're hot and cranky or hot and happy or just plain hot. Other fruits like mango will do here, but I'm partial to the sweet-tart notes of pineapple.

MAKE. Combine all the ingredients except the saffron in a blender and blend until completely smooth. Taste, adding more sugar and a splash of water, if desired. Divide among serving glasses and garnish each with a few saffron threads, if using.

Yo!

"Gold" pineapples from Hawaii, which are always ripe and ready to go, are increasingly easy to find in the produce aisle of most grocery stores.

Ice-Cold Cocoa Breeze

3 moist and sticky Medjool dates, pitted (see Yo!, page 51)

½ cup plain yogurt

1 tablespoon unsweetened cocoa powder

1½ teaspoons ground flaxseed (optional)

¼ cup ice-cold water

4 ice cubes

Yo!

If using Greek yogurt, you may want to add an extra tablespoon of ice water.

SERVES 1 (ABOUT 9 OUNCES)

A cool, chocolaty sipper with a subtle, bitter edge, this blender drink goes down smooth.

I offer two variations below: one for those with a high-speed blender and a second for those with a traditional blender or handheld immersion blender. (Either way, you'll need a model that can effectively crush ice.)

IF USING A HIGH-SPEED BLENDER: In a high-speed blender, combine all the ingredients and blend until completely smooth.

IF USING A TRADITIONAL BLENDER OR AN IMMERSION BLENDER: Finely chop the dates and set in a small bowl. Add boiling water just to cover and set aside for 5 minutes to soften. Drain. Add to the blender (or a small pitcher) with the remaining ingredients and blend until completely smooth.

SERVE. Transfer to a tall glass, pop in a straw, and serve immediately.

Ginger-Vanilla Lassi

2 cups plain whole-milk yogurt

1 tablespoon (packed) grated peeled fresh ginger

½ teaspoon pure vanilla extract

¼ cup ice-cold water

A few ice cubes (optional)

2 tablespoons sugar

SERVES 2 (10 OUNCES EACH)

Lassis are frothy yogurt drinks popular in India and some parts of Southeast Asia. Thinner than milkshakes or smoothies (thanks to the addition of water or ice), they may be sweet or savory and offer cooling refreshment in hot climates.

I return again and again to this invigorating combination of feisty ginger and floral vanilla. The yogurt pushes them into the background, where they linger softly, like a fleeting but entirely pleasant thought.

Combine all the ingredients in a blender and blend until smooth, at least 45 seconds. Serve immediately.

Yo!

Use a Microplane or the smallest holes on a box grater to grate the ginger. You want to break down its fibers completely before blending.

Savory Lassi (Chaas)

1 to 2 tablespoons cumin seeds

½ cup plain yogurt (not Greek)

½ cup ice-cold water

⅛ teaspoon kosher salt

Sprig of fresh cilantro or fresh curry leaves (see Yo!, page 113), for garnish (optional)

Yo!

Spice grinders work best with a solid tablespoon or two of spices, so I encourage you to grind more cumin seeds than you'll need for this recipe. Use the extra toasted ground cumin in future lassis or anywhere you'd use store-bought ground cumin.

SERVES 1 (8 OUNCES)

Throughout India, salty yogurt drinks hold sway as a daily tonic, and those who grew up with savory lassis will find this recipe comfortingly familiar. If you're unaccustomed to this combination, however, it may surprise the palate. On a sweltering day, give it a chance, allowing the salt and toasted cumin to work their magic.

TOAST THE CUMIN. In a small, dry skillet, toast the cumin seeds for 1 to 3 minutes, or until fragrant and one shade darker, shaking the pan constantly so they don't burn. Transfer to a spice grinder or mortar and pestle and cool completely. Grind until powdery. Transfer to a small jar or spice bottle. (A funnel may be helpful.) You'll have plenty of extra toasted cumin for future recipes.

MAKE THE LASSI. I like whisking the lassi in a 2-cup glass measuring cup, but you can also whisk it up directly in the glass. Whisk the yogurt until smooth. Then whisk in the water, salt, and ½ teaspoon of the cumin. Pour into a glass. Garnish with a cilantro sprig or a few curry leaves, if desired, and serve immediately.

Louisa Shafia, author of *The New Persian Kitchen*, and Donia Bijan, a Cordon Bleu–trained chef and former restaurateur in the San Francisco Bay Area and author of the memoir *Maman's Homesick Pie: A Persian Heart in an American Kitchen*, both painted a rich portrait of yogurt's place at the Persian table.

According to Shafia, who is the daughter of a Persian father and an American mother and grew up outside Philadelphia, yogurt is the common denominator of every Persian meal. She remembers it being on the table constantly during her childhood. "Persians don't have raw green salads," she said, "but they have yogurt salads," featuring beets, sautéed shallots, and spinach, among other vegetables. There are no smoothies, but there is *doogh* (page 138), a fizzy, salty yogurt drink often served with kebabs.

Yogurt is also closely aligned with Persian views on health. One major tenet, she explained, is that "cooling" and "warming" foods should not be mixed in a single dish. Since yogurt is a "cooling food" and soft fruits (like berries) are "warming foods,"

you won't find traditional Persian dishes combining yogurt and fruit. Indeed, yogurt is not commonly paired with sweet foods at all. Instead, yogurt is deployed as a souring agent to cut fatty foods because it is believed that its acidic properties "help flush the fat out of your system."

Unlike Shafia, who learned about her culinary heritage from her father and her own research, Bijan spent her early years in the then-bustling, cosmopolitan metropolis of Tehran. She recalled her uncle teaching her mother how to make yogurt. "I remember bowls of yogurt behind the couch with a blanket on top," she said of her childhood in prerevolutionary Iran.

The summer she turned eight, Bijan's mother turned over soup-making responsibilities to her young daughter. Preparing cucumber-yogurt soups is a memory she clearly still cherishes, even decades later. "I loved that chance," she remembers, "because I could improvise every time, sometimes with crushed rose petals, or with mint and dill, or I would freeze herbs in an ice tray and use those in the soup."

(For a similar recipe, see page 144.)

Another common dish is *ta-chin*, Bijan said, in which chicken or lamb is marinated in yogurt and saffron, then combined with a rice-yogurt mixture enriched and stabilized with egg yolks. The dish is baked like a savory cake.

Bijan agreed that yogurt's role in the country's cuisine is all about balance, "for the desire to pucker, to have something sour, and to balance the richness of whatever dish it may be."

Orange-Clove Lassi

1 cup plain low-fat or whole-milk yogurt

1 cup orange juice

1 to 2 tablespoons honey, or to taste

¼ teaspoon ground cloves

3 ice cubes

SERVES 2 (10 OUNCES EACH)

A hint of clove adds an air of sophistication to this lassi, which boosts breakfast with its mix of orange juice and yogurt. If using Greek yogurt, increase the proportion of juice to yogurt slightly to make the lassi thin and drinkable.

Combine all the ingredients in a blender and blend until smooth. Serve immediately.

Pomegranate Doogh (Yogurt Soda)

¾ cup plain yogurt (not Greek)

½ cup pomegranate juice

2 tablespoons fresh orange juice

Ice cubes

¼ cup seltzer, or more as needed

Sugar (optional)

SERVES 2 (SCANT 8 OUNCES EACH)

Prominent in Persian cuisine, doogh is a yogurt soda that's bubbly, creamy, and a touch salty. This pomegranate juice–based twist borrows conceptually from what makes doogh, and its Turkish cousin *ayran*, so popular: that yogurt drinks don't have to be sticky-sweet to quench your thirst. This one is fizzy and invigorating but not at all syrupy. (If it's too tart for you, stir in up to 2 teaspoons sugar.)

MAKE. In a 2-cup glass measuring cup, whisk the yogurt, pomegranate juice, and orange juice until smooth and mauvey pink. Pour into two ice-filled glasses. Top each off with seltzer. Taste, adding sugar if desired, and serve immediately.

Slurp

Slurp

Yogurt soups can be hot or cold, sweet or savory, extravagantly spiced or minimalist. All have a hint of luxury. When dolloped on as a garnish, a scoop of yogurt lends a touch of creaminess to an otherwise light, brothy soup; when whisked into the soup, yogurt adds thickness and body, tang and balance.

Because of yogurt's particular properties, you'll want to pay special attention to the following tips to keep the textural integrity of your soup intact:

» Adding cold yogurt to hot soup generally invites separation, so before you start chopping and cooking, remove the yogurt from the refrigerator so it can lose its chill.

» You'll often be prompted to temper the yogurt with a touch of hot soup before adding it to the soup pot. Tempering is a process of bringing two substances of unequal temperature into closer range before combining them. Doing so ensures that the yogurt will not curdle, or "break," once it hits the soup bubbling in the pot.

» Because the whey tends to weep naturally from yogurt as it stands, give your yogurt a good whisk before adding it to soup.

» When instructions call for pureeing a soup, it's generally better to do so before adding yogurt, rather than after, in order to maintain the yogurt's structural and textural qualities.

» Be safe when blending hot liquids: Never fill a blender more than three-quarters full with hot soup, always vent the hole in the lid, and place a folded kitchen towel between your hand and the hole.

I prefer soups that incorporate yogurt toward the end of cooking. The results are creamy and clean on the palate, with vivid colors and fresh, clear flavors.

The Recipes

Cold Yogurt Soup with Cucumber, Herbs, and Rose Petals

¼ cup dried rose petals (see Yo!), crushed

⅓ cup walnuts or almonds

⅛ preserved lemon (see Yo!), briefly rinsed

2 cups plain whole-milk Greek yogurt

1½ cups ice-cold water

1½ cups finely diced peeled and seeded cucumber (1 small or ⅔ large)

½ cup golden raisins, finely chopped

¼ cup finely chopped fresh mint

¼ cup finely chopped fresh dill

¼ cup finely chopped fresh chives or scallions, white and most of the green parts

Kosher salt and freshly ground pepper

Ground sumac (see Yo!, page 105) or lemon zest, for garnish

3 tablespoons coarsely chopped pistachios, for garnish

SERVES 6

The alfresco lunch my sister and I enjoyed with Greek cookbook author Aglaia Kremezi at her home on the isle of Kea will go down as one of the most memorable meals of my life. One highlight was this cold yogurt soup, so fresh and herbal, with exotic notes from rose petals, preserved lemon, and sumac. Aglaia served it in small, elegant glass bowls to show off its pink, green, and yellow specks. The soup is thick not just with yogurt but with ground nuts as well. Finely chopped raisins lend occasional bursts of unexpected sweetness.

Aglaia adapted her recipe from chef and restaurateur Hoss Zaré, whose San Francisco restaurant The Fly Trap specializes in Persian cuisine with Californian and Mediterranean influences. This soup shows off its Persian roots. Elegant and aromatic, flavorful but still understated, it appears in Aglaia's newest cookbook, *Mediterranean Vegetarian Feasts* (Stewart, Tabori & Chang, 2014).

SOAK THE ROSE PETALS. In a small bowl, soak the rose petals in lukewarm water until softened, about 20 minutes. Drain and pat dry.

TOAST THE NUTS. Preheat the oven to 350°F. Spread the walnuts or almonds on a baking sheet and toast for 8 to 10 minutes, until fragrant and lightly colored. Let cool. In a small food processor, finely chop the nuts with the preserved lemon.

(continued)

Yo!

Find dried rose petals, sumac, and preserved lemon at Middle Eastern markets or online at Kalustyans.com.

If you don't have preserved lemon, substitute the zest of 1 lemon.

MAKE THE SOUP. In a large bowl, whisk the yogurt with the ice water. Add the cucumber, raisins, mint, dill, chives or scallions, rose petals, and the nut-lemon mixture. Season with salt and pepper to taste. Cover and chill for at least 1 hour and up to 3 hours.

SERVE. Taste the soup and adjust the seasoning if needed, then serve in glasses or shallow bowls, sprinkled generously with sumac or lemon zest and the pistachios.

Springtime Asparagus-Pea Soup with Crispy Pancetta

1 tablespoon extra-virgin olive oil

4 ounces pancetta, diced

½ medium onion, diced

1 large carrot, peeled and diced

1 celery stalk, diced

1 pound asparagus, ends snapped off and discarded, stalks and tips thinly sliced

2 garlic cloves, smashed and minced

1½ teaspoons herbes de Provence, page 163

1 teaspoon kosher salt

¼ teaspoon freshly ground pepper

½ cup dry white wine

4 cups chicken stock or low-sodium chicken broth

2 cups peas (1¾ cups freshly shucked peas plus ¼ cup frozen [not thawed], or all frozen)

¾ cup (loosely packed) fresh Italian parsley leaves

(continued)

SERVES 6

This gentle, green soup delivers clean asparagus and pea flavors with a tangy back note. A piece of sandwich bread (use any kind you have, crust and all) thickens the soup in its final moments.

MAKE THE SOUP. Heat a Dutch oven or soup pot over medium-high heat. Add the oil and pancetta. Cook, stirring, until the meat is browned and crisp, 6 to 8 minutes. Remove with a slotted spoon to a paper towel–lined plate. Add the onion, carrot, celery, asparagus, garlic, herbes de Provence, salt, and pepper to the residual fat in the pot. Lower the heat to medium and cook, stirring occasionally, until tender and just beginning to color, 12 to 15 minutes. Add the wine, bring to a boil over medium-high heat, and let bubble for a minute or two until most of the liquid has evaporated and only a thin sheen remains. Add the stock and 1¾ cups of the peas and return to a boil. Reduce the heat to medium and simmer until the peas are tender, 5 minutes longer. Remove the pot from the heat. Stir in the parsley, bread, and the remaining ¼ cup frozen peas. Using caution, puree the soup in a blender in batches, or use an immersion blender in the pot. Return to the soup pot, if necessary.

(continued)

Springtime Soup (continued)

1 piece standard sandwich bread, torn into rough pieces

1 cup plain whole-milk yogurt (not Greek)

½ teaspoon cornstarch

1 tablespoon cold water

Yo!

Avoid low-fat and nonfat yogurt, which will cause the soup to break.

TEMPER THE YOGURT. Place ¾ cup of the yogurt in a small bowl. In a second small bowl, whisk the cornstarch with the water. Whisk this slurry into the yogurt to combine thoroughly. Whisk ¼ cup of the soup into the yogurt mixture to temper, then scrape the mixture into the soup pot. Whisk to combine. (Reheat gently, if necessary, but do not let the soup boil.)

SERVE. Divide the soup among six bowls. Divide the remaining ¼ cup yogurt among the bowls, in dollops. Sprinkle each dollop with the crispy pancetta. Serve immediately.

On Kea, a small island an hour's ferry ride from Athens, cookbook author Aglaia Kremezi runs the Kea Artisanal cooking school. She and her husband, Costas Moraitis, offered to teach me what they know about yogurt. But first, they wanted me to meet their neighbor, Ela Allamani, who moved to Greece from Albania fifteen years ago.

Together Allamani and Kremezi opened the door to two cultures, painting a vivid picture of how and why yogurt occupies so important a place on the vast Mediterranean table. In the kitchen, I watched Allamani make yogurt. First, she scalded milk in the microwave. She stirred some yogurt in a mug, added it directly to the hot milk, affixed a lid, draped the container with a towel, and let it sit for 3 hours.

She prepared several yogurt dishes for us, beginning with *elbasan*, a traditional Albanian lamb casserole baked in yogurt thickened with egg yolks, roux, and cooked rice. After a long, slow bake in the oven, the yogurt firms and a crust forms on top.

She stuffed oblong peppers with mint-seasoned yogurt next, frying them gently in oil until soft and yielding (see page 182 for a variation on her recipe). While she cooked, we all snacked on thickened, strained yogurt threaded with garlic and drizzled with olive oil. Slathered on bread, the spread sustained us until lunch, which we enjoyed outside on a long wooden table.

The next day, I learned about cooking with yogurt from Aglaia Kremezi herself. She greeted me with freshly baked bread dappled with tomato and smoked cheese, a jar of pickled caper vines and marinated artichokes she'd preserved, and a small bowl of thick, rust-colored *muhammara*, that Syrian-influenced red pepper dip that she flavored with hazelnuts and pomegranate molasses.

Together, we prepared an Iranian-inspired cold yogurt soup (page 144) with specks of green pistachio, pink rose petal, and maroon sumac dotting its surface.

She baked a yogurt-topped sea bass next, stabilizing the yogurt with cornstarch and egg. The fish, with its flaky, moist interior and crunchy bread-crumb cap, managed to be light and filling at the same time.

The meal ended with a comparative tasting of goat, sheep, and cow yogurt served with colorful "spoon sweets," the clean flavor of the unsweetened yogurt a fine foil for the sticky, candied fruits. (For more on spoon sweets, see pages 290 and 291.)

After Kea, we headed next to the island of Paros, where I met with two restauranteurs and learned how to make both Syrup-Drenched Orange Phyllo Cake (page 262) and the most garlicky tzatiki I've ever had (Stella's Tzatiki, page 108). I also spent an evening visiting the Lefkes Village Hotel, whose owner, a colorful character named George Pittas, gave me a lesson in Greece's Ottoman-influenced culinary history. As Pittas and I talked, the hotel's chef brought out one yogurt dish after another: a tzatziki made from cow's and sheep's yogurt, garnished with rounds of cucumber and radish; a mixed grill of pork and vegetables, sauced with yogurt and sprinkled with paprika; and veal and pork *yiaourtlou* (see page 216), a layered dish with tomato, pita, and yogurt.

Pittas said that in Greek and Ottoman cooking, yogurt should maintain its identity, remaining a discrete, discernible presence even when served with other foods. "He's not an ingredient, the yogurt," Pittas said, ascribing a gender-specific pronoun to the food we were discussing. (He used the pronoun because we communicated in French, the one language we spoke in common.) "Everything must have its identity."

In Greece, yogurt is an ingredient rich with history and significance, one prized and valued, well loved and ubiquitous. It's not just a food. It's an integral part of the country's fabric. How fortunate for the rest of us to have finally caught on to its wide-ranging pleasures.

Artichoke-Almond Soup with Chives

3 tablespoons extra-virgin olive oil

2 large globe artichokes

1 medium onion, chopped

1 celery stalk, chopped

2 medium carrots, peeled and chopped

Kosher salt and freshly ground pepper

6 cups vegetable stock, chicken stock, or low-sodium vegetable or chicken broth

½ cup almonds

1 cup plain Greek yogurt, for serving

16 chives, snipped with scissors, for serving

SERVES 8

This spring soup delivers pure artichoke flavor and substantial body, thanks not to cream but to almonds, which you puree with the soup. (If you don't have a high-speed blender, soak the almonds in cool water for several hours. Drain and rinse before use.) Yogurt peeks out from the top of each bowl, beckoning you to sweep up a bit with each spoonful.

Add the oil to a Dutch oven or 8-quart soup pot and set aside.

PREP THE ARTICHOKES. Using a large, serrated knife and working with one artichoke at a time, cut off the top half of the artichoke and discard. Cut off the stem and reserve. Invert the artichoke onto a cutting board so the stem end faces up. Working slowly but deliberately, sweep your knife along the curvature of the artichoke, top to bottom, hugging the sides and removing clumps of leaves little by little. Continue, turning the artichoke as you go, until you're left with only the pale heart. (Switch to a paring knife, if desired, toward the end to clean up the outer edges and remove stubborn dark green bits.) Discard all the leaves and green clumps. Now slice the artichoke in half top to bottom. Use a serrated spoon (or regular spoon) to scrape out the fuzzy choke and scissors to snip any spiky inner leaves. (Tender, despiked leaves may stay.) Thinly slice and then coarsely chop what's left of the artichoke. Add to the Dutch oven or soup pot. Repeat with the second artichoke. Peel the stems with your paring knife, then chop and add them to the pot along with the onion, celery, carrots, and ½ teaspoon each salt and pepper.

MAKE THE SOUP. Cover the pot and cook over medium heat for about 10 minutes, stirring a few times. Add the stock and bring to a boil. Reduce the heat and simmer, covered, until all the vegetables are completely tender, about 30 minutes. Using caution and working in batches, if necessary, combine the soup and the almonds in a blender and puree until smooth. Return to the soup pot and reheat if necessary, adjusting the seasoning to taste.

GARNISH AND SERVE. Mound 2 tablespoons yogurt into each of eight soup bowls. (An ice cream scoop works nicely.) Ladle the soup around the yogurt. Garnish each portion with chives. Serve hot.

Carrot-Cumin Soup with Cumin Seed Oil

¼ cup plus 3 tablespoons extra-virgin olive oil

4 teaspoons cumin seeds

1 large onion, diced

1½ pounds carrots (5 to 6 medium), peeled and diced

1 celery stalk, diced

1½ teaspoons kosher salt

½ teaspoon freshly ground pepper

4 cups low-sodium vegetable stock, or other stock or broth of your choice

¾ cup plain whole-milk Greek yogurt, plus (optional) 5 to 6 tablespoons for garnish

SERVES 6 TO 8

Carrots simmer up into an incredibly friendly soup. The color is vivid and bright, the flavor sweet and mellow, and the texture a smooth puree. Cumin seeds add mystery and depth, offsetting the carrots' natural sweetness and adding a top layer of warmth and crunch.

MAKE THE CUMIN SEED OIL. In a small skillet, warm ¼ cup of the oil and 2 teaspoons of the cumin seeds over medium-low heat for about 3 minutes, or until the seeds sizzle and become fragrant. Pour the oil and seeds into a small bowl and reserve for garnish. (May be made up to 2 days ahead. Keep, covered, at room temperature.)

MAKE THE SOUP. To a Dutch oven or soup pot, add the remaining 3 tablespoons oil and 2 teaspoons cumin seeds. Cook over medium-high heat, stirring constantly, until the seeds are fragrant and one shade darker, 1 to 2 minutes. Add the onion, carrots, celery, salt, and pepper. Cook, stirring occasionally and partly covered for the first half of cooking, until the vegetables are medium-tender and beginning to brown, about 15 minutes. Add the stock, raise the heat, and bring to a boil. Reduce the heat, cover partly again, and simmer to blend the flavors and soften the vegetables completely, 20 to 25 minutes. Remove from the heat. Cool slightly. Using caution, puree the soup in a blender in batches. Return to the soup pot.

(continued)

TEMPER THE YOGURT. Whisk the ¾ cup yogurt in a small bowl. Whisk ¼ cup of the hot soup into the yogurt until smooth to temper. Scrape this mixture back into the soup pot, whisking to incorporate. (Reheat gently, if necessary, but do not let the soup boil.)

SERVE. Divide among serving bowls, drizzling each portion with some of the cumin seed oil (and its attendant cumin seeds) and garnishing, if desired, with about 2 teaspoons yogurt per serving.

Yo!

If pureeing this soup with an immersion blender, wear an oven mitt and tip the Dutch oven or soup pot to one side so the liquid pools. If using a traditional blender, fill it only three-quarters full, vent the center hole, and cover the hole with a folded kitchen towel under your hand.

Don't skip the cumin seed oil. It takes just minutes to prepare, but garnishing with the spiced oil adds a special touch to what's at heart a very simple soup.

Cauliflower-Bacon Soup with Saffron Yogurt

2 teaspoons extra-virgin olive oil

3 to 5 slices thick-cut bacon, sliced crosswise

1 medium onion, diced

1 carrot, peeled and diced

1 celery stalk, diced

3 garlic cloves, smashed and minced

Freshly ground pepper

1 head cauliflower (about 2 pounds), cored and finely chopped

4 cups chicken stock or low-sodium chicken broth

4 pinches saffron threads (about ¼ teaspoon total)

1 cup plain whole-milk Greek yogurt

Squeeze of fresh lemon juice

Kosher salt

SERVES 6

A trio of ingredients—saffron, bacon, and yogurt—work intense magic on a humble head of cauliflower, transforming the ivory florets into a velvety, sun-colored elixir. Use three slices of bacon if you're feeling restrained, four or five if feeling indulgent.

CRISP THE BACON. Heat the oil in a Dutch oven or soup pot over medium-high heat. Sprinkle in the bacon. Cook, stirring frequently, until browned and crisp, about 8 minutes. Remove the pot from the heat. Using a slotted spoon, transfer the bacon to a paper towel–lined plate. Set aside. Pour off all but about 1 tablespoon fat from the pot.

COOK THE VEGETABLES. Return the pot to medium heat and add the onion, carrot, celery, garlic, and ½ teaspoon pepper. Cook, stirring occasionally, until the vegetables are beginning to brown, about 5 minutes. Add the cauliflower and cook, stirring, for a minute or two more.

SIMMER THE SOUP. Pour in the stock. Add 2 pinches of the saffron (about ⅛ teaspoon), crumbling it before dropping it into the pot. Raise the heat, bring the soup to a boil, then reduce the heat to a slow but steady simmer. Simmer the soup, partly covered, until the cauliflower is completely tender, about 20 minutes.

(continued)

PREPARE THE YOGURT. In a small bowl, whisk the remaining 2 pinches saffron into the yogurt. Transfer half of the yogurt to a medium bowl and reserve the rest. Ladle a good ½ to 1 cup broth from the soup pot into the medium bowl and whisk to temper the yogurt. Scrape this mixture back into the pot.

FINISH AND SERVE. Using caution, puree the soup, either in batches in a blender or using an immersion blender in the pot. Return to the pot if necessary. Taste, adding a bit of lemon juice and salt and pepper to taste. Divide the soup among six bowls, garnishing each serving with a dollop of the reserved saffron yogurt and a sprinkle of bacon.

Butternut Squash Soup with Toasted Seeds

2 medium butternut squash
(3½ to 4 pounds total), stems
cut off

3 tablespoons extra-virgin olive
oil

Salt and freshly ground pepper

1 medium onion, diced

⅛ teaspoon dried sage

½ teaspoon smoked paprika

½ teaspoon fennel seeds

1 large tomato, seeded and
chopped

2 cups low-sodium vegetable
stock, chicken stock, or water

½ cup plain Greek yogurt

SERVES 6

Properly roasting squash takes time, but the dividends are many:
autumnal sweetness, bold color, and smooth, almost creamy flesh that
easily purees. If you have the time and want to dress the soup up, toast
the squash seeds as directed for an addictive, crunchy garnish. (Since
the squash takes a good hour to roast, start on the soup base while it's
in the oven.)

ROAST THE SQUASH. Preheat the oven to 400°F. Line a baking sheet
with parchment or a silicone liner.

Using a heavy knife, carefully halve each squash lengthwise.
Scrape out the seeds and reserve. Place the squash cut side up on
the baking sheet. Drizzle ½ teaspoon oil over each half and season
generously with salt and pepper, rubbing in with your fingers. Turn
cut side down. Roast for 25 minutes, then flip cut side up. Continue
roasting until browned in spots and completely fork-tender, 35 to
45 minutes longer. If planning to toast the seeds, reduce the oven
temperature to 275°F.

MEANWHILE, PREPARE THE SOUP BASE. While the squash roasts, heat
2 tablespoons of the remaining oil in a Dutch oven or soup pot over
medium-high heat. Add the onion, sage, smoked paprika, ¼ teaspoon of the fennel seeds, ½ teaspoon salt, and ¼ teaspoon pepper.
Cook, stirring frequently, until very soft, 10 to 15 minutes, lowering
the heat to medium-low after about 5 minutes so the onion cooks

The squash can be roasted 1 day ahead and kept refrigerated, covered. The seeds can be toasted 1 day ahead and stored airtight at room temperature.

slowly. Add the tomato and stock, raise the heat, and bring to a boil. Reduce the heat to a gentle simmer and let bubble, uncovered, for 10 to 15 minutes longer to meld the flavors.

PUREE. When the squash finishes roasting, scoop the flesh (discard the peels) into the soup pot. Using caution, puree using an immersion blender in the pot, or in batches in a blender. Return the soup to the pot if necessary.

TEMPER THE YOGURT. Whisk the yogurt vigorously in a medium bowl. Ladle 1 cup of the hot soup into the yogurt and whisk until smooth to temper. Scrape this mixture into the soup pot. Cover and remove from the heat.

IF DESIRED, TOAST THE SEEDS. Set the reserved squash seeds in a fine-mesh strainer and discard any strings or clumps of flesh. Run under cool water, massaging until the seeds are clean. Transfer to a kitchen towel and rub dry. (You should have about ⅓ cup.) Transfer to a baking sheet and toss with the remaining 1 teaspoon oil and ¼ teaspoon fennel seeds, a scant ¼ teaspoon salt, and a large pinch of pepper. Bake for about 20 minutes, until crisp.

SERVE. Reheat the soup gently but do not let it boil. Divide among six serving bowls, sprinkling each portion with the toasted seeds, if using.

Golden Winter Vegetable Soup with Lentils and Yogurt

⅔ cup black beluga lentils or brown lentils, picked over and rinsed

1 teaspoon red or white wine vinegar

3 tablespoons drained capers

3 tablespoons extra-virgin olive oil

1 tablespoon unsalted butter

6 small shallots (or 2 or 3 large ones), cut into ½-inch dice

½ large onion, cut into ½-inch dice

3 to 3½ pounds assorted white winter vegetables (choose at least three of the following: celeriac, sunchokes, fennel, Yukon Gold potatoes, turnips), peeled and cut into ½-inch dice (9 to 10 cups)

1 teaspoon herbes de Provence (see Yo!)

SERVES 8

This mild, yellow soup showcases a slew of humble winter vegetables, from celeriac and turnips to sunchokes, fennel, and potatoes. Slowly cooking the shallots and onion at the outset provides a sweet base that is offset by acidic hits of white wine, lemon, and a generous dollop of yogurt in the soup bowl. For the best visual impact, serve in wide, shallow bowls and do not stir the yogurt through the soup.

PREPARE THE LENTILS. Place the lentils in a medium saucepan and cover with cold water by an inch or two. Bring to a boil, reduce the heat, and simmer, uncovered, until tender but not mushy, 20 to 25 minutes. Drain, then rinse briefly. Transfer to a bowl, sprinkle with the vinegar, and stir in the capers. Set aside.

MEANWHILE, MAKE THE SOUP. In a Dutch oven or soup pot, warm the oil and butter over medium heat. When the butter melts, add the shallots and onion. Cook, stirring frequently, for about 5 minutes to jump-start them, then reduce the heat to low and cook them more slowly, stirring often, until completely soft, about 15 minutes longer. Avoid overbrowning.

Add the winter vegetables, herbes de Provence, salt, and pepper and stir well. Raise the heat to medium-high and cook, stirring occasionally, for 10 minutes to develop the flavors. Add the stock and wine and bring to a boil. Reduce the heat and simmer steadily, partly covered, until the vegetables are soft, about 30 minutes. Remove from the heat. Add the lemon juice, to taste.

1½ teaspoons kosher salt

½ teaspoon freshly ground pepper

4 to 5 cups vegetable stock or low-sodium vegetable broth (depending on how brothy you like your soup)

½ cup dry white wine

1 teaspoon fresh lemon juice, or more to taste

1½ cups plain Greek yogurt, preferably whole-milk, for serving

SERVE. Scoop 3 tablespoons yogurt into each soup bowl. Top the yogurt with ¼ cup lentils, then spoon 1 cup of soup around the perimeter of the bowl.

Yo!

There's a good bit of chopping required for this recipe (try to dice the vegetables to a uniform size), so leave yourself ample time for prep. Happily, this is a toss-in-and-stir recipe once the up-front work is done.

Use any combination of white winter vegetables, and vary them each time you make the soup. I recommend including at least three different types for the best flavor and depth.

Don't have herbes de Provence (a blend of thyme, rosemary, marjoram, savory, basil, fennel seeds, and lavender)? Use 1 teaspoon total of any three or four of its components instead.

It's easiest to "peel" celeriac with a knife. It's a bit too hairy and fibrous for a vegetable peeler.

Homespun Split Pea Soup with Glossy Brussels Sprout Leaves

8 cups low-sodium vegetable stock

1 tablespoon plus 2 teaspoons extra-virgin olive oil

1 medium onion, diced

1 large carrot, peeled and diced

1 celery stalk, diced

2 garlic cloves, smashed and minced

1 pound (2 cups) green split peas, picked over and rinsed

Kosher salt and freshly ground pepper

8 Brussels sprouts, bottom third trimmed and discarded, leaves separated

½ to 1 cup plain Greek yogurt, whisked

SERVES 6 TO 8

A yogurt dollop smooths out the texture of split pea soup, a winter warmer that takes time to simmer but quiets hunger simply and effectively. This vegetarian version gets a visual lift from a fluttering of Brussels sprout leaves, a 2-minute garnish that, along with the yogurt, adds a bright note to this humble, straightforward classic. (When Brussels sprouts aren't in season, toss on a few croutons instead.)

HEAT THE STOCK. In a medium saucepan, heat the vegetable stock. Keep covered over low heat until needed.

MAKE THE SOUP. In a Dutch oven or soup pot, warm 1 tablespoon of the oil over medium heat. Add the onion, carrot, celery, and garlic and cook, stirring frequently, until tender and just beginning to brown, about 15 minutes. Ladle in 6 cups of the hot stock (keep the rest covered, off the heat). Add the split peas and bring to a low boil. Reduce the heat slightly and simmer, partly covered, at a gentle but steady bubble until the peas are completely tender, 60 to 75 minutes, adding the remaining 2 cups stock after 30 or 40 minutes to keep the pot from running dry. Stir several times during cooking so the peas don't stick to the bottom of the pot.

PUREE. When the split peas are tender, season assertively with salt and pepper. Using caution, puree half the soup in a blender and return to the pot. Keep warm.

Split peas may take more or less time to cook, depending on their age. Regardless of the times given, simmer the soup until they're completely tender.

The soup will thicken as it cools. Reheat any leftovers with additional stock or water.

COOK THE SPROUTS. Warm the remaining 2 teaspoons oil over medium heat in the same saucepan that formerly held the hot stock. Add the Brussels sprout leaves and cook, stirring frequently, until tender, glossy, and browned at the edges, about 2 minutes.

GARNISH AND SERVE. Divide the soup among bowls, spooning 1 to 2 tablespoons yogurt atop each serving and scattering with a few Brussels sprout leaves.

Afghan Beef Noodle Soup with Yogurt (Aush)

1 tablespoon extra-virgin olive oil

1 small onion, finely chopped

2 garlic cloves, smashed and minced

1 pound extra-lean ground beef (95 or 90 percent lean)

1½ teaspoons ground coriander

1½ teaspoons paprika

Kosher salt and freshly ground pepper

2 tablespoons tomato paste, whisked with 2 tablespoons hot water

10 cups beef or chicken stock, preferably low-sodium

7 to 8 ounces wide or extra-wide egg noodles

1 (15-ounce) can chickpeas, rinsed and drained

1 (15-ounce) can kidney beans, rinsed and drained

1 to 1½ cups plain whole-milk yogurt, at room temperature

Dried mint or fresh mint leaves, for garnish

SERVES 6 TO 8

Aush, a bean and noodle soup amped up with paprika-seasoned beef, is a protein-packed, family-friendly soup-as-a-meal finished with a glorious cloak of yogurt. This recipe came to me via Kabul-born, San Francisco–based writer Humaira Ghilzai and our mutual friend Katie Morford, who generously facilitated our connection.

COOK THE BEEF. In a large nonstick skillet, warm the olive oil over medium-low heat. Add the onion and cook until soft and translucent, about 10 minutes. Add the garlic and cook, stirring, for a minute or two, until fragrant. Add the ground beef, raise the heat to medium-high, and cook, breaking up the meat as it browns, for about 5 minutes. Sprinkle in the coriander, paprika, 1 teaspoon salt, ½ teaspoon pepper, and the tomato paste mixture. Reduce the heat to low and simmer gently, uncovered, for about 15 minutes so the flavors can develop.

MAKE THE BROTH. Meanwhile, bring the stock to a boil in a Dutch oven or soup pot. Drop in the egg noodles and cook at a hard simmer for 5 minutes. Add the chickpeas and kidney beans and continue simmering until the noodles are tender and the beans are heated through, 1 to 5 minutes longer.

SERVE. Ladle about 1½ cups of the noodle-bean broth into each serving bowl. Divide the meat among the bowls, scooping it generously on top. Spoon 2 to 4 tablespoons yogurt over each serving and garnish with the mint. Enjoy hot, with more salt and pepper.

For Rich and Poor Alike, A Savory Staple AFGHAN YOGURT CULTURE

Kabul-born Humaira Ghilzai fled Afghanistan when the Russians invaded in the late 1970s. She now lives in California. Still deeply tied to the culture and people of Afghanistan, both personally and professionally (she runs the website Afghancultureunveiled.com), Ghilzai explained that yogurt's use depends largely on a family's financial circumstances. Those who are more well-off drape yogurt liberally over a wide array of soups and meat- and vegetable-based stews, from *aush* (the yogurt-topped, paprika-scented beef, bean, and noodle soup on page 166) to *bourani kadoo* (sweet and salty braised pumpkin sauced with yogurt and garlic). Those from poorer Afghan families make yogurt to stretch the amount of precious milk in their diets.

Two traditional preparations illustrate yogurt's use as a food of survival for those who need to extend the fermented dairy product's longevity beyond its normal life span. The first, called *chaka*, is created by incubating yogurt in a clay pot, salting it, and hanging it in a thick cloth at room temperature so the whey can drain out. "It's a little lumpy in consistency, not as smooth as labneh," Ghilzai said. "In the villages without refrigeration, people are very poor. They may eat meat once a year, and they may not have access to much milk. Their main meal is a piece of naan with tea twice a day." When they do have milk, the salt helps to preserve the *chaka* so it lasts much longer.

The second, called *quroot*, is essentially *chaka* taken to a more extreme stage. An even heavier hand with the salt draws out even more moisture so the yogurt can be formed into little balls and left to dry in the sun. It's then completely portable, so nomads and travelers can pack it for sustenance on the go. To eat, they soak the *quroot* in hot water, softening it back into a form more like the original yogurt from which it was made. They also rub *quroot* on the bumpy-bottomed surfaces of clay pots, which crumbles the *quroot* until it falls apart. Through this process and after much stirring, it once again becomes yogurt like.

"When I was a little girl," Ghilzai told me, "I took a clump of *quroot* and sucked on it like a lollipop for days. I loved that salty taste." She surmises that pregnant women do the same, perhaps because their bodies require the extra calcium. Not reserved solely for travelers and nomads, *quroot* is popular among many Afghans as a staple part of the cuisine.

Dine

We all know that yogurt shines brightly on the breakfast table, but its potential as an afternoon and evening ingredient—in small bites, sandwiches, savory sides, and filling main dishes—has been relatively unexplored. This chapter shows just how wide-ranging a role yogurt can play.

In the form of labneh, yogurt fills beautiful sandwiches layered with raw vegetables, salad greens, thinly sliced fruit, mashed beans, or toasted nuts. It adds a luscious, moisture-sealing mantle that doesn't seep into the bread, and its mild flavor and softness welcome the addition of assertive spices and foods with crunchier textures.

Yogurt can also ooze seductively from gently fried peppers, moisten mushrooms for crostini, and whisk seamlessly into a custard for a savory pie bursting with sausage, spinach, and apples.

Its mildly acidic properties make it an excellent addition to marinades for beef, lamb, or chicken. The yogurt helps to break down tough proteins, yielding more tender meat. Seasoning these marinades with a forceful hand boosts flavor, and including a bit of oil keeps the acid in check and protects the meat from the heat of the oven, stovetop, or grill.

In sauces, yogurt adds a luxurious quality to a dish when it hits the palate. Looser sauces, like those spooned over roasted vegetables or tacos, call for thinner, traditional yogurt, while those with more body, like marinara, call for Greek yogurt.

And then there are curries. Yogurt is an essential ingredient in South Asian curries, and its compatibility with a vast array of fragrant spices helps create full-bodied stews that are rich and soulful while never feeling heavy. I've got three outstanding curries in this chapter, with shrimp, chicken, and beef. Enjoy them all, and often.

The Recipes

Starters

Main Dishes

Side Dishes

Romaine Hearts with Bacon, Tomato, and Gorgonzola Drizzle

FOR THE DRESSING

3 ounces Gorgonzola or other blue cheese, crumbled

¾ cup plain yogurt (if using Greek, see Yo!)

2 tablespoons mayonnaise

1 teaspoon fresh lemon juice

1 garlic clove, crushed

1 teaspoon Dijon mustard

¼ teaspoon kosher salt

⅛ teaspoon freshly ground pepper

FOR THE SALAD

½ pound romaine hearts, separated into individual leaves, chilled

½ cup cooked, crumbled bacon

1 cup halved cherry tomatoes

SERVES 4

It's easy to make your own blue cheese dressing, one that eases into the ruffles and grooves of each romaine leaf but still feels light on the palate. Here's a simple salad to show it off.

MAKE THE DRESSING. In a food processor, combine the Gorgonzola, yogurt, mayonnaise, lemon juice, garlic, mustard, salt, and pepper. Puree for 30 seconds, stopping the machine once or twice and scraping down the sides. (You'll have 1⅓ cups.) If time allows, refrigerate for at least 30 minutes so the flavors meld.

ARRANGE THE SALAD. On a large plate or platter, arrange the romaine leaves face up. Sprinkle with the bacon and tomatoes.

SERVE. Drizzle the salad with a bit of the dressing and pass the remaining dressing at the table.

> *Yo!*
>
> For a slightly thicker dressing, use Greek yogurt and whisk it in by hand after pureeing the other dressing ingredients.

Warm Lentil Salad with French Vinaigrette

1 cup plain low-fat or whole-milk Greek yogurt

Kosher salt and freshly ground pepper

1¼ cups green or black lentils, preferably Le Puy or beluga, picked over and rinsed

2 tablespoons minced shallot

¼ cup white wine vinegar

2 teaspoons Dijon mustard

½ teaspoon honey

½ cup extra-virgin olive oil

½ cup walnuts, toasted (see Yo!, page 95) and coarsely chopped

4 tablespoons minced fresh Italian parsley

Yo!

Le Puy are French green lentils and beluga are small black ones. Both hold their shape during cooking.

SERVES 4 TO 6

The French know their way around a warm lentil salad, usually dressing it with a classic Dijon-style vinaigrette. A generous swath of yogurt adds unexpected opulence, bringing the already compatible flavors into even more harmonious alignment.

WHISK THE YOGURT. In a medium bowl, whisk the yogurt with a pinch each of salt and pepper until light and smooth. Set aside to come to room temperature.

COOK THE LENTILS. In a medium saucepan, cover the lentils with water by 2 inches. Bring to a boil. Reduce the heat and simmer gently, covered, until tender but still firm, 15 to 20 minutes. Drain.

MAKE THE VINAIGRETTE. In a small bowl, douse the shallot with the vinegar. Let stand for 5 minutes. Whisk in the mustard, honey, and olive oil until completely emulsified. Season with salt and pepper to taste.

ASSEMBLE AND SERVE. Transfer the lentils to a shallow serving bowl. Stir in the walnuts, 3 tablespoons of the parsley, and ¼ cup of the vinaigrette. Scrape the yogurt over the lentils and pour half the remaining vinaigrette over the yogurt. Sprinkle with the remaining 1 tablespoon parsley and serve, passing the extra vinaigrette at the table. (For the prettiest presentation and most effective layering of flavors, resist the urge to stir the yogurt through the lentils.)

Little Cheddar, Chive, and Cornmeal Pancakes

¾ cup medium-grind cornmeal

¼ cup all-purpose flour

3 tablespoons minced fresh chives

¼ teaspoon baking soda

¾ teaspoon kosher salt

¼ teaspoon freshly ground pepper

¾ cup plain seltzer

¼ cup plain whole-milk or low-fat Greek yogurt

¾ cup shredded cheddar cheese

2 to 3 tablespoons melted butter, for brushing the skillet

Plain Greek yogurt, crumbled cooked bacon, and minced chives, for garnish

Yo!

For a spicy variation, drizzle the pancakes with hot sauce or fold a bit of minced chile pepper into the batter.

MAKES ABOUT 16 SMALL PANCAKES

Pancakes deserve a showcase long after the breakfast hour. These savory nibbles, topped with yogurt and sprinkled with crisp bacon, make an ideal side dish with soup. The batter can (and should) be whisked up a few hours ahead. Seltzer keeps them nice and light.

MAKE THE BATTER. In a medium bowl, whisk the cornmeal, flour, chives, baking soda, salt, and pepper. Add the seltzer and yogurt and whisk thoroughly to combine. Cover and let stand at room temperature for 1 to 3 hours. Stir in the cheese.

COOK THE PANCAKES. Heat a cast-iron skillet over medium-high heat until a drop of water on the skillet sizzles and evaporates. With a silicone pastry brush, coat the skillet generously with melted butter. Cook a test pancake to gauge the heat, using 1 scant tablespoon per pancake. (When the skillet is sufficiently hot, the batter should sizzle immediately and begin to set at the edges.) Cook the pancakes in batches until golden brown, about 1 minute per side, brushing the skillet generously with butter between each batch.

SERVE. Dollop each pancake with Greek yogurt, sprinkle with the crumbled bacon and chives, and serve hot.

Mushroom Crostini with Yogurt, Lemon, and Thyme

1¼ pounds mixed mushrooms (such as cremini, shiitake, and button)

Extra-virgin olive oil

Kosher salt and freshly ground pepper

8 to 10 sprigs fresh thyme

½-inch-thick slices of French baguette, for serving (from 1 or 2 baguettes)

1 large garlic clove, halved lengthwise

2 tablespoons plain Greek yogurt

A squeeze or two of fresh lemon juice

Zest of 1 large lemon, for garnish

MAKES 2 CUPS (PACKED) MUSHROOM TOPPING, ENOUGH FOR 15 TO 30 CROSTINI (DEPENDING ON THE SIZE OF YOUR BAGUETTE)

Roasting mushrooms for this party-ready hors d'oeuvre intensifies their meatiness by drawing out moisture and punching up already earthy flavors. Tuck leftovers into omelets or spoon onto your morning toast.

ROAST THE MUSHROOMS. Preheat the oven to 425°F, with racks in the upper and lower thirds. Line two baking sheets with parchment.

Rinse the mushrooms well, scrubbing off any grit. Leave the stems on, unless the ends are dry or cracked, in which case trim them off. Pat dry and cut into quarters. Transfer to a large bowl. Drizzle with ¼ cup oil and sprinkle with ¾ teaspoon salt and ⅛ teaspoon pepper. Strip the leaves of 2 of the thyme sprigs into the bowl. Toss well.

Divide the mushrooms evenly between the baking sheets. (Do not wash the bowl.) It may look like they all can fit on one sheet, but they need a wide berth so their liquid can release and evaporate. Spread out the mushrooms so they have plenty of space.

Roast for 25 to 30 minutes, shaking the baking sheets halfway through. Liquid will ooze during the first 20 minutes of roasting but then will disappear, leaving the mushrooms slightly shriveled and chewy. Remove from the oven and let cool on the baking sheets.

Flip on the broiler. Set the baguette slices on an unlined baking sheet and brush the tops lightly with oil. Sprinkle each with a touch of salt. Broil until golden at the edges, 1 to 2 minutes only, watching carefully. Flip and broil the other side for 30 seconds to 1 minute longer. Rub the top of each slice with the cut side of the garlic clove.

MIX. Add the yogurt to the bowl and whisk until smooth. Scrape in the mushrooms, squeeze lightly with lemon juice, stir to coat, and taste for seasoning, adding more salt, pepper, and/or lemon juice to make the flavors pop.

SERVE. Spoon 1 to 2 tablespoons of the mushroom mixture onto each baguette slice, garnish each with lemon zest and a few thyme leaves, and serve.

Mini Avocados with Yogurt, Salmon (or Trout) Roe, and Dill

6 3-inch avocados (see Yo!), halved, pits removed

½ to ¾ cup plain low-fat or whole-milk Greek yogurt

1 (1-ounce) jar salmon roe or trout roe

A big handful of fresh dill

1 lemon, halved

MAKES 12 MINI AVOCADO HALVES

A dainty, elegant, and sophisticated appetizer perfect for holiday time or any soigné party, these little bites have only five ingredients.

MAKE. Arrange the avocado halves on a platter, hollows up. Fill each hollow with a mound of yogurt (2 to 4 teaspoons). Sprinkle each mound with about ½ teaspoon of the roe. Flutter a few feathery dill fronds over each. Squeeze with lemon juice to taste and serve.

> **Yo!**
>
> If you can't find small (3-inch) avocados for hors d'oeuvres, go ahead and use the smallest full-size avocados you can find and scale up the remaining quantities as needed. (Larger avocados should be served as a first course, one half per person.)
>
> A 1-ounce (28-gram) jar of roe will contain about 6 teaspoons, enough for 12 mini avocado halves.

Labneh-Stuffed Peppers with Feta and Pistachio

½ cup labneh, homemade (page 329) or store-bought (see Yo!, page 97)

¼ cup crumbled feta

2 tablespoons finely chopped unsalted pistachios, plus 1 tablespoon pistachios for garnish

2 teaspoons finely chopped fresh mint, plus a few fresh mint leaves for garnish

Kosher salt (optional) and freshly ground pepper

½ pound Italian sweet peppers (4 large or 6 medium), any color you like

2 tablespoons extra-virgin olive oil

Warm pita, for serving

SERVES 4 AS PART OF A LARGER MEZE PLATTER

One of the most memorable dishes I tasted on the Greek island of Kea was a starter of long, colorful sweet peppers stuffed with yogurt cheese, or labneh. They were bright and bold-hued, with the pure white cheese going melty and soft thanks to a quick pan-fry in a skillet. When I returned home, I added feta for complexity, mint for freshness, and a crush of pistachios for crunch and more color.

This recipe comes to me via Ela Allamani, a warm-hearted Albanian who now lives in Greece. Served warm or at room temperature, the peppers make a vivid addition to any meze (appetizer) platter, with olives, stuffed grape leaves, and plenty of pita for sopping up the creamy filling.

MAKE THE FILLING. In a medium bowl, blend the labneh, feta, chopped pistachios, and chopped mint with a fork. Taste, seasoning lightly with salt only if necessary (some feta is very salty) and plenty of pepper.

STUFF THE PEPPERS. Slide a paring knife around the stem of each pepper and discard. Using the knife, loosen and discard the seeds. (You can also gently bang the peppers upside down on your cutting board to dislodge them.) Grab your smallest spoon—a baby spoon, ideally—and stuff each pepper with the filling to the top.

(continued)

Labneh-Stuffed Peppers *(continued)*

FRY THE PEPPERS. In a large skillet, heat the oil over medium-high heat until very hot but not smoking. Add the peppers, laying them on their sides. Partly cover the skillet and pan-fry the peppers on all sides, turning carefully, until the filling oozes and the skins char and begin to blister, about 6 minutes total.

GARNISH AND SERVE. Arrange the peppers on a platter. Mince the remaining 1 tablespoon pistachios and the mint leaves together and sprinkle over the peppers to garnish. Serve warm with plenty of pita.

Shiitake Frittata with Labneh, Kale, and Shallots

12 large eggs

¼ cup plain whole-milk or low-fat Greek yogurt

Kosher salt and freshly ground pepper

¼ cup extra-virgin olive oil, plus (optional) additional for drizzling

4 large shallots, sliced

6 shiitake mushrooms, stemmed and halved (or coarsely chopped if very large)

6 kale leaves, stems and central stalks removed, leaves chopped

½ cup labneh, homemade (page 329) or store-bought (see Yo!, page 97)

1 to 2 teaspoons dried culinary lavender (see Yo!) or snipped fresh chives

SERVES 6

Sometimes you need a big, crowd-pleasing brunch dish that can sit out and look pretty long after friends arrive. This vegetarian main will satisfy everyone—those who value good looks, those who appreciate umami, and those who know that kale in your frittata means you can nab a second scone. Creamy pools of labneh, softened shallots, and meaty shiitake mushrooms join the greens in this sophisticated main. For the best texture, do not overcook.

PREP THE OVEN. Preheat the broiler.

MAKE THE FRITTATA. In a large bowl, whisk the eggs and yogurt. Season generously with salt and pepper.

Heat a 14-inch cast-iron skillet over medium heat. Add the ¼ cup oil and the shallots. Cook, stirring frequently, until soft, about 5 minutes. Add the shiitakes cut side down and the kale. Cook, undisturbed, for 5 minutes. Pour the egg mixture around the mushrooms and, using a small scoop or tablespoon, dollop the labneh on top in little mounds. Cook for 5 minutes longer, sliding a spatula under the frittata to let the liquid eggs flow underneath as large swaths begin to set. (If using a 12-inch skillet, cook for a minute or two longer.)

(continued)

BROIL AND SERVE. Slip the pan under the broiler and broil until the frittata is golden and set, 2 to 3 minutes, watching carefully. Serve warm or at room temperature, garnished with the lavender or chives and drizzled sparingly with additional olive oil, if desired.

Yo!

Grab your biggest cast-iron skillet—14 inches, preferably, but 12 inches will do (just cook a 12-inch frittata a bit longer). In a pinch, use a nonstick skillet with an oven-proof handle. You can also make this recipe in two smaller skillets. Each frittata will be thicker and will therefore take a bit longer to set, both on the stovetop and under the broiler.

Look for culinary lavender in natural foods stores or order it online from Kalustyans.com or Worldspice.com. If you can't find it, you can omit it.

If you have truffle oil or truffle salt, dig it out for a light drizzle or sprinkle right before serving. (Or keep things simple and drizzle with a bit more olive oil instead.)

Potato-Leek Tart with Parmesan and Thyme

Ice cubes

About 1 cup cold water

2 cups all-purpose flour

1¼ cups finely shredded Parmesan

Kosher salt and freshly ground pepper

12 tablespoons (1½ sticks) very cold unsalted butter, cut into cubes

5 or 6 sprigs fresh thyme

½ pound red or Yukon Gold potatoes (2 or 3 medium), scrubbed

2 medium leeks, trimmed, white and pale green parts only, halved lengthwise and rinsed thoroughly

2 tablespoons extra-virgin olive oil

1 garlic clove, smashed and minced

1 cup plain whole-milk yogurt, at room temperature

3 large eggs, at room temperature

MAKES TWO 9-INCH TARTS; EACH TART SERVES 6

Yogurt replaces heavy cream in a custard filling that cradles potatoes, leeks, and shreds of nutty Parmesan. Savory tarts take a bit of up-front work—chilling the dough, cooking the filling—but the extra effort pays off. I recommend dividing this recipe into phases: boil and cool the potatoes, prep and chill the tart dough, and even cook the leeks a few hours or up to 1 day ahead, if you like. (Refrigerate the components separately, covered.) The rest of the recipe goes quickly.

MAKE THE TART DOUGH. Fill a liquid measuring cup halfway with ice cubes and add the cold water. (You won't use it all.) In a food processor, combine the flour, ⅓ cup of the Parmesan, 1¼ teaspoons salt, ¼ teaspoon pepper, the butter, and the stripped leaves of 2 of the thyme sprigs. Pulse in bursts until the butter is the size of peas. With the machine on, gradually add 5 tablespoons of the ice water through the feed tube. Let the machine run just until the dough forms a ball. Remove the dough, divide in half, and press each half into a thick disk. Wrap separately in plastic wrap and refrigerate for at least 30 minutes.

MEANWHILE, BOIL THE POTATOES. Place the potatoes in a medium saucepan and cover with cold water by 2 inches. Bring to a boil. Reduce the heat and boil gently until a skewer comes out with no resistance, 20 to 30 minutes. Cool completely (plunge in ice water, if you like), then peel, if desired, and cut in ¼-inch-thick slices.

COOK THE LEEKS. Slice the leeks thinly crosswise. In a large skillet, warm the oil over medium-low heat. Add the leeks, season generously with salt and pepper, and cook, stirring frequently, until very tender, 6 to 8 minutes. Add the garlic and cook for about 30 seconds. Remove from the heat and let cool completely.

MAKE THE CUSTARD. In a large bowl, whisk the yogurt vigorously with ¾ teaspoon salt and ¼ teaspoon pepper. Whisk in the eggs one at a time until completely incorporated.

LINE THE TART PANS. Preheat the oven to 425°F, with one oven rack in the bottom position and a second one just above. Working with one dough disk at a time (keep the second one refrigerated), roll out the dough on a floured surface into a 12-inch round. (If the dough is too cold, you may need to leave it at room temperature for a few minutes before rolling.) Transfer to a 9-inch tart pan with a removable bottom, easing the dough into the fluted edges and folding down any overhang to create double-thick sides. (Avoid stretching the dough.) Set on a baking sheet and refrigerate until needed. Repeat with the remaining tart dough and pan.

FILL AND BAKE THE TARTS. Sprinkle the bottom of each tart shell with ⅓ cup of the remaining Parmesan. Divide the potato slices and leek mixture between the tart shells. Carefully pour the custard over the vegetables, dividing evenly. Sprinkle each tart with 2 tablespoons Parmesan. Garnish with the remaining whole thyme sprigs. Bake until the filling is set, golden, and slightly puffed, 25 to 30 minutes, switching the position of the tarts halfway through to ensure even baking. Serve warm.

Eritrean Spicy Tomato Bread Salad with Yogurt (Fata)

½ medium red onion, finely chopped

4 garlic cloves, smashed and minced

¼ cup plus 1 tablespoon extra-virgin olive oil or vegetable oil

4 good-sized plum tomatoes

⅔ cup water

2 teaspoons tomato paste

½ to ¾ teaspoon hot Hungarian paprika, or more, to taste

⅛ to ¼ teaspoon cayenne pepper, or more, to taste

Big pinch of ground allspice

Kosher salt

6 small crusty rolls (plain or sourdough)

Diced red onion, diced jalapeño, and diced tomato, for garnish

Plenty of plain low-fat or whole-milk yogurt (not Greek), for serving

SERVES 2 OR 3

Fata mis celeste banee, a dish of spicy tomato sauce spooned over three torn rolls (*celeste* means three, *banee* means bread) and drizzled with yogurt was my husband's favorite lunch for the two years we worked as Peace Corps volunteers in Eritrea.

Cracking the code on a beloved dish from long ago isn't easy. Fortunately we have a large network of friends from our Eritrea days, all of whom piped up via email to help us recall the basic elements of this simple, peasant-like meal. Since *berbere*, a complex spice mixture in Eritrean cooking, is difficult to come by, I've called for a mix of Hungarian hot paprika, cayenne, and allspice, plus tomato paste for color, all of which can be easily found in major grocery stores.

MAKE THE SAUCE. In a medium saucepan, combine the onion, garlic, and oil. Cook, stirring occasionally, over medium heat for about 10 minutes to soften and develop flavor. If the mixture begins to brown, reduce the heat a bit, but try to maintain a gentle, audible sizzle. Meanwhile, break down the tomatoes on a cutting board with a large, heavy knife. Chop them as fine as possible, turning them basically into a mass of seedy, watery pulp without discrete chunks. When the onion mixture is ready, add the chopped tomatoes to the saucepan along with the water, tomato paste, paprika, cayenne, and allspice. Season generously with salt. Simmer gently, uncovered, for

20 to 25 minutes, reducing the heat to as low as possible about halfway through. You want to cook off much of the water but still have a fairly fluid sauce.

FINISH AND SERVE. If the rolls are soft, toast them for a few minutes so they develop a nice crustiness. (If they're already crusty, don't bother.) Tear the rolls into medium pieces and divide among two or three serving bowls. When the sauce is ready, taste and adjust the seasoning with additional salt, paprika, and/or cayenne, if necessary. (The heat should be prominent.) Ladle the sauce over the bread, dividing evenly. Garnish each portion with the red onion, jalapeño, and tomato and add plenty of yogurt to cool things down. Serve immediately, before the bread gets too mushy.

Creamy Pasta Marinara

3 tablespoons extra-virgin olive oil

1 medium onion, grated or finely chopped

2 garlic cloves, smashed and minced

1 24- to 28-ounce jar or can tomato puree

Kosher salt and freshly ground pepper

½ cup plain whole-milk Greek yogurt, at room temperature

Crushed red pepper, to taste (optional)

1 pound pasta, for serving

Torn fresh basil, for garnish

Yo!

You can leave the sauce a bit chunky, or puree it before adding the yogurt.

For a meaty twist, sprinkle the finished sauce with ½ cup crisp, cooked diced pancetta.

SERVES 6 TO 8

I first tasted vodka sauce, the pinkish tomato- and cream-based concoction whose vodka was tough to pinpoint but nevertheless added a special mystery, at a pastacentric restaurant in New York City. That sauce inspired this vodka-free one, with yogurt taking the place of cream. If you're not serving children, go ahead and kick things up with an extra clove of garlic and a generous pinch (or three) of crushed red pepper.

MAKE THE SAUCE. In a large saucepan, warm 2 tablespoons of the oil over medium-low heat. Add the onion and cook, stirring occasionally, until soft and translucent, 8 to 10 minutes. Toss in the garlic and cook, stirring constantly, until fragrant, about 30 seconds. Pour in the tomato puree and season generously with salt and pepper. Bring to a bubble, then reduce the heat and maintain a low simmer so the flavors can fully develop, 30 to 40 minutes, giving a stir when you think of it. Remove from the heat and let cool for about 10 minutes.

TEMPER THE YOGURT. In a small bowl, whisk the remaining 1 tablespoon oil into the yogurt. Whisk in ½ cup of the warm sauce to temper the yogurt. Scrape the yogurt mixture back into the saucepan, whisking to incorporate fully. Taste, adding more salt and pepper and the crushed red pepper, if desired.

SERVE. Boil the pasta in plenty of salted water according to the package instructions. At the end of cooking, set aside ½ cup of the pasta water. Using a slotted spoon or tongs, slowly transfer the hot pasta to the tomato sauce, tossing to coat. Drizzle in a tablespoon or two of the reserved pasta water, or more if desired, to loosen. Serve hot, garnished with the basil.

Chickpea-Quinoa Bowl with Harissa Yogurt

1¾ cups water

1 cup quinoa, preferably red

¼ cup plus 1 tablespoon extra-virgin olive oil

2¾ to 3 cups rinsed and drained cooked or canned chickpeas (see Yo!), patted dry

¾ teaspoon salt

¼ teaspoon freshly ground pepper

2 tablespoons fresh lemon juice, plus lemon wedges for serving

¼ cup finely chopped fresh cilantro or Italian parsley

¾ cup plain whole-milk yogurt (not Greek)

1 tablespoon plus 1 teaspoon harissa (see Yo!)

SERVES 4 AS A MAIN COURSE OR 6 AS A SIDE DISH

Chickpeas are true chameleons. Pureed with garlic and tahini, they become soothing, filling hummus. Tossed into salads, they offer mild, nutty flavor and tender texture—a nice counterpoint to crunchy vegetables and leafy greens. In this main dish, they're sautéed in a skillet so their exteriors brown in spots, making them gently crisp but still yielding to the bite. A bed of fluffy quinoa and a lively harissa-yogurt sauce complete the picture. When eating, I recommend scooping up the harissa and yogurt with each forkful rather than stirring it throughout the dish.

COOK THE QUINOA. Bring the water to a boil in medium saucepan. Place the quinoa in a fine-mesh strainer and rinse well. Add it to the saucepan and return to a boil. Lower the heat, partly cover, and simmer gently for 10 to 15 minutes, until the seeds shoot out a thread-like curlicue. Remove from the heat. Let stand, covered, until needed. (Makes 2 cups cooked quinoa.)

CRISP THE CHICKPEAS. Heat ¼ cup of the oil in a large nonstick skillet over medium-high heat. When the oil is hot enough that a single chickpea sizzles on contact, add the chickpeas, salt, and pepper. Cook, shaking the pan frequently, until the chickpeas are deeply browned in spots and nicely crisp, about 8 minutes. Remove from the heat.

SERVE. Transfer the quinoa to a serving bowl. Sprinkle with 1 tablespoon of the lemon juice and the remaining 1 tablespoon oil. Give it a stir. Tumble the chickpeas over the quinoa. Shower with the herbs. In a small bowl, stir the yogurt with the remaining 1 tablespoon lemon juice. Scrape the yogurt over the chickpeas. Dollop the harissa into the center of the yogurt and swirl a bit with a fork, but do not whisk. (Whisking will make the yogurt turn salmony pink.) Serve immediately, passing lemon wedges at the table.

Yo!

Harissa is a brick-red, chile-based condiment common in North Africa and the Middle East. Look for it in tubes or cans in Middle Eastern or international markets (or see Sources).

You'll need two 15-ounce cans of chickpeas (garbanzo beans) for this recipe. Or, do what I do and cook them up yourself: In a large bowl, cover 1 cup dried chickpeas with plenty of cold water. Soak overnight. Rinse and drain. Transfer to a medium saucepan, cover with cold water by 2 inches, and add ½ teaspoon baking soda. Bring to a boil, skimming off the white foam that rises to the surface. Reduce the heat and simmer vigorously, uncovered, until very tender, 30 to 40 minutes, depending on the age of the beans. Drain. Use right away, or cool, pat dry, and refrigerate for a few days, until ready to proceed. (Makes 2¾ cups cooked chickpeas.)

Middle Eastern Eggplant Casserole (Fatet Makdous)

1 tablespoon extra-virgin olive oil

1 small onion, diced

2 garlic cloves, smashed and minced, plus 2 whole garlic cloves

1 globe eggplant (1 to 1¼ pounds), cut into ½-inch cubes

1 28-ounce can diced or crushed tomatoes with juice, or tomato puree

½ cup plus 2 to 4 teaspoons water

¾ teaspoon ground cumin

Kosher salt and freshly ground pepper

1 tablespoon pomegranate molasses (optional; see Yo!, page 50)

1½ cups plain whole-milk yogurt (not Greek)

3 tablespoons tahini

2 large or 3 small pita, toasted

⅓ cup lightly toasted slivered almonds and/or pine nuts, for garnish

Minced fresh parsley and/or mint, for garnish

SERVES 6 AS A MAIN COURSE OR 12 AS A SIDE DISH

This rustic, vegetarian casserole, called *fatet makdous* in Arabic, is composed of layers of torn, toasted pita, tomato-stewed eggplant, and yogurt-tahini sauce. Sprinkled with an almond-herb topping, it was served to me by Balkees Abu-Rabie in Nazareth, Israel, when I went to her house for lunch. Though this particular version is vegetarian, *fatet makdous* can also include meat.

Nazareth is the largest city in Israel's Northern District, with curvy roads and houses built on hillsides. Through the windows, the city splayed out dramatically. In front of us, on a low table, was a shellacked bowl that looked like a small, hollowed-out log, full of almonds in their shells.

Beside the nuts were wooden paddles, some for molding cookies, others for stamping designs on loaves of bread. Each had ornate, deep-set grooves. Abu-Rabie grabbed a mound of dough, made a fist, and pressed it into a paddle. She brought out more seed-speckled dough so my fellow travelers and I could try the technique ourselves.

Soon, it was time for lunch. We ate the bread, which Abu-Rabie had baked in a small stairwell oven, with bowls of lentil soup, a cress and sumac salad, chicken with freekeh, and the *fatet makdous*. From Abu-Rabie, we learned the history behind each dish. In the distance, fireworks popped. We jumped, and Abu-Rabie smiled, explaining that the sound was one of celebration not alarm, commemorating the return of the pilgrims from Mecca.

When lunch ended, I wanted to stay and learn more about Abu-Rabie and her family and their everyday lives. Her good will and generosity, and the memory of that meal, have stayed with me ever since.

MAKE THE EGGPLANT AND SAUCE. In a Dutch oven or large skillet, heat the oil over medium heat. Add the onion and cook, stirring occasionally, until soft and just beginning to brown, 8 to 10 minutes. Add the minced garlic and stir for about 30 seconds, until fragrant. Stir in the eggplant, tomatoes, the ½ cup water, the cumin, 1 teaspoon salt, and ½ teaspoon pepper and bring to a simmer. Reduce the heat to low, cover, and simmer gently for 30 minutes, until the eggplant is tender. Remove the lid, add the pomegranate molasses, if using, and continue to simmer until the sauce has thickened and most of the excess liquid has cooked off, about 15 minutes longer. The sauce should be loose but not at all watery.

Preheat the oven to 350°F, with a rack in the center position.

MAKE THE YOGURT SAUCE. Whisk together the yogurt, tahini, and the remaining 2 to 4 teaspoons water. (If the yogurt was very thick to start, use 4 teaspoons water.) Grate the whole garlic cloves directly into the yogurt sauce, then season with a pinch each of salt and pepper. Whisk until smooth.

ASSEMBLE AND SERVE. Break the toasted pita into large, irregular pieces and lay them on the bottom of a 13-by-9-inch baking dish. Top with the eggplant sauce. Scrape the yogurt sauce on top, spreading gently to smooth and leaving a slight border around the edges so the red sauce peeks through. Bake for 5 minutes only, just to set and warm the yogurt. Scatter the toasted nuts and minced herbs on top. Serve hot or warm.

Cast-Iron Chicken with Barberry (or Cranberry) Gremolata over Freekeh

1 cup plain whole-milk yogurt (not Greek)

1 teaspoon ground allspice

1 teaspoon ground cardamom

1 teaspoon kosher salt

½ teaspoon freshly ground pepper

3 to 4 tablespoons extra-virgin olive oil

1 lemon

1 whole chicken (4 to 5 pounds, preferably organic), cut into 10 pieces, or 6 bone-in, skin-on chicken thighs, very large thighs cut in half

(continued)

SERVES 6 TO 8

This chicken supper benefits from an overnight marinade. It's served on a bed of toasted grain called freekeh, with a topping of chopped parsley, lemon zest, and sweet-and-sour barberries (or cranberries). It's a comforting family meal with an irresistible flavor profile.

Freekeh is a popular, jagged-edged Middle Eastern grain, a roasted form of durum wheat that's harvested early. With a subtle, nutty taste, it develops a tempting crust when baked in the oven. Soaking the freekeh isn't obligatory, but doing so ensures that the meat and grains will cook through simultaneously.

Ask your butcher to halve larger chicken breasts or thighs for you, if necessary, so that all the pieces are roughly the same size. (I ask whoever's behind the meat counter to break down a whole organic chicken into 10 parts.)

MARINATE AND SOAK. In a medium bowl, whisk together the yogurt, allspice, cardamom, salt, pepper, and 2 tablespoons of the oil. Finely zest the lemon, wrap the zest in a bit of plastic wrap, and reserve it in the refrigerator for the gremolata. Juice the lemon into the yogurt mixture and whisk to combine. Transfer the marinade to a gallon-size zip-top bag and add the chicken, pressing out any air. Massage well and refrigerate overnight, turning it a few times if you think of it.

(continued)

1½ cups freekeh (see Yo!), picked over and rinsed

¼ cup dry wine, preferably white, but red's fine

1 large onion, diced

3½ cups chicken stock or low-sodium chicken broth

½ cup plus 1 tablespoon dried barberries (see Yo!, page 71) or unsweetened dried cranberries

½ cup (loosely packed) fresh Italian parsley

In a separate bowl, cover the freekeh with cool water by 2 inches. Refrigerate, covered, overnight. (The grains will absorb most of the water.)

COOK THE CHICKEN AND FREEKEH. Preheat the oven to 375°F.

Drain the chicken, discarding the marinade. Separately, drain the freekeh, if necessary. In your largest cast-iron skillet (see Yo!), heat 1 tablespoon oil over medium-high heat until very hot but not smoking. Brown the chicken, skin side down only, in two batches (adding a second tablespoon of oil between batches, if necessary), until the skin is deeply colored. Remove to a large plate or tray. Drain off all but 1 tablespoon fat from the skillet, if desired.

Maintaining medium-high heat, add the wine and onion, scraping the skillet with a wooden spoon. Cook, stirring frequently, until the onion is softened, about 4 minutes. Add the freekeh, season with salt and pepper, and cook, stirring, for 2 minutes to lightly toast the grains. Add the chicken stock and ½ cup of the barberries or cranberries and bring to a boil. Simmer vigorously until about three quarters of the liquid has been absorbed, about 10 minutes.

Nestle the chicken skin side up in a single layer on the freekeh. Transfer to the oven and bake, uncovered, for 45 to 50 minutes, until the freekeh has absorbed about 90 percent of the stock, the top of the grains looks dry, and the chicken has cooked through. (If you nudge the grains aside, a bit of lovely gravy should be visible underneath.)

MAKE THE GREMOLATA AND SERVE. Heap the parsley, the reserved lemon zest, and the remaining 1 tablespoon barberries or cranberries on a cutting board and chop finely. Sprinkle the gremolata over the chicken and freekeh. Serve hot or warm.

Yo!

Look for both freekeh and barberries in an international or Middle Eastern grocery.

If you have the space, you'll find a 14-inch cast-iron skillet indispensable for paella, fried chicken, scrambled eggs or corned beef hash for a crowd, large cobblers, and both the Shiitake Frittata with Labneh, Kale, and Shallots (page 185) and this recipe. But not everyone cooks for large groups. If you don't have one, substitute a 12-inch skillet or Dutch oven and simmer the freekeh for a few extra minutes on the stove before transferring to the oven.

Twice-Cooked Yogurt-Marinated Chicken

8 garlic cloves, coarsely chopped

1 1½-inch piece fresh ginger, peeled and coarsely chopped

½ cup plain whole-milk yogurt (not Greek)

1 tablespoon extra-virgin olive oil

1 tablespoon fresh lemon juice

2 teaspoons sumac (see Yo!, page 105) or lemon zest

1 teaspoon kosher salt

½ teaspoon freshly ground pepper

1 (4- to 4½-pound) chicken, preferably organic, cut into 8 to 10 pieces

SERVES 6

Two special features make this dish stand out. First, an overnight garlic-yogurt soak infuses the chicken with big flavor and keeps it juicy and tender under heat. Second, a two-stage cooking process calls for first baking and then grilling the meat. This baking-grilling process was inspired by a chicken recipe in Heidi Insalata Krahling's wonderful cookbook, *Insalata's Mediterranean Table.* Happily, the yogurt marinade makes this dish difficult to overcook.

MARINATE THE CHICKEN. In a food processor, combine the garlic and ginger and process until very finely chopped. Add the yogurt, oil, lemon juice, sumac or lemon zest, salt, and pepper and process for about 1 minute. Stop the machine, scrape down the sides, and then process for about 1 minute longer, until very well blended. (The mixture may still be a bit chunky.) Put the chicken pieces in a gallon-size zip-top bag and pour in the marinade. Press out the air, seal the bag, massage it well, and refrigerate for 24 hours.

BAKE THE CHICKEN. Preheat the oven to 375°F, with a rack in the center position. Line a baking sheet with foil and set an ovenproof (uncoated) metal cooling rack on top. Lift the chicken from the marinade and lay the pieces skin side up on the rack. (The air circulation will help crisp the bottom.) Bake for 30 to 40 minutes, depending on the size and thickness of the pieces, until the meat firms, the marinade sets, and everything but the skin looks cooked.

PREP THE GRILL. About 10 minutes before removing the chicken from the oven, prepare a grill for direct cooking over medium-high heat (about 400°F). Scrape the grates clean.

GRILL THE CHICKEN. When the chicken has finished baking, transfer the pieces skin side up to the hot grill. Grill the chicken, keeping the lid closed as much as possible, flipping with tongs a few times, for anywhere from 8 to 20 minutes, until the meat is done and the skin is crisp but not burned. The wings will finish first; whole breasts, thighs, and drumsticks may take the full 20 minutes. Transfer the chicken pieces to a serving platter.

Yo!

Because chickens these days vary enormously in size, add or reduce the grilling time if your chicken is larger or smaller than the 4 pounds called for. If the breasts are especially large, ask your butcher to halve them so the marinade can best penetrate the meat. Smaller pieces, such as wings, will finish cooking before the larger breasts, thighs, and drumsticks.

I sometimes remove everything but the breasts (if whole) after 10 to 15 minutes, turn off the grill, and then let the residual heat finish cooking the breasts for a few more minutes while I go inside and gather the plates.

Coriander-Lime Grilled Chicken

½ cup (loosely packed) fresh cilantro leaves with tender stems attached

½ cup plain yogurt

1 tablespoon extra-virgin olive oil

1½ teaspoons ground coriander

Juice of ½ small lime, plus (optional) lime wedges for serving

1 garlic clove, coarsely chopped

1 teaspoon kosher salt

½ teaspoon freshly ground pepper

1½ pounds boneless, skinless chicken breasts, patted dry and sliced into cutlets (see Yo!)

Olive oil spray (optional)

Yo!

To make the cutlets, press your palm on top of each, and carefully slide a knife parallel to the cutting board, dividing each breast into two thinner cutlets.

SERVES 4

One of my favorite marinades for weeknight grilling, this vibrant green yogurt soak thoroughly pervades quick-cooking chicken breast cutlets. Start them a good 6 hours ahead for the biggest flavor payoff. Chicken cutlets grill in under 10 minutes.

MARINATE THE CHICKEN. In a food processor, combine the cilantro, yogurt, oil, coriander, lime juice, garlic, salt, and pepper and puree until smooth, stopping the machine a few times to scrape down the sides.

Place the chicken in a gallon-size zip-top bag. Pour the marinade over the chicken, squeeze out any excess air, and seal the bag. Refrigerate flat for 6 hours (a bit longer is fine), flipping and massaging the bag a few times if you think of it. Remove the chicken from the refrigerator 20 minutes before grilling.

PREP THE GRILL. Preheat the grill for medium-high direct heat (400 to 450°F). Scrape the grates clean.

GRILL THE CHICKEN. Transfer the cutlets to a baking sheet, letting the marinade drip away. (Discard the marinade, but do not pat the cutlets dry.) Coat both sides of the cutlets with olive oil spray, if desired. Grill, turning once, until deeply marked and cooked through, 8 to 10 minutes total.

SERVE. Let the chicken rest for 5 to 10 minutes. Slice into strips and serve with lime wedges, if desired.

Chicken Curry with Almond Cream

FOR THE MARINADE AND CHICKEN

⅔ cup plain low-fat or whole-milk yogurt (not Greek)

¼ cup ginger-garlic paste (see page 207)

1¼ teaspoons turmeric

1¼ teaspoons ground coriander

1 teaspoon garam masala

1 teaspoon red chile powder or ½ teaspoon cayenne pepper

Kosher salt

1 tablespoon extra-virgin olive oil

2 pounds boneless, skinless chicken thighs, cut into 1½-inch chunks

(continued)

SERVES 10 TO 12

An opulent almond cream serves as the spectacular finishing touch to this generously portioned chicken curry, one bathed in yogurt and heady with Indian spices. It came my way via Nayaki Nayyar, an executive at a major Silicon Valley software company who was raised in Hyderabad, India. Nayyar cooks big meals on the weekends to sustain her husband and two sons during her frequent spates of international travel. She walked me through the preparation of this classic dish, one I now make for my own family as often as possible.

MARINATE THE CHICKEN. In a large bowl, whisk together the yogurt, ginger-garlic paste, turmeric, coriander, garam masala, chile powder or cayenne, 1 tablespoon salt, and the oil until smooth. Season the chicken with a touch more salt and add it to the marinade, tossing to coat. Cover and refrigerate for several hours or overnight.

(continued)

> ### Yo!
>
> This curry has moderate heat, which my family and I love. To tone it down, halve the amount of red chile and serrano.

FOR THE CURRY

¼ cup extra-virgin olive oil

2 medium red onions, diced

2 serrano chiles, cut into large chunks

2 tablespoons ginger-garlic paste (see below)

2 plum tomatoes, coarsely chopped

1 teaspoon turmeric

1 teaspoon red chile powder or ½ teaspoon cayenne pepper

1 teaspoon ground coriander

1½ teaspoons kosher salt

2 medium russet potatoes, peeled and cut into ¾-inch dice

1¾ cups water, or more if needed

¾ cup raw unsalted almonds

Plenty of steamed rice, for serving

Fresh cilantro, for garnish

MAKE THE CURRY. In a Dutch oven or large saucepan, preferably nonstick, heat the oil over medium-high heat. Add the onions and chiles. Cook, stirring occasionally, until tender and nicely browned, 10 to 15 minutes. Add the ginger-garlic paste and stir constantly for 30 seconds. Stir in the tomatoes. Bring to a simmer, reduce the heat to medium-low, cover, and cook for 5 minutes. Mash the tomato mixture lightly with a wooden spoon. Stir in the turmeric, chile powder or cayenne, coriander, and salt. Add the chicken, all the marinade, the potatoes, and 1 cup of the water and stir well. Cook, covered, stirring occasionally, at a gentle but steady simmer until the chicken is cooked through and the potatoes are tender, about 45 minutes. If the liquid starts to run dry, add a touch more water.

MAKE THE ALMOND CREAM. In a blender, puree the almonds with the remaining ¾ cup water until foamy and as smooth as possible. Stir into the chicken curry. Continue to cook until warmed through.

SERVE. Spoon the chicken curry over steamed rice and garnish with cilantro. The curry will thicken as it stands and upon storage; leftovers can be refrigerated, covered, for several days.

Ginger-Garlic Paste

Ginger-garlic paste is a foundational ingredient in Indian curries. It's easy to make your own. Blitz one 3-inch knob peeled fresh ginger and 1 medium head garlic, cloves peeled and smashed, in a mini food processor until smooth, about 1 minute. You'll have about ½ cup, twice as much as you need for this recipe. It will keep in a tightly sealed jar for several weeks.

Yogurt-Plumped Lamb Kebabs

¾ cup plain low-fat or whole-milk yogurt

1 tablespoon extra-virgin olive oil

1½ teaspoons smoked paprika

½ teaspoon turmeric

Juice of ½ lemon

1¼ teaspoons kosher salt

½ teaspoon freshly ground pepper

2 to 2½ pounds lamb kebab meat, or boneless leg of lamb cut into 2-inch cubes

Olive oil spray

Lemon wedges, for serving

Yo!

If using wooden skewers, soak them for at least 30 minutes before grilling.

SERVES 4

Alternating meat and vegetables on skewers has understandable appeal: You get your main and side on a single stick, with colorful produce lending visual punch. But in many countries, meat kebabs are just that: meat on a stick, with salads and vegetables served separately, alongside. Cubed lamb (sold as "kebab meat" at some meat counters) enjoys a seasoned-yogurt soak, then is grilled until charred. Served simply with lemon or—better yet—with Turkish-Style Spinach Dip (page 102), it's a caveman-like dinner that's weeknight friendly.

MARINATE THE LAMB. In a large bowl, whisk the yogurt, oil, paprika, turmeric, lemon juice, salt, and pepper until smooth. Add the lamb and toss to coat. Cover and refrigerate for 4 to 12 hours. Remove the lamb from the refrigerator 30 minutes before grilling to come to room temperature.

PREP THE GRILL. Preheat the grill for medium-high direct heat (400 to 500°F). Scrape the grates completely clean.

ASSEMBLE THE KEBABS. Set a colander in the sink. Turn the meat and marinade out into the colander so the excess marinade can drain away. Thread the lamb onto skewers, dividing evenly. Coat on all sides with olive oil spray.

GRILL AND SERVE. Grill the skewers for 10 to 16 minutes total (depending on the size of your kebab meat), turning two or three times, until evenly charred on all sides and cooked through. Serve hot, with lemon wedges.

Lamb Kefte Sandwiches with Middle Eastern Yogurt Salad

1 cup diced English cucumber

1 cup diced red onion

1¼ cups plain yogurt (not Greek), preferably whole-milk

3 garlic cloves, smashed and minced

¼ teaspoon sumac (optional; see Yo!, page 105)

Kosher salt and freshly ground pepper

1 pound ground lamb

5 tablespoons tahini

⅓ cup finely chopped yellow onion

2 tablespoons soaked bulgur (see Yo!)

¾ teaspoon ground cumin

½ teaspoon ground cinnamon

½ teaspoon paprika

¼ teaspoon cayenne pepper

½ cup chopped tomato or quartered cherry or grape tomatoes

4 rectangles lavash bread

4 cups shredded lettuce

MAKES 4 LARGE SANDWICHES OR 8 HALF SANDWICHES

Several staples of Middle Eastern cuisine come together in this substantial sandwich: huge rectangles of pliable lavash bread; ground lamb meatballs fragrant with cumin, cinnamon, and paprika; and a yogurt-drenched cucumber, tomato, and red onion salad. Traditionally, the yogurt sauce and vegetables are added separately, but I like mixing them together so the flavors marry as the kefte cooks.

MAKE THE YOGURT SALAD. In a medium bowl, combine the cucumber, red onion, 1 cup of the yogurt, one third of the garlic, and the sumac, if using. Season lightly with salt and pepper. Cover and refrigerate until needed.

MAKE THE KEFTE. Preheat the oven to 450°F with a rack in the upper third. Line a baking sheet with foil.

In a large bowl, combine the lamb, 1 tablespoon of the tahini, the yellow onion, the soaked bulgur, cumin, cinnamon, paprika, cayenne, the remaining ¼ cup yogurt, and the remaining garlic. Season with 1 teaspoon salt and ½ teaspoon pepper. Mix gently but thoroughly with a fork. Scoop the meat into 20 to 24 mounds on the prepared baking sheet. (You can use a 1½-inch ice cream scoop or a spoon, doling out roughly 1½ tablespoons per kefte.) Lightly roll each mound in your hands to form ovals.

(continued)

BAKE FOR ABOUT 8 MINUTES, OR UNTIL SLIGHTLY PINK INSIDE. Tip off any liquid into the sink, then flip on the broiler and broil for 2 minutes, until the kefte brown a bit on top.

MAKE THE SANDWICHES. Stir the tomatoes into the yogurt salad. Make one sandwich at a time: Warm the lavash (if desired, see Yo!), spread with 1 tablespoon of the remaining tahini across the bottom third, sprinkle with 1 cup of the lettuce, top with 5 or 6 kefte in a horizontal line, and spoon one quarter of the yogurt salad over the kefte. Roll up, pinching the sides so the contents don't escape. Cut in half on the diagonal. Repeat with the remaining lavash and fixings.

Yo!

If desired, you may warm the lavash briefly just before rolling, either directly over the flame of a gas burner or on a baking sheet in a low oven for 3 to 5 minutes. If your lavash has been refrigerated, warming it will make it easier to roll.

To soak the bulgur, place 1 scant tablespoon quick-cooking bulgur in a small bowl. Cover with boiling water. Let stand until tender, 10 to 20 minutes. Drain. (Makes 2 tablespoons.)

Chorizo-Black Bean Tacos with Avocado-Lime Crema

8 ounces bulk fresh (Mexican) chorizo or hot Italian sausage

2 or 3 teaspoons extra-virgin olive oil

1 small onion, chopped (about 1 cup)

2 cups cooked black beans (or one 15-ounce can, rinsed and drained)

½ teaspoon ground cumin

¼ teaspoon ground chipotle chile

Kosher salt and freshly ground pepper

Juice of 1 lime (about 2 tablespoons)

½ avocado, pitted and peeled

½ cup plain yogurt (not Greek)

10 taco shells, warmed

Optional accompaniments: Shredded lettuce, diced avocado, chopped tomatoes, lime wedges, fresh cilantro, shredded cheddar or Jack cheese

SERVES 4 OR 5 (10 TACOS)

Yogurt and avocado are perfect partners. When blended together and kicked up with lime, they create a smooth, green sauce, perfect over spicy tacos or tostadas. This simple crema can also double as a dressing. Try it with a chopped summer salad of romaine, cherry tomatoes, fresh corn, and bacon.

MAKE THE FILLING. Set a large skillet over medium-high heat. Once hot, add the chorizo, breaking it up with the back of a wooden spoon. Cook, stirring occasionally and breaking up clumps, until the fat renders and the meat browns, about 5 minutes. Remove to a plate with a slotted spoon.

Reduce the heat to medium. Add 2 or 3 teaspoons oil to the skillet (depending on how much fat was released by the meat). Add the onion and cook, stirring occasionally, until soft, about 5 minutes. Return the chorizo to the skillet and add the beans, cumin, chipotle, ¼ teaspoon each salt and pepper, and half the lime juice (about 1 tablespoon). Reduce the heat to low, cover, and simmer gently for 5 minutes, until the flavors meld.

MAKE THE CREMA. In a mini food processor, puree the avocado, yogurt, the remaining lime juice, and ⅛ teaspoon salt.

SERVE. Fill each taco shell with about ¼ cup of the chorizo mixture and drizzle with a generous spoonful of crema. Top with any of the optional accompaniments.

Skillet Pork Chops with Quick Mustard Sauce

FOR THE SAUCE

2 to 3 tablespoons apricot or peach preserves

¼ cup Dijon mustard

¼ cup plain Greek yogurt

¾ teaspoon white wine vinegar

Kosher salt and freshly ground pepper

Stripped leaves from a few sprigs fresh thyme

FOR THE PORK CHOPS

4 bone-in pork chops (2½ pounds total), each 1 inch thick

2 tablespoons plus 1 teaspoon olive oil

¼ teaspoon kosher salt

¼ teaspoon freshly ground pepper

1 tablespoon unsalted butter

Few sprigs fresh thyme

A few crushed pink peppercorns, for garnish (optional)

SERVES 4

A speedy mustard sauce glosses juicy pork chops in this low-effort week-night meal. Fresh thyme and optional pink peppercorns add a splash of color before serving. Serve with rice or noodles to lap up the extra sauce.

MAKE THE SAUCE. Warm 2 tablespoons of the preserves gently in the microwave (30 seconds on 50 percent power) or in your smallest skillet just to loosen. Whisk until smooth. Cool slightly. In a small bowl, whisk the warm preserves with the remaining sauce ingredients, adding more preserves, if you like.

COOK THE CHOPS. Preheat the oven to 350°F.

Set the pork chops on a baking sheet. Drizzle ½ teaspoon of the oil over each chop. Season with the salt and pepper and rub in with your fingers. Flip the chops and oil and season them.

Place your largest, ovenproof skillet (cast-iron is best) over high heat. Swirl in the remaining 1 tablespoon oil and the butter. When the butter foams, add the chops. Sear, undisturbed, until a dark crust forms, 4 to 6 minutes. Flip the chops and cook for about 1 minute on the second side. Transfer the skillet to the oven to finish cooking, 5 to 7 minutes longer. The centers should be juicy and slightly pink, but cooked through. Remove from the oven and let stand, covered loosely with foil, for 3 to 5 minutes.

GARNISH AND SERVE. Dollop a bit of sauce on each chop. Garnish with additional thyme sprigs and the pink peppercorns, if using. Pass the remaining sauce at the table.

Sausage, Spinach, and Apple Pot Pie

FOR THE DOUGH

1¼ cups all-purpose flour

½ teaspoon kosher salt

8 tablespoons (1 stick) cold unsalted butter, cut into ¾-inch cubes

2½ tablespoons plain low-fat or whole-milk yogurt, kept cold

FOR THE FILLING

1 teaspoon extra-virgin olive oil

1 pound bulk sweet Italian sausage

1 large onion, diced

2 teaspoons apple cider vinegar

1 large apple, unpeeled, cored and diced

4 cups (packed) baby spinach, coarsely chopped

MAKES ONE 9-INCH PIE; SERVES 6

Yogurt adds richness to this savory pie's pastry and filling. Featuring Italian sausage, warm pantry spices, fresh spinach, and sweet apple, the pie can be made ahead, in whole or in part, and baked right before serving.

MAKE THE DOUGH. In a stand mixer fitted with the paddle, mix the flour and salt briefly to combine. Add the butter and mix on low speed until the pieces are reduced to the size of large peas. Add the yogurt. Mix on the lowest speed until the dough just comes together in a single mass around the paddle, 1 to 2 minutes. Transfer to a large square of plastic wrap, flatten into a ¾-inch-thick disk, and wrap tightly. Refrigerate for at least 30 minutes. (The dough can be made up to 2 days ahead and refrigerated, well wrapped in plastic. Let it sit at room temperature for a bit so it becomes pliable.)

MEANWHILE, MAKE THE FILLING. Heat the oil in a large skillet over medium-high heat. When it starts to shimmer, add the sausage and cook, stirring and breaking up clumps, until the sausage is browned and cooked through, 8 to 10 minutes. With a slotted spoon, remove the sausage to a large bowl.

To the residual fat, add the onion and cook, stirring and scraping up the brown bits, until almost soft, 5 to 10 minutes. Add the vinegar and apple; cook, stirring frequently for 5 minutes longer. Add the spinach, cumin, nutmeg, and thyme; toss through until the spinach is wilted, 1 to 2 minutes. Scrape into the bowl with the sausage, tossing

¼ teaspoon ground cumin

¼ teaspoon freshly grated nutmeg

¼ teaspoon dried thyme

½ cup low-fat or whole-milk Greek yogurt, plus (optional) additional for garnish

FOR ASSEMBLING

1 large egg yolk, beaten with a splash of milk or cream, for egg wash

Yo!

If using sausage links, slit them and remove the meat from the casings.

to combine. Let cool for 15 minutes. Stir in the yogurt. (The filling can be made 1 to 2 days ahead. Refrigerate, covered, until ready to use.)

ASSEMBLE AND BAKE. Preheat the oven to 375°F.

Mound the filling in a standard 9-inch pie plate. Roll out the dough to an 11-inch round and drape over the filling, taking care not to stretch the dough. Fold the overhanging dough under itself to make double-thick edges, pressing them against the rim and scalloping them, if desired. Brush all over with the egg wash. Cut a few slits in the top to vent steam.

Bake the pie until golden brown all over, 30 to 40 minutes. Cool slightly and enjoy hot or warm, with an extra dollop of yogurt beside each serving, if desired.

Baked Veal and Pork Meatballs (Yiaourtlou)

1½ cups plain Greek yogurt

Kosher salt and freshly ground pepper

1 tablespoon extra-virgin olive oil

1 medium onion, finely chopped

2 garlic cloves, smashed and minced

2 cups (16 ounces) fresh tomato puree (see Yo!) or jarred

1 tablespoon plus 1 teaspoon smoked paprika, plus more for garnish

Pinch of cayenne pepper, or more, to taste

½ pound ground veal

½ pound ground pork

2 teaspoons ground cumin

4 teaspoons chopped fresh mint

2 pitas, split in half to yield 4 thin rounds and toasted

SERVES 4

During my visit to the Greek island of Paros, proprietor George Pittas of the charming Lefkes Village Hotel educated me about yogurt over glasses of *suma*, a local spirit. During our conversation, he instructed his chef to bring out plate after plate of yogurt-based specialties for me to try. One of them was a rustic plate of pita smothered with tomato sauce, lightly spiced meatball kebabs, and a paprika-sprinkled yogurt sauce. Though you may be accustomed to eating pita with your hands, this is messy knife-and-fork food at its best.

SEASON THE YOGURT. In a large bowl, whisk the yogurt vigorously with a generous pinch each of salt and pepper. Let stand at room temperature until needed.

MAKE THE TOMATO SAUCE. In a small saucepan, warm the oil over medium-low heat. Add half the onion (save the rest for the kebabs) and the garlic and cook, stirring occasionally, until soft, about 10 minutes. Add the tomato puree, 1 teaspoon of the smoked paprika, the cayenne, and a generous pinch each of salt and pepper. Simmer for 20 to 25 minutes over low heat while you make the kebabs. Taste, adding additional cayenne if desired for a more pronounced kick.

MAKE THE MEATBALLS. Preheat the oven to 450°F, with a rack in the center position. Line a baking sheet with parchment.

In a large bowl, combine the remaining onion, the veal, pork, the remaining 1 table-spoon smoked paprika, the cumin, 2 teaspoons of the mint, 1½ teaspoons salt, and ¾ teaspoon pepper. Mix gently but thoroughly with a fork. Use a 1½-inch ice cream scoop or a spoon to portion the mixture into about 20 mounds on the baking sheet. With moist hands, roll each mound gently between your palms into 2-inch ovals. Bake until cooked through, 10 to 12 minutes. Blot on paper towels to remove excess fat, if desired.

ASSEMBLE AND SERVE. Set each toasted pita round on a plate. Divide the meatballs among the pitas. Top generously with the tomato sauce (don't drown them, but give them more than a drizzle), then with the yogurt. Garnish with a sprinkle of smoked paprika and the remaining 2 teaspoons mint.

Yo!

Six (18 ounces) good-size ripe plum tomatoes, halved and seeded, will yield 16 to 18 ounces to make puree, perfect for this recipe. Puree them in a blender or food processor (no need to strain). While Pittas prefers veal and pork in this dish (as do I), beef and lamb are perfectly acceptable substitutes.

Dry-Rubbed Skirt Steak with Caramelized Onion Yogurt

2 teaspoons granulated onion or onion powder

1 tablespoon minced fresh sage, plus 4 small leaves for garnish

Kosher salt and freshly ground pepper

1¼ pounds skirt steak, cut into 4 pieces of roughly equal length and trimmed of any excess fat (leave the natural marbling intact)

3 tablespoons plus 2 teaspoons extra-virgin olive oil

2 large onions (1½ pounds total), halved and sliced

2 teaspoons sherry vinegar, apple cider vinegar, or white wine vinegar

2 teaspoons brown sugar

½ cup plain Greek yogurt

Olive oil spray or additional olive oil

¼ teaspoon cornstarch

1½ teaspoons cold water

Lime wedges, for serving

SERVES 4

When I was a kid, skirt steak was my dad's beef cut of choice. He'd sear the outside, leaving the inside nice and pink, and serve canned creamed corn alongside. Skirt steak's nostalgia factor for me is still high. I serve it with a sauce of yogurt and deeply caramelized onions.

MAKE THE DRY RUB. In a small bowl, stir the granulated onion or onion powder, minced sage, 1½ teaspoons salt, and ½ teaspoon pepper together. Lay the steaks side by side on a baking sheet or in a rectangular baking dish. Pat dry with paper towels and rub both sides evenly with the spice mix. Cover and refrigerate for 1 hour.

FRY THE SAGE. Heat a large skillet over medium-high heat for 2 minutes. Add 2 teaspoons of the oil. When the oil is shimmering but not smoking, add the whole sage leaves and fry until crisp and glossy, about 1½ minutes, flipping halfway through. Transfer the sage to paper towels to drain. Sprinkle with salt. Set aside for the garnish. Remove the skillet from the heat and let it cool slightly.

CARAMELIZE THE ONIONS. Add the remaining 3 tablespoons oil to the skillet, along with the onions, 1 teaspoon salt, and ¼ teaspoon pepper. Cook over medium heat, tossing occasionally with tongs, for about 15 minutes. Add the vinegar and brown sugar and toss well. Continue cooking, tossing frequently, until the onions soften completely and take on a deep, rich golden color, lowering the heat if they start to burn, 20 to 25 minutes longer. Remove from the heat. Taste, adding a bit more salt if desired. Cover to keep warm.

GRILL OR BROIL THE STEAK. When the onions are about halfway done, remove the steaks and the yogurt from the refrigerator and bring to room temperature. Preheat the grill for direct cooking over medium-high heat (400 to 450°F). Scrape the grates clean.

Coat the steaks with olive oil spray (or brush lightly with oil). Grill the steaks until dark grill marks appear on the outside and the inside is done to your liking, 3 to 4 minutes per side for medium-rare. (Alternatively, broil the steaks about 5 inches from the heating element for 3 to 4 minutes per side.) Let rest for 5 to 10 minutes. Slice against the grain.

FINISH THE SAUCE. In a small bowl, combine the cornstarch and water and stir to dissolve. Add the yogurt, stirring to combine completely. Add the yogurt mixture to the onions. Cook, stirring, over low heat for just a minute or two to warm through.

GARNISH AND SERVE. Divide the steaks among four plates. Top with the caramelized onion yogurt and garnish each steak with a fried sage leaf. Serve lime wedges alongside.

Beef-Stuffed Swiss Chard Rolls with Yogurt Sauce

1½ cups plain whole-milk or low-fat yogurt (not Greek)

10 large Swiss chard leaves

2 teaspoons extra-virgin olive oil

½ medium onion, diced

⅔ cup water, plus 1 tablespoon for the filling if needed

1 pound lean ground beef

1 tablespoon tomato paste

4 teaspoons paprika

½ teaspoon ground cinnamon

Kosher salt and freshly ground pepper

SERVES 4 OR 5 (10 ROLLS)

Greeks and Turks have dolmas (stuffed grape leaves) and Serbs have *sarmicas*, leafy parcels stuffed with paprika-seasoned beef and sauced with yogurt. This dish was inspired by Svetlana Watkins (see page 300), a Serbian who now lives in Southern California. Since grape leaves weren't available in her Yugoslavian youth, her mother used wild sorrel instead. I opt for chard leaves and add a touch of cinnamon to the paprika-scented filling.

PREP. Place the yogurt in a medium bowl and keep at room temperature until ready to serve.

Swish the chard leaves in a large bowl of cool water to clean. Pat dry. Fold each leaf in half and slice out the bottom and central portions of the stem, working from the center of the leaf downward. (You want the two halves to stay connected up top.) When unfolded, each leaf should look like an upside-down V. Finely chop the stems you just removed.

MAKE THE FILLING. In a large skillet, heat the oil over medium heat. Sauté the chard stems and onion until tender, about 10 minutes, adding 1 tablespoon water if the skillet runs dry. Add the beef, tomato paste, 3 teaspoons of the paprika, the cinnamon, 1½ teaspoons salt, and ½ teaspoon pepper. Raise the heat to medium-high and cook until the beef loses its pink color, breaking it up as it cooks, about 5 minutes. Remove from the heat.

MAKE THE ROLLS. Work with one chard leaf at a time. Lay a leaf on a work surface, with the slit ends at the top so it now resembles a regular V. The bumpy side of the leaf should face down and the concave part should face up. Scoop ¼ to ⅓ cup filling onto the leaf near the bottom, then tightly roll it up burrito style, pushing in the sides and forcing the slit top together as you encase the filling. Tuck back any filling that pops out. Transfer seam side down back to the skillet next to the remaining filling. Repeat with the remaining chard and filling.

STEAM THE ROLLS. Sprinkle the remaining 1 teaspoon paprika and a scant ¼ teaspoon each salt and pepper into the ⅔ cup water. Pour into the skillet around the rolls. Bring to a simmer, cover, reduce the heat to medium-low, and cook until the rolls are very tender, 20 to 25 minutes. Use a slotted spoon to remove the rolls to a platter. Whisk the yogurt vigorously, then spoon over the rolls. Serve immediately.

Regal Creamy Beef Curry (Shahi Korma)

2 tablespoons vegetable oil

2 large red onions, halved and thinly sliced

8 whole green cardamom pods

½ cinnamon stick

2 pounds lean or extra-lean beef stew meat, cut into 1-inch pieces

1 teaspoon ginger-garlic paste (see page 207), or ½ teaspoon each grated peeled fresh ginger and minced garlic

½ teaspoon ground cumin

½ teaspoon ground coriander

1¾ teaspoons kosher salt

½ teaspoon red chile powder or cayenne pepper (see Yo!), or to taste

3 tablespoons slivered almonds

2 tablespoons golden raisins

SERVES 4

The "regal" ingredients—saffron, almonds, raisins, and cream—in this fragrant Pakistani curry were historically reserved for important occasions or special guests. Combined, they elevate beef stew to great elegance. Aisha Piracha-Zakariya, a Pakistani-born friend who lives in Palo Alto, California (see page 229), taught me this dish, which she learned from her mother, who learned it from *her* mother. Now you too can enjoy this festive celebration dish, traditionally served during the Muslim holiday of Eid-ul-Azha (*Eid al-Adha* in Arabic) to mark the end of the Hajj, or pilgrimage to Mecca. This dish simmers for almost 2 hours, so plan accordingly.

MAKE THE CURRY. Heat a large saucepan, preferably nonstick, over medium heat. Add the oil. When it starts to shimmer, add the onions and cook, stirring occasionally, until they deepen in color and begin to brown, about 15 minutes. Add the cardamom and cinnamon, stirring to coat. Add the beef and raise the heat to medium-high as it begins to release its juices. After 2 minutes or so, add the ginger-garlic paste, cumin, coriander, salt, chile powder or cayenne, almonds, and raisins. Simmer steadily for 10 minutes, stirring occasionally. Reduce the heat to low.

1 cup heavy cream, at room temperature

Pinch of saffron

1 cup plain yogurt (not Greek), at room temperature

1 cup water

Warm naan or steamed basmati rice, for serving

Yo!

Remove the cream and yogurt from the refrigerator before starting to cook.

Indian and Pakistani red chile powder is fiery, closer to cayenne pepper than to what's labeled "chili powder" in U.S. grocery stores (don't use the latter). Cayenne is a fine substitute.

ADD THE YOGURT AND CREAM. Warm 2 to 4 tablespoons of the cream in the microwave or a small skillet. Off the heat (if using a skillet), add the saffron and let stand until needed. Whisk the yogurt until very smooth. Slowly add the yogurt, just a little at a time, to the saucepan with the beef, stirring slowly to incorporate. Add the remaining cream (not the saffron cream). Raise the heat to medium, cover, and simmer for about 10 minutes. Add the saffron cream and water to the curry.

SIMMER. Return to a simmer, then reduce the heat to as low as possible and simmer, covered, stirring occasionally, until the meat is completely tender, 75 to 90 minutes longer. (The longer it cooks, the more tender the meat will be.) The natural fat from the beef will dot the top of the sauce in little pools and the sauce will be loose and soupy, not thick like an American beef stew.

SERVE. Serve hot, with plenty of warm naan or steamed rice. (If guests are unfamiliar with cardamom pods, advise them to pluck them out; they're not meant to be eaten.) Leftovers reheat beautifully over low heat.

Golden Curry with Shrimp and Peas

FOR THE CURRY

2 cups plain whole-milk or low-fat yogurt (not Greek)

3 tablespoons chickpea flour (see Yo!)

1½ teaspoons kosher salt

1 teaspoon turmeric

½ teaspoon cayenne pepper

1 medium red onion, cut into small dice

1 tablespoon vegetable oil

½ teaspoon whole cumin seeds

5 fresh curry leaves (optional; see Yo!, page 113)

1¾ cups water

Yo!

Find chickpea flour (also labeled garbanzo flour, *gram* flour, or *besan*) and fresh curry leaves at Indian markets or well-stocked natural foods stores.

SERVES 4

Thickened with chickpea flour, this golden Pakistani curry combines yogurt and aromatics in a bright simmer-sauce for pink shrimp and emerald peas. Drizzling the finished dish with a high-impact spiced oil—called a *tarka*—adds a dramatic final touch. My friend Aisha Piracha-Zakariya (see page 229) taught me a traditional version of this dish made with chickpea fritters: This is a streamlined adaptation. Steam the rice while the sauce simmers.

PREP THE YOGURT. Whisk the yogurt in a large bowl until smooth. Add the chickpea flour, 1 tablespoon at a time, whisking aggressively to dissolve any lumps. Whisk in the salt, turmeric, and cayenne. Stir in the onion.

MAKE THE SAUCE. Warm the oil in a medium saucepan over medium-low heat for a minute or two. Add the cumin seeds and curry leaves, if using, and cook, stirring, until they sizzle. Lower the heat and whisk in the yogurt mixture and water. Bring to a simmer, whisking occasionally, then simmer gently for 45 minutes to 1 hour, whisking frequently to prevent lumps. (Start out over medium-low heat, then reduce the heat to low about halfway through. You want to maintain a steady bubble.) The final consistency should be thicker than when you started, but still loose and saucy.

1 pound large shrimp, peeled and deveined

2 cups fresh or frozen (not thawed) peas

FOR THE FINISHING OIL (*TARKA*)

1 tablespoon vegetable oil

1 garlic clove, thinly sliced

5 fresh curry leaves (optional)

3 to 5 dried whole red chiles (optional)

½ teaspoon whole cumin seeds

FOR SERVING

Kosher salt

Steamed rice

ADD THE SHRIMP AND PEAS. When the sauce has reached the desired consistency, add the shrimp, stir gently, and simmer until cooked through, about 5 minutes. Add the peas and simmer for 2 to 3 minutes longer. Cover and remove from the heat.

MAKE THE FINISHING OIL (*TARKA*). In a small skillet, heat the oil briefly over medium heat. Drop in the garlic, curry leaves (if using), chiles (if using), and cumin seeds. Sizzle for a minute or two, then immediately pour the oil and seasonings over the shrimp curry. (Don't leave them in the skillet or they'll burn.)

SERVE. Add a touch of salt, to taste, and spoon the curry over steamed rice.

Cilantro Shrimp with Tomatillo–Tomato Salsa

FOR THE SHRIMP

1½ pounds large shrimp, peeled and deveined, tails left on

Coriander-lime yogurt marinade (see page 204)

FOR THE SALSA

1 pound tomatillos, peeled, scrubbed, and quartered

½ small red onion, halved

1 tablespoon extra-virgin olive oil

Kosher salt and freshly ground pepper

Olive oil spray

(continued)

SERVES 4 TO 6

An herbal, citrusy marinade flavors shrimp before they hit the grill. Once cooked, the shrimp are served with a bold, colorful salsa, showcasing roasted tomatillos, fresh tomatoes, and a kick of piquant serrano chile, and with lime wedges for squeezing.

MARINATE THE SHRIMP. Place the shrimp in a gallon-size zip-top bag and add the marinade. Squeeze out any excess air and seal the bag. Leave at room temperature for 30 minutes, massaging the bag a few times. (Or refrigerate the bag for up to 1 hour. Bring to room temperature for 10 minutes before grilling.)

MAKE THE SALSA. Preheat the oven to 425°F. Line a baking sheet with parchment.

Tumble the tomatillos and onion onto the sheet and drizzle evenly with 1 teaspoon of the oil. Season with salt and pepper. Spread them out so there's a bit of space between them. Roast for 18 to 22 minutes, until darkened in spots. Cool.

(continued)

It was early afternoon when I finally tasted the *shahi korma*, a Pakistani celebration curry of long-simmered beef, yogurt, and cream. Aisha Piracha-Zakariya, who was born in Lahore, Pakistan, and I were sitting on the back patio of her Palo Alto, California, home, and having just spent close to three hours in her kitchen, I should have known the results would be good. Great, even. But this dish stilled me with its delicate flavors and gentle spicing. It was comforting yet elegant, creamy yet light, a seeming contradiction in a bowl.

Yogurt plays a starring role in the Pakistani kitchen, from its raitas and lassis to its marinades and sauces. To those familiar with North Indian cuisine, in particular, the food of Pakistan will feel familiar—lots of heady spices; dishes served with basmati rice or tandoori naan; an emphasis on bold color; legumes, long-simmered sauces, and stews; and the frequent and generous use of yogurt. The similarity is undoubtedly because Pakistan became independent of India only in 1947, with most Muslims and some Sikhs settling in what is now Pakistan and the Hindus remaining in India.

Yogurt is used on the side in raitas, as a dip for fried breads, and on top of rice. It adds creaminess to curry dishes and acts as a marinade for lamb and beef.

Lassis, thin, quaffable yogurt drinks, are also common. "Lassi is a drink of the farmers," Piracha-Zakariya explained. "They've been working all day, they come in and have lost all their electrolytes, and the salt in the lassi replenishes that. In countries where the water isn't potable, eating lots of yogurt can counteract the effects of unhealthy water and help develop good gut bacteria in a medicinal way." At 4:00 p.m. in Pakistan, she added, "Grandma will call you in to drink your lassi."

As she spoke, Piracha-Zakariya cooked a second yogurt-simmered curry, called *karhi*, made with fried chickpea flour *pakoras*, or fritters. (I adapted the *karhi* to make a speedier dish with shrimp and peas; see page 224.) Though the yogurt simmered for a long time, it never curdled or broke. The results were beautiful, showing off yogurt in ways I'd never considered.

½ pound tomatoes (Green Zebras keep the salsa green, or choose red ones), seeded and coarsely chopped

1 serrano chile, seeded if you want less heat, coarsely chopped

2 tablespoons chopped fresh cilantro

¾ teaspoon ground cumin

¼ teaspoon brown sugar

Juice of 1 lime, plus lime wedges for serving

Yo!

You will have plenty of salsa left over. Refrigerate, covered, for 2 to 3 days.

Transfer the roasted vegetables to a food processor or blender. Add the tomatoes, chile, cilantro, cumin, brown sugar, lime juice, the remaining 2 teaspoons oil, ¼ teaspoon salt, and ⅛ teaspoon pepper. Pulse or puree until mostly but not completely smooth. Taste, adjusting the seasoning, if desired.

GRILL THE SHRIMP. Preheat the grill for medium-high direct heat (400 to 450°F). Scrape the grates clean. Or heat a grill pan over medium-high heat.

Remove the shrimp from the marinade, place them on a baking sheet, and coat them generously with olive oil spray on both sides. Grill the shrimp until they turn pink, dark grill marks appear, and the flesh is opaque, 2 to 3 minutes per side. Serve hot, warm, or at room temperature, with lime wedges and the salsa.

1 pound large shrimp, peeled and deveined

2 cups fresh or frozen (not thawed) peas

FOR THE FINISHING OIL (*TARKA*)

1 tablespoon vegetable oil

1 garlic clove, thinly sliced

5 fresh curry leaves (optional)

3 to 5 dried whole red chiles (optional)

½ teaspoon whole cumin seeds

FOR SERVING

Kosher salt

Steamed rice

ADD THE SHRIMP AND PEAS. When the sauce has reached the desired consistency, add the shrimp, stir gently, and simmer until cooked through, about 5 minutes. Add the peas and simmer for 2 to 3 minutes longer. Cover and remove from the heat.

MAKE THE FINISHING OIL (*TARKA*). In a small skillet, heat the oil briefly over medium heat. Drop in the garlic, curry leaves (if using), chiles (if using), and cumin seeds. Sizzle for a minute or two, then immediately pour the oil and seasonings over the shrimp curry. (Don't leave them in the skillet or they'll burn.)

SERVE. Add a touch of salt, to taste, and spoon the curry over steamed rice.

Cilantro Shrimp with Tomatillo-Tomato Salsa

FOR THE SHRIMP

1½ pounds large shrimp, peeled and deveined, tails left on

Coriander-lime yogurt marinade (see page 204)

FOR THE SALSA

1 pound tomatillos, peeled, scrubbed, and quartered

½ small red onion, halved

1 tablespoon extra-virgin olive oil

Kosher salt and freshly ground pepper

Olive oil spray

(continued)

SERVES 4 TO 6

An herbal, citrusy marinade flavors shrimp before they hit the grill. Once cooked, the shrimp are served with a bold, colorful salsa, show-casing roasted tomatillos, fresh tomatoes, and a kick of piquant serrano chile, and with lime wedges for squeezing.

MARINATE THE SHRIMP. Place the shrimp in a gallon-size zip-top bag and add the marinade. Squeeze out any excess air and seal the bag. Leave at room temperature for 30 minutes, massaging the bag a few times. (Or refrigerate the bag for up to 1 hour. Bring to room temperature for 10 minutes before grilling.)

MAKE THE SALSA. Preheat the oven to 425°F. Line a baking sheet with parchment.

Tumble the tomatillos and onion onto the sheet and drizzle evenly with 1 teaspoon of the oil. Season with salt and pepper. Spread them out so there's a bit of space between them. Roast for 18 to 22 minutes, until darkened in spots. Cool.

(continued)

Oven-Baked Tarragon-Scented Salmon

1 tablespoon fennel seeds

½ teaspoon kosher salt

⅛ teaspoon freshly ground pepper

½ cup plain yogurt (not Greek), preferably whole-milk

1½ teaspoons Dijon mustard

1 teaspoon white wine vinegar

1 tablespoon plus 1 teaspoon minced fresh tarragon

6 to 8 (5- to 6-ounce) wild salmon fillets, 1 inch thick, or 1 (2- to 2½-pound) salmon fillet (see Yo!), pin bones removed

1½ tablespoons extra-virgin olive oil

¾ cup panko bread crumbs

SERVES 6 TO 8

Fennel seeds and fresh tarragon quietly infuse a yogurt marinade in this delicate fish supper. After it has spent a few hours in the fridge, slide the salmon into the oven and stir together the golden bread-crumb topping. You'll be rewarded with a meal completely out of proportion to the amount of effort expended.

MARINATE THE SALMON. In a spice grinder or with a mortar and pestle, grind the fennel seeds, salt, and pepper together until powdery. Transfer to a small bowl. Whisk in the yogurt, mustard, vinegar, and 1 teaspoon of the tarragon.

Line a baking sheet with parchment. Place the salmon on the parchment and spread the yogurt marinade thickly and evenly over the top. Refrigerate, covered, for 2 to 4 hours.

BAKE THE SALMON. Preheat the oven to 375°F, with a rack in the center position.

Bake the salmon until cooked through but still moist, about 15 minutes for individual fillets or 20 minutes for one large fillet.

(continued)

MAKE THE TOPPING. While the fish bakes, or just after you pull it from the oven, heat the oil in a small skillet over medium heat. Add the panko. Season generously with salt and pepper and cook, stirring, until golden. Remove from the heat and stir in the remaining 1 tablespoon tarragon.

SERVE. Sprinkle the panko over the salmon and serve.

Yo!

If you don't have a spice grinder or a mortar and pestle, bash the cooled, toasted fennel seeds in a zip-top bag with a meat mallet.

This dish is equally elegant with a single 2- to 2½-pound fillet you portion out after baking. If baking a large fillet, you'll have one thinner end that's flakier and better done and one thicker end that's rarer. This is ideal for diners with different taste preferences. I like my salmon pretty rare. You can also use salmon steaks, if you like.

If you can get your hands on Alaskan king salmon—a high-oil variety also called Chinook—I recommend it because of its rich flavor and texture. Sockeye and coho will also taste great, but you'll want to check for done-ness a few minutes earlier so the salmon doesn't dry out. This is especially important if your fillets are less than 1 inch thick.

Where Simple Is Best ISRAELI YOGURT CULTURE

In October 2012, several chefs and I spent the night at a family-run inn called Pausa in Israel's Galilee region. Proprietors Einat and Avigdor Rothem grow everything from kiwis to eggplants to stevia leaf in their fertile gardens and colorful orchard. Underfoot, a dachshund named Pizza Pepperoni ran about, setting the tone for this warm, magical place.

In the morning, Einat laid out a breakfast buffet loaded with homemade granola, fruits, salads, and cured meats and fish. One of the dishes I liked best was a shallow bowl of strained yogurt topped with a shimmering pool of bright lemon vinaigrette. Sweeping the dip with triangles of warm, fluffy pita, I loved the bracing, energizing flavors first thing in the morning. (The recipe appears on page 111.)

I followed up with Avigdor after I'd returned to the United States. He told me that labneh (which he spells *labane*) is "the most famous yogurt dish in Israel," noting that it "comes from the Arabic kitchen" and is a common staple on the breakfast table. "It is yogurt with reduced liquid so it is like soft cheese and more sour."

He uses yogurt to marinate grilled meats, a tradition he attributes to Balkan and Turkish kitchens. He also adds it to bind casseroles of meat and rice. His favorite dish, though, is a simple one: split, grilled eggplant, with yogurt, lemon juice, and olive oil drizzled luxuriously on top (see page 240).

Trout with Tahini–Lemon Yogurt and Baby Arugula

FOR THE SAUCE

½ cup plain yogurt (not Greek), preferably whole-milk

3 tablespoons tahini

3 to 4 tablespoons fresh lemon juice

1 tablespoon water

½ cup (loosely packed) fresh Italian parsley leaves, minced

1 garlic clove, grated

½ teaspoon kosher salt

¼ teaspoon freshly ground pepper

FOR THE SALAD

6 cups (loosely packed) baby arugula

1 tablespoon extra-virgin olive oil

1½ teaspoons fresh lemon juice

Kosher salt and freshly ground pepper

SERVES 4

Tahini brings depth and complexity to a lemon-yogurt sauce for crispy trout fillets. Mounding a pile of peppery arugula on top adds a final hit of freshness. This is quick-fix weeknight fare, casual and gloriously messy. You'll need napkins.

MAKE THE SAUCE. In a medium bowl, whisk the yogurt, tahini, 3 tablespoons lemon juice, the water, parsley, garlic, salt, and pepper until smooth. Taste, adding up to 1 tablespoon more lemon juice, if desired.

MAKE THE SALAD. Toss the arugula in a large bowl with the olive oil and lemon juice. Season with salt and pepper.

FOR THE TROUT

1¾ to 2 pounds boneless trout fillets (4 to 6 fillets)

2 tablespoons plus 2 teaspoons extra-virgin olive oil

Kosher salt and freshly ground pepper

2 teaspoons unsalted butter

FOR SERVING

Extra-virgin olive oil, fleur de sel, and cracked black pepper (optional)

Lemon wedges

COOK THE TROUT. Place the trout fillets on a baking sheet. Sprinkle both sides with oil (using 2 teaspoons total) and season with salt and pepper. Heat a large cast-iron skillet over medium-high heat. Work in two batches: Add 1 teaspoon of the butter and 1 tablespoon oil to the skillet. When the butter foams and the oil starts to shimmer, add 2 or 3 trout fillets skin side down. Cook for 3 to 4 minutes, until the underside is crisp. Flip and cook for 2 to 3 minutes longer, until the flesh is opaque and flaky. Transfer to a large platter and tent with foil to keep warm. Repeat with the remaining butter, oil, and trout.

SERVE. Nap the trout with the sauce and pile some of the salad right on top. If desired, drizzle with oil and sprinkle with fleur de sel and cracked pepper. Serve with lemon wedges.

Yo!

Don't make the sauce ahead of time. Refrigeration makes it too thick.

Roasted Cauliflower with Tahini Yogurt and Pomegranate

½ cup plain Greek yogurt, preferably whole-milk

2 teaspoons tahini

1 teaspoon fresh lemon juice

½ teaspoon honey

Kosher salt and ground white or freshly ground black pepper

1 head cauliflower (about 1¾ pounds)

1 tablespoon extra-virgin olive oil

Large pinch of turmeric, for color (optional)

3 tablespoons pomegranate seeds, for serving

SERVES 4 TO 6

Cauliflower nirvana is a careful calibration of texture (tender but not mushy), bright-hued accompaniments (because it's so pale), and flavorful saucing to give it some zip and zing. This dish, inspired by one I enjoyed at my sister-in-law Jessie's bridal shower, pairs florets with a smooth, creamy yogurt-tahini sauce. It's a hint exotic but still comforting and easy to pull off. Pomegranate seeds add visual flair and a burst of tart juice.

MAKE THE YOGURT SAUCE. In a large bowl, vigorously whisk the yogurt, tahini, lemon juice, honey, and ⅛ teaspoon each salt and pepper. Continue whisking for 30 seconds to loosen the sauce. Set aside at room temperature until needed.

ROAST THE CAULIFLOWER. Preheat the oven to 400°F, with a rack in the upper third. Cut the cauliflower into 1½-inch florets (see Yo!) and pile in the center of a baking sheet. In a small bowl, whisk the oil, turmeric (if using), ½ teaspoon salt, and ⅛ teaspoon pepper. Scrape the seasoned oil over the cauliflower and rub it in to coat. (It won't seem like you have enough oil, but you do.) Spread the florets evenly on the baking sheet so they have a bit of breathing room. Roast for 20 to 25 minutes, until browned in spots and tender but not mushy, flipping once with a spatula halfway through. Let cool to room temperature.

DRESS AND GARNISH. Scrape the cauliflower into the bowl with the yogurt sauce. Stir gently to combine. Transfer to a serving platter, sprinkle with the pomegranate seeds, and serve immediately.

Yo!

To get the texture of the cauliflower just right, be sure to break down the florets so they're roughly 1½ inches long. If they're larger or smaller, increase or decrease the roasting time by a few minutes.

When pomegranates aren't available, substitute soaked dried barberries (see Yo!, page 71) or minced soaked dried cranberries.

Roasted Vegetables with Spiced Yogurt, Pistachio, and Lemon

1 cup plain whole-milk or low-fat yogurt

¾ teaspoon dried mint

⅛ to ¼ teaspoon cayenne pepper

2¼ teaspoons kosher salt

1 large or 2 small celeriac (2 to 2½ pounds total)

4 to 6 carrots (about 1 pound)

1 large or 2 medium leeks, trimmed, halved, and thoroughly rinsed

¼ cup extra-virgin olive oil

½ teaspoon ground coriander

½ teaspoon freshly ground pepper

⅓ cup unsalted pistachios, finely chopped, for garnish

½ lemon, for serving

SERVES 8

Celeriac, or celery root, may be the world's ugliest vegetable, but it roasts up beautifully and adds herbal notes to sweet carrots and tender leeks. A drizzle of yogurt spiced with mint and cayenne lends a secondary layer of flavor and texture, as does a crush of pistachios. Because this side dish is rather high yield, it's perfect for holidays or parties, especially when served with lentils or a roast.

MAKE THE YOGURT SAUCE. In a medium bowl, whisk the yogurt vigorously with the mint, cayenne, and ¼ teaspoon of the salt until light and smooth. Set aside at room temperature.

PREP AND ROAST THE VEGETABLES. Preheat the oven to 400°F, with racks in the upper and lower thirds. Line two baking sheets with parchment.

Peel the celeriac with a heavy knife, squaring the round corners, then sweeping down the sides to remove the hairy, gnarly exterior. Halve, then cut each half into ¾-inch-wide slices. Cut those into sticks and then into ¾-inch dice. Peel the carrots, quarter lengthwise, and cut into ¾-inch pieces. Halve each leek again lengthwise so you have 4 long quarters. Cut at rough ¾-inch intervals. Transfer the celeriac to one lined baking sheet and the carrots and leeks to the other. Divide the oil and coriander evenly between the baking sheets and sprinkle each sheet with 1 teaspoon salt and ¼ teaspoon pepper. Massage the seasonings in with your hands and spread the vegetables into a single layer.

Roast, stirring at 15-minute intervals, until the vegetables are deeply caramelized. The carrots and leeks should take 25 to 30 minutes and the celeriac a bit longer, 30 to 40 minutes. Proceed immediately if planning to serve the dish hot, or cool the vegetables briefly to serve warm or at room temperature. (They're delicious all three ways.)

GARNISH AND SERVE. Tumble the vegetables onto a large platter. Immediately before serving, drizzle with the yogurt sauce, sprinkle with the pistachios, and spritz with lemon juice.

Israeli-Style Grilled Eggplant with Roasted Garlic and Yogurt

2 medium heads garlic, left intact

Extra-virgin olive oil

Kosher salt

2 eggplants (about 1 pound each) of relatively consistent thickness from end to end (not Japanese)

Freshly ground pepper

4 to 8 tablespoons plain whole-milk yogurt (not Greek), at room temperature

1 or 2 lemons

Finishing salt, such as Maldon

Fresh mint or Italian parsley leaves, for garnish

SERVES 4

A close cousin of baba ghanouj (page 104) but in fork-and-knife form, this dish takes a straightforward concept—grilling eggplant and drizzling it generously with yogurt—a bit further, adding copious amounts of roasted garlic for a sweet, intoxicating earthiness. The original blueprint, without the garlic, came to me from Avigdor Rothem, co-owner with his wife, Einat, of Israel's beautiful, serene Pausa Inn in the Upper Galilee.

ROAST THE GARLIC. Prepare a grill for direct medium-high heat (450 to 500°F). Brush the grates completely clean.

Slice off the top fifth of each garlic head to expose the tops of the cloves. Place each head on a separate 8-inch square of foil. Drizzle each with 1 teaspoon oil and sprinkle generously with kosher salt. Pinch the tops of the foil closed to create two bundles. Tuck toward the back of the grill. (The garlic and eggplant should finish cooking simultaneously, or thereabouts.)

GRILL THE EGGPLANT. Meanwhile, halve the eggplants lengthwise. Make long, shallow crosshatches in the flesh up and down each half. Brush the cut sides generously with oil and sprinkle liberally with salt and pepper. Grill the eggplant flesh side down until dark grill marks appear and the skin begins to shrivel, about 15 minutes. Turn with a spatula (try not to tear the flesh) and continue grilling flesh side up until very tender and nearly collapsed, 15 to 25 minutes longer. Remove the eggplant from the grill.

CHECK THE GARLIC. Carefully open the garlic bundles (watch out for steam). If the cloves feel soft when pressed with tongs and are browned in spots, remove from the grill. Otherwise, grill for a few more minutes until the garlic is soft.

COMBINE AND SERVE. Open the garlic bundles carefully so they can cool. When cool enough to handle, squeeze the soft cloves over all 4 eggplant halves, mashing the garlic lightly into the eggplant with a fork. Drizzle each eggplant with the yogurt, a thin stream of oil, and a hearty squeeze of lemon juice. Season with the finishing salt and pepper and garnish with plenty of mint or parsley.

Tangy Potato Mash with Scallions

1¼ cups plain yogurt (not Greek), preferably whole-milk

¼ cup extra-virgin olive oil, plus more for drizzling

Kosher salt

2½ to 3 pounds Yukon Gold or other creamy potatoes (about 8 medium), peeled

Freshly ground pepper

2 scallions, trimmed, white and green parts thinly sliced

Yo!

I usually save the ricer, which makes silky smooth mashed potatoes, for holidays and fancy guests. A handheld potato masher does the job quickly and easily, and a few bumps and lumps don't offend me.

SERVES 8 (MAKES 7½ CUPS)

I tend to be a traditionalist when it comes to mashed potatoes: I don't want to ruin their inherent simplicity with too many strong flavors or distracting embellishments. That said, yogurt—like buttermilk—enhances them with a subtle tang. And because onions and potatoes are lifelong friends, I can't resist capping the creamy mass with a pile of scallion ringlets.

PREP THE YOGURT. In a medium bowl, whisk the yogurt with the olive oil and 1 teaspoon salt. Set aside at room temperature until needed.

COOK AND MASH THE POTATOES. Fill a large saucepan (at least 4½ quarts) with cool water. Coarsely dice each potato into about ¾-inch pieces, transferring them to the saucepan as you go. Once you've added all the potatoes, add or subtract water from the saucepan so the potatoes are covered by 1 to 2 inches of water. Bring to a boil.

Skim off any foam that rises to the top. Lower the heat to medium and cook at a hard simmer until the potatoes are completely tender, 12 to 15 minutes. Drain, then immediately return to the saucepan with a bit of water still clinging. Mash until the potatoes are about halfway smooth. Scrape in the yogurt mixture and continue mashing until they're as smooth as you like them. (I like them to have a bit of texture.) Adjust the salt and add pepper, to taste. (You'll likely need more salt.)

SERVE. Transfer to a serving bowl and smooth the top. Pile with the scallions and drizzle with oil just before serving.

Where Homemade is King ERITREAN YOGURT CULTURE

Though she now lives in Virginia, Mebrat Ibrahim grew up in Eritrea in East Africa. She recalled yogurt's role in her native land when I spoke with her by phone.

"As a small, undeveloped country," Ibrahim said, "we're still old-fashioned. Everything is homemade, natural, and organic." During Ibrahim's youth, homemade yogurt—called *rug'o*—was a staple. "My mother and grandmother and aunt would make it together every day," she said. "You can eat it throughout the day, not just at breakfast. You have to eat it within a day because there was no refrigeration."

As a starter, Eritreans add yogurt from the prior day's batch or else a piece of *injera*, the spongy, fermented flatbread made from teff, the nation's staple grain. "Leave it overnight, and it will start tasting like yogurt." The following day, she'd remove the *injera*, add more milk, and leave it overnight a second time, this time in a cold spot covered with a cloth or towel. Sometimes, she'd add a local herb called *chena adam*, for a basil-like flavor.

"We still don't have commercial yogurt in Eritrea," Ibrahim said, though she noted that some imported brands may be sold in the capital. "People still make it themselves. Sometimes, if there's a shortage of fresh milk, Eritreans will use NIDO," (powdered milk from Nestlé sold in cans).

Several traditional Eritrean dishes are served with yogurt, including *ga'at*, a mix of barley or wheat flour that's kneaded with water until it comes together in a ball. It's then pressed into a volcano-shaped mound, which may be filled with butter, spicy *berbere*, yogurt, or even—for children—sugar. Yogurt can also be poured around the edges, creating a sort of moat. During the Muslim holy days of Ramadan, *ga'at* may be served with yogurt as a predawn meal. "You'll eat *ga'at, rug'o*, and a few more things to help you get through the long, hot days," said Ibrahim.

But yogurt isn't reserved for special occasions or holy days. It's an everyday food, one kids pair with honey and adults prefer in more savory dishes. It's especially nice alongside *fata*, a rustic bread salad sauced with tomato and spiked with rounds of fiery jalapeño (see page 190).

Bake

Bake

Flavor enhancer. Leavening activator. Moisture deliverer. Luxe filling. Yogurt contributes so much value to such a wide variety of baked goods that you'll want copious amounts on hand for everything from tarts and galettes to flatbreads and cakes. Its versatility in the baker's pantry can't be overstated.

Like its friends sour cream and buttermilk, yogurt has acidic properties and, when combined with baking soda, releases carbon dioxide and causes baked goods to swell and rise. It also adds moisture, and—so long as you're using yogurt with some fat—tenderness as well.

When yogurt joins forces with other dairy stars—like heavy cream, butter, ricotta, and goat cheese—desserts take on special opulence. Flatbreads, quick breads, and cakes across the spectrum—from a petite batch of Mocha Cupcakes to a fruit-dappled sheet cake that feeds a small army—all shine brighter with yogurt in the batter.

Although it's true that oven temperatures kill off the live, active cultures in yogurt, eliminating its probiotic health benefits, all of yogurt's other nutritive contributions—significant protein and calcium, plus vitamins and minerals—remain present. But these are treats, so let's stop the health talk. Let's indulge.

The Recipes

Iced Almond-Lemon Loaf Cake

FOR THE CAKE

10 tablespoons (1¼ sticks) unsalted butter, at room temperature, plus soft butter for greasing the pan

2 cups all-purpose flour

2 teaspoons baking powder

¼ teaspoon baking soda

1 teaspoon kosher salt

½ cup almond meal (see Yo!, page 250)

Zest of 2 large lemons

1 cup granulated sugar

2 large eggs, at room temperature

2 teaspoons pure almond extract

1 cup plain whole-milk or low-fat yogurt (not Greek)

(continued)

MAKES ONE 9-INCH LOAF

Yogurt appears twice in this sunny loaf cake: A full cup of it gives the batter tenderness and moisture, and a spoonful in the icing delivers tang and shine. Bold lemon and almond flavors play off the yogurt beautifully, enhancing and deepening its impact.

PREP. Preheat the oven to 350°F, with a rack in the center position. Generously butter a 9-by-5-inch loaf pan.

MIX THE BATTER. Into a large bowl, sift the flour, baking powder, baking soda, and salt. Whisk in the almond meal and lemon zest. In a stand mixer fitted with the paddle, cream the butter and granulated sugar until light and fluffy, about 5 minutes. Reduce the speed to low and add the eggs one at a time, beating well after each addition and scraping down the sides as needed. Beat in the almond extract. Slowly beat in half the dry ingredients, then the yogurt, then the remaining dry ingredients until incorporated. Raise the speed to medium and beat for 1 to 2 minutes to develop some structure.

BAKE THE CAKE. Scrape the batter into the prepared pan and smooth the top. Bake until risen and lightly browned and a skewer inserted in the center comes out clean, 50 to 60 minutes. Cool in the pan on a rack for 15 minutes. Slide a knife around the perimeter and invert the cake onto the rack. Cool completely, then flip right side up.

(continued)

Loaf Cake (continued)

FOR THE ICING

½ cup confectioners' sugar

1 tablespoon plain whole-milk or low-fat yogurt (not Greek)

1 tablespoon fresh lemon juice

Yo!

If you can't find almond meal, grind about ½ cup almonds in a food processor as finely as possible.

ICE THE CAKE. Sift the confectioners' sugar into a medium bowl. Whisk in the yogurt and then the lemon juice, 1 teaspoon at a time, until the icing is smooth, thick, and drips slowly from the whisk. Wave the whisk over the cake to drizzle lines of icing, or scrape the icing over the cake and smooth with an offset spatula.

STORE. Once the icing firms, cover the cake with plastic wrap. It can be kept at room temperature for up to 48 hours, or covered with a layer of foil and refrigerated for up to 5 days.

Frosted Mocha Cupcakes (A Small Batch)

FOR THE CUPCAKES

1 cup all-purpose flour

¾ cup granulated sugar

¼ cup unsweetened cocoa powder

1½ teaspoons instant espresso powder (see Yo!, page 67)

1 teaspoon baking powder

¼ teaspoon baking soda

¼ teaspoon kosher salt

3 tablespoons unsalted butter, melted about halfway

⅔ cup plain yogurt (if using Greek, see Yo!)

1 to 2 tablespoons milk

1 large egg

1 teaspoon pure vanilla extract

(continued)

MAKES 9 CUPCAKES

With this speedy recipe on hand, you may never visit your neighborhood bakery again. The batter whips up quickly with a wooden spoon, and the fluffy frosting takes just 2 minutes with an electric mixer. The 9-cupcake yield makes this recipe equally accessible for a weeknight family dessert or a special afternoon snack. Or scatter on some sprinkles, tuck in a few candles, and you're birthday ready.

MAKE THE CUPCAKES. Preheat the oven to 325°F, with a rack in the lower third. Line a 12-cup muffin tin with 9 cupcake liners.

Into a large bowl, sift together the flour, sugar, cocoa powder, espresso powder, baking powder, baking soda, and salt. Stir in the butter, yogurt, 1 tablespoon milk, the egg, and vanilla. Beat well with a wooden spoon or silicone spatula. It's fine if the batter's thick and a bit lumpy, but make sure to dissolve any floury pockets hiding on the bottom and sides of the bowl. If the batter is too dry to moisten all the dry ingredients, add the second tablespoon of milk.

BAKE. Divide the batter evenly among the cupcake liners and bake until a skewer inserted in the center of a cupcake comes out clean, 22 to 27 minutes. Cool completely on a rack.

(continued)

FOR THE FROSTING

½ cup plus 1 tablespoon cold heavy cream

3 tablespoons plain low-fat or whole-milk Greek yogurt

1 tablespoon very soft unsalted butter

2½ to 3 tablespoons granulated sugar, or to taste

1 tablespoon plus ½ teaspoon unsweetened cocoa powder

¼ teaspoon instant espresso powder

¼ teaspoon pure vanilla extract

Pinch of kosher salt

Sprinkles or colored sugar, for decorating (optional)

MEANWHILE, MAKE THE FROSTING. Combine all the frosting ingredients (starting with 2½ tablespoons sugar) in a stand mixer fitted with the whisk attachment or in a bowl with a handheld mixer. Whip on high speed until thick, creamy, and peaked, 1 to 2 minutes, scraping down the sides of the bowl halfway through. Taste, adding a bit more sugar if desired. (The frosting may be made up to 1 hour ahead and refrigerated. Whisk to return it to the proper consistency, if necessary.)

FROST AND SERVE. Dollop a thick frosting cap on each cupcake. Scatter with sprinkles or colored sugar, if desired, and serve.

> **Yo!**
>
> Have only Greek yogurt on hand? Whisk an extra 2 tablespoons milk into the yogurt to loosen, then go ahead and use it in the batter.

Walnut Cake with Rum-Soaked Currants

Soft unsalted butter, for the pan

¾ cup dried currants

2 tablespoons dark rum or very hot water

1 cup walnuts

1 cup all-purpose flour

¾ teaspoon baking soda

¼ teaspoon baking powder

¼ teaspoon salt

4 large eggs, at room temperature

¾ cup plain low-fat or whole-milk yogurt (not Greek)

½ cup extra-virgin olive oil

1 cup granulated sugar

Confectioners' sugar, for serving

MAKES ONE 9-INCH CAKE

A full cup of ground, toasted walnuts flavors this cake, which is liberally strewn with rum-drunk currants. Yogurt and olive oil join forces to moisten the cake's crumb. I was inspired by a slightly more labor-intensive yogurt cake in Ayla Algar's informative book *Classical Turkish Cooking*.

PREP THE CURRANTS AND NUTS. Preheat the oven to 350°F, with a rack in the lower third. Line a 9-inch springform pan with parchment and generously butter the sides. Set aside.

In a small bowl, toss the currants with the rum or hot water and set aside until needed. Toast the walnuts on a baking sheet for 8 to 12 minutes, until one shade darker. Leave the oven on. Let the nuts cool.

PROCESS THE DRY INGREDIENTS. In a food processor, combine the walnuts, flour, baking soda, baking powder, and salt. Process until powdery, about 20 seconds. Remove the blade and, with your fingers, fluff the ingredients lightly up from the bottom to evenly distribute any floury particles hiding underneath.

MIX THE BATTER. In a large bowl, whisk the eggs until thoroughly combined. Whisk in the yogurt and oil, beating until emulsified and lemon yellow. Slowly stream in the granulated sugar, whisking all the while. Scrape the dry ingredients over the wet and fold to combine. Make sure no dry, floury pockets remain, but do not overmix. The batter may be a bit lumpy.

BAKE THE CAKE. Transfer the batter to the prepared pan. Scatter the currants and any residual liquid evenly over the batter. Bake for 35 to 40 minutes, until the cake has risen, is firm, and a skewer inserted in the center comes out clean. Cool for 10 minutes on a rack, then remove the sides of the pan and cool to room temperature.

SERVE. Sift with confectioners' sugar and cut into wedges.

STORE. Store the cake at room temperature, wrapped in plastic, for the first 24 hours, then refrigerate it, well wrapped. It will keep for up to 3 days.

Mixed Fruit and Yogurt Sheet Cake for a Crowd

Nonstick cooking spray

4 cups mixed summer fruit (see opposite), any combination of 3 or more, berries left whole, larger fruits pitted and coarsely chopped

2 tablespoons fresh lemon juice

1¼ cups plus 3 tablespoons granulated sugar

½ teaspoon ground cloves

2 cups all-purpose flour

2 teaspoons baking powder

½ teaspoon baking soda

1¼ teaspoons ground cardamom

¾ teaspoon kosher salt

8 tablespoons (1 stick) unsalted butter, melted and cooled slightly

1 cup plain yogurt (not Greek)

4 large eggs

1 tablespoon pure vanilla extract

Confectioners' sugar, for serving

Plain Greek yogurt, for serving (optional)

MAKES ONE 18-BY-13-INCH SHEET CAKE; SERVES 24

Bookmark this no-mixer-required, cardamom-forward sheet cake for all your casual entertaining needs—picnics, potlucks, and barbecues especially. It's completely flexible (use cherries, apricots, peaches, blueberries, blackberries, and/or raspberries, preferably in combination), takes just minutes to whisk together, and feeds more than twenty people. A half sheet pan (18 by 13 by 1 inches) is perfect here.

PREP. Preheat the oven to 350°F, with a rack in the center position. Line an 18-by-13-inch rimmed baking sheet with parchment. Coat the sides and corners with nonstick cooking spray.

PREP THE FRUIT. In a medium bowl, toss the fruit with the lemon juice, 2 tablespoons of the granulated sugar, and ¼ teaspoon of the cloves.

MIX THE BATTER. Into a large bowl, sift together the flour, baking powder, baking soda, 1 teaspoon of the cardamom, and the salt. Add the butter, yogurt, eggs, vanilla, and 1¼ cups of the granulated sugar and whisk well to combine. Sweep the bottom and sides of the bowl with a silicone spatula to dissolve any hidden pockets of flour.

(continued)

BAKE THE CAKE. Scrape the batter into the prepared baking sheet (it will be a very thin layer), smoothing the top and working the batter into the corners. Scatter the fruit in big spoonfuls evenly over the batter, drizzling any residual juice onto the cake. In a small bowl, stir together the remaining 1 tablespoon granulated sugar and the remaining ¼ teaspoon each cloves and cardamom. Sprinkle evenly over the batter. Bake for 35 to 45 minutes, until nicely browned and a skewer inserted in the center comes out clean. Cool completely on a rack.

SERVE. Cut into 24 squares. Dust each square lightly with confectioners' sugar just before serving. Spoon a dollop of Greek yogurt alongside each slice, if desired.

STORE. Store leftover cake in the refrigerator, covered tightly with plastic wrap, for up to 3 days.

Goat Cheese Cheesecake

FOR THE CRUST

28 chocolate wafer cookies (such as Nabisco Famous Chocolate Wafers), or 6.25 ounces (176 grams) other chocolate wafer cookies (2 cups crushed)

4 tablespoons (½ stick) unsalted butter, melted

1 tablespoon honey

¼ teaspoon kosher salt

(continued)

MAKES ONE 8-INCH CHEESECAKE; SERVES 8 TO 16

Goat's milk yogurt and goat cheese produce a cheesecake that is both delicately flavored and rich tasting. This recipe can be made entirely in a food processor.

MAKE THE CRUST. Preheat the oven to 350°F, with a rack in the center position. Line the bottom of an 8-inch springform pan with parchment.

In a food processor, grind the cookies until uniformly pebbly. Add the butter, honey, and salt and pulse about 10 times, until finely ground and evenly moistened. Transfer to the prepared pan. Press evenly onto the bottom (not up the sides), tamping gently. Bake for 18 to 20 minutes, until firm. Remove from the oven. Reduce the oven temperature to 325°F. Cool the crust for 5 minutes.

PREP THE PAN. Wrap the entire outside of the pan with two layers of foil. Fill a kettle and set over high heat. (You'll use this for the water bath.)

(continued)

FOR THE FILLING

8 ounces soft goat cheese, at room temperature

1½ cups goat's milk yogurt, at room temperature

5 large eggs, at room temperature

¾ cup sugar

1½ teaspoons pure vanilla extract

Raspberries, blueberries, and/or sliced strawberries, for topping

MEANWHILE, MAKE THE FILLING. Wipe the food processor clean. Rinse and dry the blade. Add all the filling ingredients to the food processor and process for 1 minute, or until completely smooth. Pour over the crust. Bang the pan against the counter once to dissolve any air bubbles.

BAKE THE CHEESECAKE. Place the springform pan in a large roasting pan and set it in the oven. Pour the hot water from the kettle into the roasting pan so it reaches between one-third and halfway up the sides of the springform pan. Bake until the filling is set, 70 to 80 minutes. Turn off the oven, open the oven door, and let the cheesecake cool slowly in the oven for 1 hour. Refrigerate for at least 3 hours.

SERVE. Slide a hot knife along the inside of the springform pan, then remove the sides. If desired, transfer the cheesecake to a cake plate (leaving the parchment behind). Top with the berries and serve.

STORE. Cover loosely with plastic wrap and refrigerate (without the berry topping), for up to 5 days.

Yo!

The cheesecake takes more than 1 hour to bake, another 1 hour to cool in the oven, and at least 3 hours to chill in the refrigerator, so plan ahead.

My favorite brand of goat's milk yogurt is made by Redwood Hill Farm in Sonoma County, California (Redwoodhill.com).

Syrup-Drenched Orange Phyllo Cake

MAKES ONE 13-BY-9-INCH CAKE; SERVES 12 TO 16

If I were ever caught without heat, I'd want Anna Vlachogianni by my side. The slim proprietor of Restaurant Anna on the Greek isle of Paros has a smile so bright it radiates. On the day of my visit, the restaurant was a beehive of activity, a chaos just barely controlled by Anna herself, who flitted from stove to counter to my table, where she told me she couldn't chat until later, until close to midnight, when she'd finally have a chance to sit still. It was before noon when she said this, but I hung around a while anyway, taking in the scene and drinking in Anna's energy.

As I sat, Anna kept popping back to me, sharing bits of yogurt know-how. Suddenly, she ran over and handed me a sweet, thick slice of syrup-drenched cake. Off she went, then back she came, once more, twice more, talking me through the recipe in fits and starts as I frantically scrawled in my notebook. Using hand gestures more than words, Anna pantomimed each step, at one point grabbing my arm and walking me back to the freezer so she could point out the phyllo dough at the center of the recipe.

This cake used phyllo in a way I'd never seen. Rather than thawing the dough and brushing each papery sheet with butter, Anna minced the stacked layers and used the shreds in place of flour to structure and bind the cake.

Anna's recipe relied on measurements like teacups and soupspoons, and when she told me she mixes the batter by hand, she literally meant by using her hand (not a whisk or spoon).

I've recreated Anna's cake using standardized (and boring) quantities and a spoon. If you'd like to mix this cake by hand, by all means, go ahead. You'll be in excellent company.

(continued)

Orange Phyllo Cake *(continued)*

FOR THE CAKE

1½ cups vegetable oil

All-purpose flour, for dusting the pan

1½ cups sugar

4 large eggs

2 cups plain whole-milk yogurt

¼ cup plus 1¼ teaspoons baking powder

Zest of 2 large or 3 medium oranges (2 packed tablespoons) (see Yo!)

½ teaspoon pure vanilla extract

1 (1-pound) box phyllo dough, not thawed

FOR THE ORANGE SYRUP

¾ cup sugar

1½ cups water

¾ cup fresh orange juice (see Yo!)

MAKE THE CAKE. Preheat the oven to 350°F, with a rack in the center position and a baking sheet on the rack below to catch any drips. Using a brush, coat a 13-by-9-inch metal baking pan with a thin film of the oil, then dust lightly with flour.

In your largest bowl, stir the remaining oil and the sugar until thoroughly combined. Add the eggs one at a time, stirring well to incorporate each one before adding the next. (The texture will become thick and gelatinous.) Stir in the yogurt, mixing well. Add the baking powder, then the orange zest and vanilla and mix well.

Unroll the phyllo and, keeping the layers stacked, use the tip of a sharp knife to slice the stack into long, thin ribbons. Mince these still-stacked ribbons into confetti-like bits. They should be roughly the same size, but you don't have to be precise. Stir the phyllo into the batter a little at a time until it is completely incorporated.

Bake until golden brown and a skewer inserted in the center comes out clean, about 45 minutes.

MEANWHILE, MAKE THE SYRUP. In a medium saucepan, bring the sugar, water, and orange juice to a rolling boil over medium-high heat, stirring for the first minute to dissolve the sugar. Boil vigorously, without stirring, for 5 to 7 minutes. Let cool for 15 minutes.

DRENCH THE CAKE AND SERVE. When the cake comes out of the oven (it's okay if it sits a bit while the syrup cools), ladle the syrup evenly over the cake, letting each ladleful absorb before adding the next. Let cool completely. Serve at room temperature, or cover tightly and refrigerate for a few hours (or overnight) for a damper consistency. Serve in generous squares.

STORE. Refrigerate the cake, tightly covered, for up to 3 days.

Yo!

Like many syrup-soaked cakes, this one is sweet and damp, not fluffy and light like American cakes. It changes over time, becoming denser and moister as it settles in the refrigerator.

This cake includes an unusually large amount of baking powder—the amount given is not a mistake. Although baking powder can sometimes impart a bitter taste, mysteriously, in this cake, it does not.

Go ahead and juice the zested oranges for the syrup, but you'll also need an extra orange or two. For a twist, add the juice and zest of a lemon to the syrup as well.

Plum Tart in a Date-Nut Crust

1½ cups plain whole-milk Greek yogurt

Nonstick cooking spray

¼ cup chopped, pitted Medjool dates (about 4) (see Yo!, page 51)

1½ cups sweetened flaked coconut

2 cups hazelnuts (with or without skins)

¼ teaspoon kosher salt

2 tablespoons unsalted butter, melted

3 tablespoons apricot preserves

2 teaspoons hot water

2 tablespoons honey

¼ teaspoon pure vanilla extract

3 medium plums, pitted and thinly sliced, or other fruit of your choice (about 2½ cups)

¼ cup large shreds unsweetened coconut, toasted (see Yo!), for garnish (optional)

MAKES ONE 9½-INCH TART; SERVES 8

A tender, macaroon-like crust of pulverized dates, coconut, and hazelnuts supports juicy plums and creamy yogurt in a unique, summery tart. The brightness and natural acidity of the fruit, the mild yogurt layer, and the chewy, nutty base make for an intriguing and beautifully balanced triad.

Note that you'll want to make this tart a good 7 hours before you plan to serve it. You'll need an hour to drain the yogurt (while you make the crust) plus 6 hours for the tart to chill before slicing. This tart happens to be gluten free.

DRAIN THE YOGURT. Line a fine-mesh strainer with a paper towel or cheesecloth and set it over a bowl. Spoon in the yogurt and refrigerate for 1 hour to drain some of the whey.

MEANWHILE, MAKE THE CRUST. Preheat the oven to 300°F, with a rack in the bottom position. Fit a parchment round in the bottom of a 9½-inch metal tart pan with a removable bottom. Coat the sides with nonstick cooking spray.

In a food processor, pulse the dates, sweetened coconut, hazelnuts, and salt in 10 to 15 bursts, until finely ground. With the machine on, slowly add the butter through the feed tube. Continue processing for about 30 seconds. (When you press a bit of the mixture between your thumb and forefinger, it should hold together.)

Dump the mixture into the prepared tart pan. If you like (it's not strictly necessary), lay a sheet of waxed paper over the crumbles to act as a nonstick barrier. Using your fingers or the flat bottom of a dry measuring cup, press and compact the crumbles into the bottom and up the sides of the tart pan. Move slowly, as the structure of the crust relies on tamping it down and building cohesive sides. Move up to the rim of the tart pan and gently compact this as well. Set on a baking sheet. (Discard the waxed paper, if you used it.) Bake until the crust is dry and the edges are golden brown, 20 to 25 minutes.

SEAL THE CRUST. While the crust is still warm, whisk together the apricot preserves and water in a small bowl until smooth. Scrape the preserves into the crust. Using a pastry brush, ease the preserves across the crust in an even layer. Cool completely, still in the tart pan, before filling.

FILL THE TART. In a small bowl, stir together the drained yogurt, honey, and vanilla. Scrape into the crust and smooth the top. Cover loosely and refrigerate for at least 6 hours to set.

SERVE. Just before serving, remove the sides of the tart pan and carefully slide a thin spatula under the parchment to loosen. Transfer the tart to a cake plate or stand. Top the tart with the plums, garnish with the toasted coconut, if using, and serve.

Yo!

You can substitute any seasonal fruit—alone or in combination—for the plums in this recipe. Berries, any pitted stone fruits, and poached pears work well. Pomegranate seeds and blood oranges are great in winter.

You'll find the dates, both kinds of coconut, and the hazelnuts in the bulk bins of most natural foods stores, so you can buy just what you need.

Toast the unsweetened coconut in a small, dry skillet over medium heat for 1 to 2 minutes, shaking the skillet and stirring constantly so it doesn't burn. Immediately transfer to a plate to cool.

Cherry Galettes with Yogurt-Ricotta Cream

FOR THE DOUGH

2½ cups all-purpose flour, plus more for rolling

1 teaspoon kosher salt

14 tablespoons (1¾ sticks) cold unsalted butter, cut into large cubes

⅓ cup ice-cold water

1 teaspoon white vinegar

FOR THE FRUIT

1½ pounds cherries (about 4½ heaping cups), stemmed, pitted, and halved

¼ cup granulated sugar

1 tablespoon plus 1½ teaspoons cornstarch

FOR THE YOGURT-RICOTTA CREAM

2 large eggs

1 cup whole-milk yogurt (not Greek)

1 cup whole-milk ricotta cheese

¼ teaspoon pure almond or vanilla extract

(continued)

MAKES FOUR 6-INCH GALETTES

Lightly scented with almond extract, this galette, with its barely sweet, almost blintz-like dairy filling, showcases juicy summer cherries at their finest. I assemble four miniature galettes—each one serves three or four people—and freeze two for later, even if later is just later that same week.

MAKE THE DOUGH. In a food processor, combine the flour and salt. Distribute the butter evenly atop the flour. Pulse for eight 1-second bursts, until the butter is reduced to the size of peas. Combine the water and vinegar. With the machine on, slowly stream the liquid through the feed tube. Process just until the dough forms a ball. Remove to a lightly floured work surface.

Divide the dough into 4 equal pieces. Flatten each piece into a 4-inch disk, wrap well with plastic wrap, and refrigerate for at least 30 minutes.

PREP THE FRUIT AND CREAM. In a large bowl, stir together the cherries, granulated sugar, and cornstarch. In a second large bowl, whisk the eggs, then whisk in the yogurt, ricotta, and almond or vanilla extract.

(continued)

FOR FINISHING

1 large egg yolk, whisked with 1 tablespoon cream or milk, for egg wash

2 teaspoons coarse or granulated sugar, for sprinkling

Confectioners' sugar, for serving

Yo!

To make two large galettes, divide the dough in half rather than in quarters and proceed as directed, dividing the filling proportionally. The baking time will be roughly the same.

If freezer space is limited, assemble and freeze the final two galettes once the first ones are in the oven. Once frozen, you can slide them on a lower rack to bake with the first two. (Set a separate timer so you don't get confused.)

MAKE THE GALETTES. Line two baking sheets with parchment. Remove one disk of dough from the refrigerator. Using a floured rolling pin, roll the disk into a rough 10-inch round. Transfer to a lined baking sheet, positioning it as close to one end as possible. Scoop ½ cup of the yogurt-ricotta cream into the center of the dough. Smooth lightly with an offset spatula, leaving a 1-inch border. Top with 1 generous cup of the fruit mixture. Gently fold in the perimeter of the dough (you'll be pushing some of the cream toward the center, which is fine), pleating as you go. Leave a 3-inch peekaboo window in the center of the galette, but don't be too fussy about it—it should look rustic. Repeat with the second dough disk on the same baking sheet.

Once you have assembled two galettes, pop the baking sheet into the freezer for at least 20 minutes. Repeat to form the second two galettes on the second baking sheet, then freeze for at least 20 minutes (see Yo!). Leave the galettes in the freezer until just before you're ready to bake.

BAKE AND SERVE. Preheat the oven to 400°F, with a rack in the center position (and one in the lower third if you're baking both sheets at once).

Quickly brush the edges of the galettes on one baking sheet with egg wash and sprinkle the crusts lightly with half of the coarse or granulated sugar (about ½ teaspoon per galette). Bake in the center of the oven if baking one sheet at a time or in the center and lower third if baking both sheets at the same time, switching the positions of the sheets halfway through, for about 45 minutes, until the crust is deep golden brown and the filling bubbles vigorously.

COOL COMPLETELY. Dust with confectioners' sugar just before serving.

Labneh-Dimpled Brownie Tart

8 tablespoons (1 stick) unsalted butter, plus soft butter for greasing the pan

6 ounces dark chocolate (72% cacao preferred), finely chopped

½ cup labneh, homemade (page 329) or store-bought (see Yo!, page 97)

3 large eggs, at room temperature

¾ cup sugar

½ teaspoon pure vanilla extract

½ teaspoon pure almond extract

½ cup whole-wheat flour

¼ cup almond meal (see Yo!, page 250)

¼ teaspoon kosher salt

Ice cream, Greek yogurt, or whipped cream, for serving (optional)

MAKES ONE 9-INCH TART; SERVES 8

The cream cheese brownie's older, more elegant cousin, this dinner-party dessert is supremely rich, dark, and chocolaty, with large polka dots of labneh and a hint of almond. It comes together quickly.

PREP. Preheat the oven to 350°F, with a rack in the center position. Generously butter the fluted sides of a 9-inch tart pan with a removable bottom, working the butter into each nook and cranny. Line the bottom with a parchment round. Set on a baking sheet.

MAKE THE TART. In a large saucepan, melt the butter and chocolate over low heat, stirring frequently with a wooden spoon. When completely smooth, remove from the heat and stir in ¼ cup of the labneh. (You may have a few small lumps.) Let cool to lukewarm. Meanwhile, in a medium bowl, whisk together the eggs, sugar, vanilla, and almond extract. When the chocolate mixture has cooled, stir in the egg mixture until no yellow streaks remain. Sprinkle the flour, almond meal, and salt on top and stir just until incorporated. (Do not overmix.)

BAKE AND COOL. Scrape the batter into the prepared pan. Dot with the remaining ¼ cup labneh in teaspoon-size dollops. Bake until the tart just loses its sheen and a skewer comes out of the center with a few moist crumbs attached, 20 to 25 minutes. Cool on a rack for 15 minutes, then pop up the removable bottom and remove the metal ring. Let cool completely.

SERVE. When ready to serve, slide a thin spatula between the tart and the parchment and lift carefully onto a serving plate. Serve alone or with ice cream, Greek yogurt, or whipped cream.

STORE. Keep in the refrigerator, tightly wrapped, for up to 4 days.

Blueberry-Topped Pavlovas

4 large egg whites

Pinch of cream of tartar

1 scant cup sugar

½ teaspoon cornstarch

½ teaspoon white vinegar

½ teaspoon pure vanilla extract

Yogurt Whipped Cream
(page 301)

2 to 2½ cups fresh blueberries
(with no moisture on them), or
other fruit of your choice

Honey or Red Wine Syrup
(page 291), for drizzling

MAKES TWO 8-INCH PAVLOVAS; SERVES 6 EACH

A study in textural contrast, the pavlova is light and crisp outside and chewy, marshmallowy inside. A variation on a classic dessert wildly popular in Australia and New Zealand, this one is heaped with berries and yogurt cream. Pavlovas are prone to cracking, so don't worry if yours show a few imperfections. Avoid making pavlovas on humid days, as the meringue won't be as crisp. Note that the meringue shells should be made 1 day ahead.

MAKE THE MERINGUE SHELLS. Preheat the oven to 250°F, with racks in the center position and the lower third. Line two baking sheets with parchment.

With an electric mixer, whisk the egg whites and cream of tartar until cloudy and foamy. On medium-high speed, slowly stream in the sugar, then crank the speed up high and continue to whip until you have stiff, glossy peaks. Sift in the cornstarch, drizzle in the vinegar and vanilla, and whip for a few more seconds to incorporate. Divide the meringue evenly between the baking sheets, using a silicone spatula or wooden spoon to spread it into two 8-inch rounds. Make a wide, shallow depression in the center of each meringue, which you will later fill with cream and berries. Bake for 1 hour. Turn off the oven. Leave the pavlovas overnight either in the oven or at cool room temperature.

MAKE THE YOGURT WHIPPED CREAM. Prepare according to the instructions on page 301, decreasing the cream and yogurt to ¾ cup each, the vanilla to ¼ teaspoon, and the sugar to 1 tablespoon. (The whipped cream may be made several days ahead and refrigerated, tightly covered.)

(continued)

ASSEMBLE AND SERVE. Carefully slide a wide spatula or two under each meringue shell and transfer to a platter or cake stand. Just before serving, scrape the Yogurt Whipped Cream into each indentation, gently smoothing the top. Top with the blueberries and drizzle lightly with honey or a bit of Red Wine Syrup. Serve immediately.

> ### Yo!
>
> Both the meringue shell and the yogurt whipped cream may be made ahead of time and stored separately. Assemble the pavlova moments before serving.
>
> If you prefer to make one large pavlova instead of two smaller ones, go ahead. You may want to serve it directly from the baking sheet, however, as it will be quite a feat to move it to a platter without incident.

Raisin-Poppy Seed Flatbreads with Cardamom-Honey Butter

FOR THE CARDAMOM-HONEY BUTTER

6 tablespoons (¾ stick) unsalted butter, at room temperature

1 tablespoon honey

¼ teaspoon ground cardamom

Pinch of kosher salt

FOR THE FLATBREADS

¼ cup golden raisins, coarsely chopped

¼ cup warm (about 100°F) water

2¼ teaspoons (one ¼-ounce packet) active dry yeast

½ cup plain low-fat or whole-milk yogurt (not Greek), at room temperature

¼ cup honey

1½ cups all-purpose flour, plus more for kneading and rolling

¾ cup whole-wheat flour

3 tablespoons poppy seeds

1 tablespoon kosher salt

2 to 4 tablespoons coconut oil (see Yo!, page 91), melted, for brushing

MAKES EIGHT 6-INCH FLATBREADS

If you're going to make homemade flatbread, make one whose dough is tender with yogurt, sweet with honey, chewy with raisins, and charming with itty-bitty poppy seeds. Griddling them in coconut oil adds both flavor and crispness, and serving them warm with a fast-fix cardamom-honey butter gilds the lily.

MAKE THE CARDAMOM-HONEY BUTTER. In a small bowl, beat the butter, honey, cardamom, and salt with a spoon until smooth. Cover and set aside at room temperature. (May be made several days ahead and refrigerated. Bring to room temperature before using.)

MAKE THE DOUGH. In a small bowl, cover the raisins with boiling water. Let stand until needed.

Meanwhile, add the ¼ cup warm water to a large bowl. Sprinkle with the yeast, swirl with a fingertip to moisten, and let stand for 5 minutes, until foamy. Add the yogurt and honey and whisk until the honey dissolves. Drain the raisins, reserving the liquid; pat dry. To the yeast mixture, add the raisins, all-purpose flour, whole-wheat flour, poppy seeds, and salt. Stir with a wooden spoon until a dough forms. (If the dough is too dry to come together, add a few teaspoons of the reserved raisin liquid.) Turn out onto a lightly floured work surface and knead until smooth, 3 to 5 minutes. Place in a greased bowl, cover with plastic wrap, and let rise in a warm spot for 2 hours, until lightly puffed. (The dough will not double.)

(continued)

GRIDDLE AND SERVE. Return the dough to the floured surface and cut into 8 equal wedges. Working with one wedge at a time (keep the rest covered), roll the dough nice and thin into a rough 6-inch round.

Heat a cast-iron skillet over medium-high heat. After a minute or two, when a drop of water on the skillet sizzles and evaporates, brush the skillet with oil. Add the dough round and cook until the underside is golden brown, about 2 minutes. Brush the top with more oil, flip, and cook the other side for another 2 minutes. Stack the flatbreads, wrapped in a kitchen towel, while you cook the remaining breads.

SERVE. Serve the flatbreads with the cardamom-honey butter.

Parmesan and Sun-Dried Tomato Quick Bread

¼ cup extra-virgin olive oil, plus additional for greasing the pan

2 cups all-purpose flour

1¼ cups whole-wheat flour or white whole-wheat flour

1 cup plus 2 tablespoons shredded Parmesan cheese (about 3 ounces)

2 teaspoons baking powder

¼ teaspoon baking soda

1½ teaspoons kosher salt

½ teaspoon freshly ground pepper

1½ cups plain whole-milk or low-fat yogurt (not Greek)

⅔ cup finely chopped oil-packed sun-dried tomatoes (it's fine if oil clings to them)

3 tablespoons milk

2 teaspoons unsalted butter, melted

MAKES ONE 9-INCH LOAF

With big, pizza-like flavors, this savory quick bread benefits from a long bake but little up-front work. Drizzling the bread during the final minutes with melted butter and sprinkling it with a little more Parmesan creates a cheesy top. Pair the warm, fat slices with bowls of soup.

PREP. Preheat the oven to 350°F, with a rack in the center position. Line a 9-by-5-inch loaf pan with a large piece of aluminum foil, allowing plenty of overhang. Grease the foil-lined pan with oil.

MAKE THE BATTER. In a large bowl, whisk together the all-purpose flour, whole-wheat flour, 1 cup of the cheese, the baking powder, baking soda, salt, and pepper. In a separate bowl, whisk together the yogurt, oil, and sun-dried tomatoes. Pour the wet ingredients over the dry and begin to fold, adding the milk slowly as you work to moisten the dough. The dough will start out quite dry, but keep folding and eventually it will all come together in a well-moistened mass.

BAKE. Transfer the batter to the prepared loaf pan. Bake until risen, golden brown, and firm, about 1 hour. (Do not underbake.) Carefully drizzle the melted butter over the top and sprinkle with the remaining 2 tablespoons cheese. Return to the oven for 5 to 10 minutes, until the top is golden, the cheese has melted, and an instant-read thermometer inserted into the center of the bread reads about 190°F or until it sounds hollow when carefully turned out of the pan and thumped.

COOL AND SERVE. Use the foil to lift the bread out of the pan. Cool completely on a rack. Remove the foil, slice thickly, and serve.

"Yogurt is one of the basic ingredients in our cuisine," wrote Hande Bozdoğan, with whom I corresponded by email. "It is indispensable."

Bozdoğan, founding director of the Istanbul Culinary Institute, said yogurt is enjoyed throughout Turkey.

Today's Turkish cooks are rediscovering the joys of foods and production methods once dismissed as old-fashioned. In large cities, it's now chic to make yogurt at home, using modern yogurt makers or the traditional methods still common in rural villages. Markets offer a wide variety of yogurts to increasingly discerning consumers. Sheep's, cow's, and goat's milk are all used, with sheep's milk being dominant.

With widespread application in savory cooking, yogurt pairs often in Turkey with kebabs, like in the regional specialty *iskender kebab*—sliced spit-cooked meat served on pita bread with yogurt and tomato sauce—and *ali nazik kebab*—chargrilled eggplant topped with chunks of meat and either plain or garlic-flecked yogurt. In both cases, the yogurt is often dusted with dried mint, sumac, or crushed red chile pepper just before serving.

Thickened, strained yogurt makes a popular addition to a Turkish meze (appetizer) platter, and dips that feature yogurt and garlic, with or without other vegetables, are widely consumed as well. (See Turkish-Style Spinach Dip, page 102.) A classic comfort food called *manti* features meat-stuffed dumplings sauced with garlicky yogurt, melted butter, and mint.

Particularly in hot regions, Turkey's most refreshing yogurt beverage, *ayran*, made with water, yogurt, and salt, is served. Big city cafés now offer yogurt shakes or frozen yogurt or yogurt with fruits, things that did not exist in Turkish culinary culture twenty years ago. Other trends, including a new emphasis on nonfat and reduced-fat yogurt, probiotics, and high-protein foods, have also taken hold.

Whether past or present, in cities or the countryside, yogurt's primacy on the country's culinary landscape isn't ebbing. It's a central ingredient, one whose diverse uses continue to delight and sustain the Turkish people.

Chill

Whether molded into panna cotta, layered into tiramisu, or whisked into a simple sauce for fresh sliced fruit, yogurt makes the ultimate chilled dessert.

The flavors in this chapter—citrusy, chocolaty, caramelly, or boozy—all complement rather than overshadow yogurt's telltale tang. If you prefer a bit more sweetness than called for, go ahead and add more sugar to taste. These desserts are flexible enough to handle a range, so feel free to customize them to suit your own palate.

And do plan ahead. Chilled treats like these need to hang out in the refrigerator for a few hours to firm up and develop maximum flavor. Make them early in the day or even the day before you plan to serve them and keep them cold. Happily, this means that you can pull them out on a warm afternoon or at the end of a summer dinner party with minimal last-minute fuss.

The Recipes

Lemon-Poppy Seed Mousse with Raspberries and Amaretti

FOR THE LEMON-POPPY SEED CURD

Zest and juice of 2 to 4 lemons (Meyer, if available) (⅓ cup juice)

2 large eggs

⅓ cup sugar

3 tablespoons unsalted butter, cut into cubes

1 teaspoon poppy seeds

⅛ teaspoon pure vanilla extract

Pinch of kosher salt

FOR SERVING

½ recipe Yogurt Whipped Cream (page 301), made without any sugar

1⅓ cups fresh raspberries (one 6-ounce basket)

12 amaretti (see Yo!, page 64) cookies or other small cookies, crushed

SERVES 6

With its airy texture, clear lemon flavor, and pop of bright raspberry, this mousse gets its crunch from crumbled amaretti cookies. If you can't find them or don't appreciate their bitter edge, use any cookies you like (graham crackers will be milder for kids) or opt for chopped, toasted nuts.

MAKE THE CURD. Set aside a good pinch of the lemon zest for the curd; wrap the remaining zest in plastic wrap and refrigerate for the garnish. Place a fine-mesh strainer over a medium bowl.

In a medium saucepan, off the heat, whisk the eggs and sugar until well combined and light, about 1 minute. Slowly whisk in the lemon juice, drizzling it in bit by bit, whisking constantly. Scatter the butter on top. Set the pan over medium-low heat. Swapping the whisk for a wooden spoon, begin making figure eights along the bottom of the saucepan. Stir like this constantly as the curd cooks and thickens (don't let it boil).

FINISH THE CURD. After 3 to 4 minutes of constant stirring, swipe an index finger quickly along the back of the spoon. If it holds the line without drips, the curd has thickened sufficiently. If not, continue cooking and stirring until the line holds. Remove from the heat and immediately pour through the strainer into the bowl. Stir in the poppy seeds, vanilla, salt, and the pinch of lemon zest. Press a piece of plastic wrap directly on the surface of the curd and refrigerate until cold, several hours or overnight.

(continued)

Yo!

Make the lemon–poppy seed curd and Yogurt Whipped Cream up to several days ahead. Refrigerate separately, covered.

ASSEMBLE AND SERVE. In a large bowl, fold the lemon–poppy seed curd into the Yogurt Whipped Cream to create a mousse. Refrigerate for 15 minutes to firm up. Dollop a spoonful of mousse on the bottom of each of six glasses. Top with a few raspberries and a good sprinkle of cookie crumbs. Repeat (you should have two layers of mousse, berries, and crushed cookies). Garnish each glass with a pinch of the reserved lemon zest and serve.

Stripy Fruit Gelées

FOR THE JUICE LAYERS

2 packets (4¾ teaspoons total) unflavored powdered gelatin

2 tablespoons sugar

1½ cups orange juice, preferably fresh

1½ cups pomegranate juice

FOR SERVING

¾ cup plain whole-milk Greek yogurt

1 tablespoon sugar, or to taste

2 kiwis, peeled and diced, or other colorful diced fresh fruit of your choice

Yo!

Plan ahead. The gelées take at least 3 hours to chill.

SERVES 4 TO 6

In this sophisticated take on an old-fashioned classic, layers of firmed-up orange juice, pomegranate juice, and yogurt combine in a refreshing and eye-popping finale to a meal.

MAKE THE ORANGE LAYER. In a small bowl, stir together the gelatin and sugar until well combined. You'll have about a scant 4 table-spoons. Pour the orange juice into a small but wide saucepan. Sprinkle 2 tablespoons of the gelatin mixture evenly over the orange juice. Let stand off the heat for 2 minutes to soften. Set the saucepan over low heat and cook, stirring, for about 2 minutes, until the gelatin dissolves. Pour into a liquid measuring cup. Divide the orange juice mixture among four 8-ounce or six 6-ounce juice glasses, jars, or small, clear bowls. Set the glasses on a small tray. (A toaster oven tray works well.) Freeze for exactly 10 minutes, then transfer to the refrigerator and chill for at least 1 hour before proceeding.

MAKE THE POMEGRANATE LAYER. Wash and dry the saucepan. Pour in the pomegranate juice. Sprinkle evenly with the remaining gelatin mixture. Let stand off the heat for 2 minutes to soften. Set the saucepan over low heat and cook, stirring, for about 2 minutes, until the gelatin dissolves. Let cool to room temperature, at least 15 minutes. Transfer to a clean liquid measuring cup. Retrieve the glasses from the refrigerator and slowly pour the pomegranate mixture on top, dividing evenly. Return to the refrigerator for about 2 hours, or until fully set.

SERVE. In a small bowl, gently stir together the yogurt and sugar, adding more sugar to taste, if desired. Divide the yogurt among the gelées, dolloping it on top. Scatter with the kiwi or other fruit and serve.

Candied Kumquat Spoon Sweets

1 pound kumquats, well scrubbed

¾ cup sugar

¼ cup honey

1 tablespoon fresh lemon juice

½ cup water

½ cup plain whole-milk Greek yogurt per serving

Yo!

Kumquats have tiny seeds, but they soften and become relatively unobtrusive in the candying process.

A candy thermometer is crucial for gauging the doneness of the syrup and making sure it reaches the proper stage. Always use special caution when working with hot sugar.

MAKES 2 CUPS CANDIED KUMQUATS

For dessert, Greeks often enjoy thick yogurt topped with colorful "spoon sweets," candied fruits in sticky syrup. When I was in Greece, this golden kumquat version stole my heart with its balance of sweet, tart, and pleasantly bitter flavors. Start 1 day ahead.

BLANCH THE KUMQUATS. In a large, heavy (4½- to 5-quart) saucepan with tall sides, bring 6 cups water to a rolling boil. Add the kumquats and blanch for 1 minute. Drain.

CANDY THE KUMQUATS. Dry the pot, then add the sugar, honey, lemon juice, and water. Set over medium-high heat and cook, stirring, until the sugar dissolves. Clip a candy thermometer to the side of the saucepan. Add the kumquats and bring to a rolling boil.

Boil until the syrup reaches exactly 230°F, swirling the saucepan occasionally or stirring to ensure all the fruits are evenly coated. This may take anywhere from 8 to 15 minutes, depending on the size and weight of your saucepan. The syrup will become very foamy. Remove the saucepan from the heat and let the foam settle. Cover and let stand overnight at room temperature.

The next day, the syrup should be thick and sticky and the kumquats shriveled and glossy. Transfer the fruit and syrup to a 2-cup glass jar (or other container), cover, and refrigerate.

SERVE. For each serving, stir the yogurt in a small bowl until smooth, then make a wide, shallow indentation with the back of the spoon. Spoon 1 to 2 tablespoons of the candied kumquats and their syrup into the indentation and serve.

STORE. The candied kumquats may be stored, covered, for up to 2 weeks in the refrigerator.

Fig Spoon Sweets in Red Wine Syrup

13 dried figs, hard tips trimmed off (see Yo!)

1½ cups red wine

½ cup sugar

1 cinnamon stick

3 cloves

½ cup plain whole-milk Greek yogurt per serving

MAKES ABOUT 2 CUPS FIGS

This chilled spoon sweet, equally at home in summer and winter, falls squarely in the camp of low-effort, high-impact, make-ahead desserts. Swirling the scarlet syrup into yogurt creates a gorgeous, spiraled effect that screams fancy. I'm partial to Mission figs, which become glossy and almost onyx colored in the syrup, but tan-colored Greek figs are also wonderful. Use Syrah for the syrup, like I do, or any red wine you have on hand.

BLANCH THE FIGS (OPTIONAL). Taste one fig. If its skin is thin and it isn't too hard or chewy, skip this step and move on to the red wine syrup. If it's hard and chewy, with thick skin, blanch the figs before proceeding: Bring a small saucepan of water to a boil, drop in the figs, and simmer for exactly 2 minutes. Drain.

MAKE THE RED WINE SYRUP. Have a 1- or 2-cup heatproof glass measuring cup close at hand. In a medium saucepan with tall sides, combine the wine, sugar, cinnamon, and cloves. Bring to a moderate boil over medium heat, stirring for the first minute until the sugar dissolves. Continue to simmer until reduced to about ⅔ cup. Depending on your heat and your saucepan, this may take anywhere from 7 to 20 minutes. Keep an eye on it, as you don't want the syrup to boil over.

(continued)

Yo!

I tend to leave smaller Mission figs whole and quarter the flatter, thicker-skinned Greek figs.

DOUSE THE FRUIT. Set the figs in a bowl or heatproof jar just large enough to hold the figs and syrup. Pour the hot syrup over the figs and let cool to room temperature. Cover and refrigerate until needed. (May be made several days ahead. Leave the cinnamon stick and cloves in the syrup as it chills, but don't spoon them out when serving.)

SERVE. Whisk the yogurt to loosen, then divide among serving bowls. Swirl a bit of the red wine syrup into each bowl and top with the figs.

VARIATION

For a flavor twist, spoon these sweets over Coffee Yogurt (page 67) instead of plain.

Milk Chocolate Yogurt Pots with Salted Peanut Crush

8 ounces high-quality milk chocolate, finely chopped (do not use chocolate chips)

2 cups plain Greek yogurt, preferably whole-milk

½ teaspoon pure vanilla extract

Pinch of kosher salt

Confectioners' or granulated sugar, to taste (optional)

2 tablespoons salted roasted peanuts, finely chopped

Yo!

If you don't have a double boiler, set a large, heat-proof bowl (metal or glass) over a smaller saucepan filled with about 2 inches of barely simmering water. The bottom of the bowl should not touch the water or the chocolate will seize. Keep the heat as low as possible.

SERVES 5

On a visit to 31st Union, a bustling restaurant in San Mateo, California, my family and I ended our meal in the best way possible: with a rich chocolate panna cotta dusted with salty, spicy peanuts. In my version, I've omitted the spice and turned to yogurt instead of gelatin for body to create a lighter, more mousse-like dessert.

MELT THE CHOCOLATE. Stir the chocolate slowly in a double boiler (see Yo!) over barely simmering water until completely smooth. Turn off the heat, but leave the double boiler in place over the still-warm burner so that the residual heat keeps the chocolate warm.

MIX. Slowly whisk the yogurt into the chocolate, stirring with a spoon at first and then switching to a whisk. The goal here is twofold: to warm the yogurt slightly so it marries completely with the chocolate and to prevent the chocolate from seizing back up and becoming gritty. Once you've got a completely smooth texture, whisk in the vanilla and salt. Taste, and if it's not sweet enough for you, add a bit of sugar (confectioners' sugar will dissolve most easily, but you can also use granulated). Pour the mixture into five 4-ounce ramekins or little jars.

CHILL, GARNISH, AND SERVE. Refrigerate for at least 1 hour to set. Dust with the salted peanuts just before serving.

STORE. The chocolate pots can be refrigerated, covered with plastic wrap, for up to 8 hours.

Salted Caramel Panna Cottas

1 cup sugar

⅓ cup water

¾ cup plus ⅓ cup heavy cream

½ cup cold whole milk

1 packet unflavored powdered gelatin (about 2⅛ teaspoons)

1¼ cups plain whole-milk Greek yogurt

1½ teaspoons pure vanilla extract

¼ teaspoon kosher salt

Fleur de sel, for garnish

Yo!

Don't neglect the fleur de sel on top when serving. Caramel is very sweet, and the salt provides an important contrast.

SERVES 6

My version of this cool Italian dessert offsets deep caramel notes with the refreshing taste of yogurt. For the ideal texture and flavor, make the custards the night before serving so they can properly set up.

MAKE THE CARAMEL. In a small, heavy saucepan, combine the sugar and water. Cook, stirring constantly, over low heat until the sugar dissolves, 3 to 5 minutes. If you have a candy thermometer, affix it to the inside of the pot. Raise the heat to medium-high and slowly bring the mixture up to between 320 and 350°F without stirring, though you may swirl the pan slightly now and again. Watch carefully. The liquid will first turn golden, then amber, then finally a deep, caramelly brown. Once you've reached the target temperature range and color, remove the saucepan from the heat. Stand back and slowly add ⅓ cup of the cream. The caramel will bubble vigorously. Stir with a silicone spatula until smooth. Let stand while you bloom the gelatin.

MAKE THE PANNA COTTA. Pour the milk into a wide, shallow bowl. Sprinkle the gelatin on top and let stand for 5 minutes to bloom. Whisk the milk mixture into the hot caramel until very smooth. Return to very low heat just for a minute as you whisk in the remaining ¾ cup cream, the yogurt, vanilla, and kosher salt. (You will have 3 cups panna cotta.)

CHILL. Divide the panna cotta among six 4-ounce ramekins. Refrigerate until set and very cold, at least 6 hours but preferably overnight.

UNMOLD, GARNISH, AND SERVE. Run a thin knife along the inside rim of each ramekin to loosen. Briefly dip the ramekin in a shallow bowl of hot water, up to the lip. Remove. Set a plate over the top of the ramekin, then invert. (You may have to repeat this process.) Garnish panna cottas with a generous sprinkling of fleur de sel. Serve cold.

Tiramisu

½ cup cold heavy cream

1¼ cups cold coffee concentrate (see Coffee Yogurt, page 67)

¼ cup dark rum

About 30 ladyfingers (see Yo!)

2 cups plain whole-milk Greek yogurt

Sugar, to taste (optional)

Sifted unsweetened cocoa powder, melted or shaved dark chocolate, or crushed chocolate-covered espresso beans, for garnish

SERVES 8 TO 10

Spiked with booze, rich with mascarpone, and doused with espresso, tiramisu ranks high on the list of beloved Italian desserts, and with good reason: It's relatively easy to make and surprisingly light tasting, given its indulgent profile. With no raw eggs to cause worries (most recipes call for beating eggs with the sugar) and yogurt ousting mascarpone, this tiramisu is airier but no less special—still creamy, rummy, and espresso toned, but with less cloying sweetness.

WHIP THE CREAM. Whip the cream to firm peaks. Refrigerate until needed.

DUNK HALF THE LADYFINGERS. In a medium bowl, combine the coffee concentrate and rum. One by one, dip half of the ladyfingers in the coffee-rum mixture for a few seconds per side. You want the ladyfingers to barely soften. (If they're rock hard, give them a slightly longer dip.) Place rounded side up in a 2-quart serving bowl or dish. (I generally choose a shallow bowl and assemble two layers each of ladyfingers and yogurt cream.) Continue dipping, placing the ladyfingers side by side without overlapping, in a single layer to cover the bottom of the bowl. You can break a few to fit them in like puzzle pieces, if you like.

MAKE THE COFFEE YOGURT CREAM AND ASSEMBLE THE TIRAMISU. In a large bowl, whisk ½ cup of the remaining coffee-rum mixture into the yogurt. Fold in the whipped cream, taking care not to deflate it too much. Taste, adding up to 2 tablespoons sugar, if desired. Spread half the yogurt cream over the ladyfingers. Dip the remaining ladyfingers in the remaining coffee-rum mixture, arrange them on top of the yogurt cream, and then top with the remaining yogurt cream. Smooth the top.

CHILL, GARNISH, AND SERVE. Cover tightly with plastic wrap and refrigerate for at least 3 hours. Just before serving, cover the top with the garnish of your choice. To serve, use a slotted spoon to scoop into shallow bowls.

STORE. The tiramisu can be refrigerated, covered with plastic wrap, for up to 8 hours.

Yo!

You may make the coffee concentrate a day or two ahead. (You won't need the full recipe; save the rest to make the Coffee Yogurt, page 67.)

Depending on the size and shape of your serving dish, you'll need about 30 ladyfingers, perhaps a few more. I advise you to buy at least 6 ounces (170 g) to be sure you'll have enough.

Once assembled, the tiramisu needs about 3 hours to chill before serving, so plan accordingly.

Serbia is a mélange of Italian, Austrian, Hungarian, Turkish, and Greek influences, all of which are evident in the culture's food. And one of its most prominent ingredients is yogurt.

Serbian yogurt comes in two distinct forms: thick and thin, said Svetlana Watkins, who was raised in the city of Čačak, about two hours southwest of Belgrade, and now lives in California. The thicker version is "so thick you can cut it with a spoon," Watkins said. Serbs call this yogurt "sour milk" (*kiselo mleko*) and women throughout the country make it from sheep's or cow's milk.

When making yogurt, Watkins's mother would boil the milk, cool it "to the temperature of your skin," stir in yogurt from a prior batch, wrap the pot in a blanket, and let it sit on a radiator that had been turned off but still retained heat. In the morning, Watkins said, "we'd just eat it plain with our savory breakfast."

The second type of yogurt is drinkable, acidic, and slightly salty. Called *jogurt*, it is closer to buttermilk. *Jogurt* is now sold in cartons at the grocery store, but when Watkins was growing up, it came in glass bottles.

Both styles of yogurt are consumed on their own, but they are also incorporated into recipes. In May or June, for example, Watkins's mother would make small, savory, yogurt-sauced parcels, gathering large, thin leaves of sorrel (an edible weed), stuffing them with a ground beef filling seasoned with paprika and onions, and simmering the rolls in a light broth before spooning yogurt over the top. Called *sarmica*, the dish is a Serbian take on the Turkish dolma or Greek *dolmada* (page 220).

Yogurt also featured in her mother's spanakopita, which had a filling of yogurt, eggs, cheese, and spinach. "Ours is thicker and softer than the Greek version," Watkins explained. "It's not crispy."

Watkins misses the yogurt of her childhood. "When I go home, the first thing I do is go to the corner bakery and get a *borek* (phyllo stuffed with meat or cheese) and a nice glass of yogurt, because that's not something I can get here," she said wistfully.

Yogurt Whipped Cream

1 cup cold heavy cream

1 cup plain whole-milk Greek yogurt

½ teaspoon pure vanilla extract

2 to 3 tablespoons sugar

Yo!

This full process should take 1 to 2 minutes total. Do not overwhip, or you'll lose the smooth texture you've created.

Use yogurt whipped cream anywhere you'd use regular whipped cream: atop pies and cakes, alongside brownies or ice cream, as a frosting, or dolloped over fresh berries.

MAKES 3½ CUPS

There is perhaps no more versatile accompaniment to any dessert than fluffy whipped cream. What makes it so special—its lightness, its airiness—is also, however, its greatest drawback. On its own, whipped cream is highly unstable, deflating quickly and losing its structure. It also cannot be made in advance. Whipping a bit of yogurt into it solves these problems, creating a light, sweet, and still-fluffy topping that has enough structure and stability to last for days in the refrigerator.

MAKE. Using an electric mixer with the whisk attachment, whip the cream on medium speed until soft peaks form. Add the yogurt and vanilla, then continue to whip, slowly streaming 2 tablespoons sugar down the sides of the bowl. Continue whipping until the peaks hold when the whisk is lifted. Taste, whipping in up to 1 tablespoon more sugar, if desired.

STORE. Store, tightly covered, in the refrigerator for up to 1 week. No rewhipping is required.

Lick

Lick

Though it's easier than ever to get your frozen-yogurt fix at nearly any airport, strip mall, or street corner in America, churning your own is worth the effort. There's pleasure to be had in macerating fresh-from-the-market fruit, plucking herbs, toasting spices, and grinding nuts to create homemade frozen yogurts that taste like no one else's. Textures are smooth and luscious but not unnaturally "whipped" or so uniform you forget you're eating a homemade treat.

In the recipes that follow, fat and sugar play an important role not just in flavor, but in the mouthfeel of the frozen yogurt. Reducing the fat or sugar may make your frozen yogurts icy, hard, or "flaky" instead of creamy. (Keep this in mind if you're tempted to veer off from the quantities provided in each recipe.) Just as I make ice cream with real cream and whole milk, I opt for whole-milk yogurt in my frozen yogurts.

Here are a few tips for making frozen yogurt.

» Pressing a layer of parchment directly on the surface of frozen yogurt is the best way to preserve its flavor and textural integrity and to prevent an icy layer from forming on top.

» Most homemade frozen yogurt will get quite hard after a few hours or a few days in the freezer. To return it to optimal texture, always leave the container—I like using a metal loaf pan—at room temperature for at least 20 to 30 minutes before serving, until it looks creamy around the edges.

» The best way to scoop frozen yogurt is to use a hot, dry scoop. Heat the scoop by running it under hot tap water. Dry it quickly and thoroughly. Drag it across the top of the partially thawed yogurt until beautiful, round scoops form. Repeat the process between scoops.

Ready?

The Recipes

Ultimate Strawberry Frozen Yogurt

1 pound strawberries, preferably organic

½ cup plus 2 tablespoons sugar

2 tablespoons balsamic vinegar

2½ cups plain whole-milk yogurt (not Greek) or 1½ cups plain whole-milk Greek yogurt

1 tablespoon light corn syrup

1 tablespoon plus 1 teaspoon finely minced fresh rosemary, plus (optional) additional minced rosemary for garnish

Yo!

A standard-size green plastic basket of strawberries like you'll find in grocery stores and farmers' markets is generally a pint. You'll need about 1¼ of those baskets to equal 1 pound.

MAKES 1 GENEROUS QUART

Balsamic vinegar and minced rosemary lend subtle notes that heighten the berry essence without overshadowing it.

PREP THE BERRIES. In a food processor, pulse the strawberries, sugar, and vinegar in five 1-second bursts. Let stand at room temperature (go ahead and keep it in the food processor), covered, for 1 hour.

MEANWHILE, PREP THE YOGURT. If using traditional yogurt, spoon it into a fine-mesh sieve set over a deep bowl. Refrigerate to drain off the whey for 1 hour only. Discard the whey or reserve it for another use (see page 331). Add the yogurt to the food processor with the strawberries. (If using Greek yogurt, do not strain, but do not add the yogurt to the berries until after they have stood for 1 hour.)

PUREE AND CHILL. Add the corn syrup to the yogurt mixture. Process until nearly smooth. Transfer to a covered container and refrigerate for at least 4 hours or overnight.

FREEZE. Freeze the mixture in an ice cream maker according to the manufacturer's instructions. After 20 minutes, add the rosemary. Continue churning until the mixture has fully thickened and is nearly scoopable. You may eat it now, soft-serve style, but I recommend transferring it to a metal loaf pan to further chill and develop deeper flavor. Press a sheet of parchment directly on the surface of the frozen yogurt, then cover tightly with aluminum foil. Freeze for several hours.

SERVE. Let the yogurt stand at room temperature at least 20 minutes before scooping with a hot, dry scoop. Garnish sparingly with rosemary.

Blackberry-Lavender Frozen Yogurt *(pictured on page 307)*

10 ounces blackberries (about 2¼ cups), rinsed, with some water still clinging

⅔ cup sugar

1½ teaspoons dried culinary lavender (see Yo!, page 187), plus a few optional petals for garnish

2 tablespoons raspberry vinegar (see Yo!, page 50)

2½ cups plain whole-milk yogurt (not Greek) or 1½ cups whole-milk Greek yogurt

1 tablespoon light corn syrup

MAKES 1 SCANT QUART

With its glorious, royal color and deep summer flavor, this frozen yogurt showcases blackberries' sweet side and tempers their occasional astringency. The raspberry vinegar adds color and flavor and improves scoopability.

PREP THE BERRIES. In a large bowl, stir together the blackberries, sugar, lavender, and vinegar. Set aside at room temperature. After 10 minutes, hit the berries a few times with a potato masher to break them down ever so slightly. Let stand, uncovered, for 1 hour total, stirring a few times.

MEANWHILE, PREP THE YOGURT. If using traditional yogurt, spoon it into a fine-mesh sieve set over a deep bowl. Refrigerate to drain off the whey while the berries macerate. Discard the whey or see page 331 for uses. (If using Greek yogurt, do not strain.)

PUREE AND CHILL. Combine the berries and their juices and the corn syrup in a blender or food processor and puree until smooth. (Strain out the seeds, if desired.) Return the berries to their macerating bowl and whisk in the strained or Greek yogurt. Cover and refrigerate for at least 4 hours or overnight.

FREEZE. Churn the mixture in an ice cream maker according to the manufacturer's instructions until thick and scoopable, about 30 minutes. You may eat it now, soft-serve style, but I recommend transferring it to a metal loaf pan to further chill and develop deeper

I don't bother straining out the blackberry seeds because I hate washing extraneous dishes and don't mind the textural flecks. If you prefer a smoother consistency, then by all means strain away.

flavor. Press a sheet of parchment directly on the surface of the frozen yogurt, then cover tightly with aluminum foil. Freeze for several hours.

SERVE. Let the yogurt stand at room temperature until scoopable, at least 20 minutes, before scooping with a hot, dry scoop. If desired, garnish each serving sparingly with a few lavender petals.

VARIATION

Blackberry-Pinot: My friend Melissa Shafer created a terrific variation on this recipe. To make 1 pint (2 cups) Blackberry-Pinot Frozen Yogurt, use 5 ounces blackberries (about 1⅛ cups), 6 tablespoons sugar, 1 tablespoon chia seeds, 1 tablespoon Pinot Noir, 1½ teaspoons agave nectar, and 1¼ cups plain whole-milk yogurt. Proceed as directed.

Marbled Concord Grape Frozen Yogurt

1½ pounds (4 to 5 cups) Concord grapes (weighed without stems), rinsed well and patted dry

2 scant tablespoons sugar

1 tablespoon chia seeds (see Yo!)

2 tablespoons fresh lemon juice

2 cups plain whole-milk Greek yogurt

½ cup heavy cream

¼ cup honey

MAKES 1 QUART

Run, don't walk, to the farmers' market when purple Concord grapes come into season, generally in late summer and early fall. Their flesh packs more grape flavor than any other variety and their royal color shines especially bright when marbled through creamy frozen yogurt. The only drawback? Seeds, but they are a small price to pay for flavor this good. A food mill, which is essential here, makes easy work of getting rid of them (and the skins).

ROAST THE GRAPES. Preheat the oven to 300°F, with a rack in the center position. Line a baking sheet with parchment.

Tumble the grapes onto the prepared sheet in a single layer. Sprinkle with the sugar. (Much of the sugar will fall onto the parchment; carry on.) Roast for 70 to 90 minutes, until most of the skins have burst and the juices pool thickly on the parchment. (Check at the 1-hour mark to make sure neither the grapes nor the juices are burning. If they're getting close, reduce the temperature to 275°F for the last 10 to 30 minutes.) Cool to room temperature. Refrigerate, covered, for at least 2 hours and up to 1 day.

PUREE. Pass the grapes through the medium holes of a food mill to remove the skins and seeds. (You should have 1¼ cups grape puree.) Return to the refrigerator until needed.

SOFTEN THE CHIA. In a small bowl, stir the chia seeds into the lemon juice. Let stand for 10 minutes, then stir the chia mixture into the grape puree and return to the refrigerator.

MIX. In a medium bowl or large liquid measuring cup, whisk together the yogurt, cream, and honey until incorporated. Refrigerate for at least 30 minutes.

FREEZE. Churn the yogurt mixture (not the grape puree) in an ice cream maker according to the manufacturer's instructions until thick and scoopable, about 15 minutes. Scrape half the yogurt into a metal loaf pan and smooth the top. Scrape or dollop half the grape puree on top of the yogurt and smooth lightly. Repeat with one more layer each of yogurt and puree. (The top layer will be grape.) Press a sheet of parchment directly on the surface, then cover tightly with aluminum foil. Freeze for 3 hours for optimal scooping consistency.

SERVE. If the yogurt was frozen for longer than 3 hours, let stand for at least 20 minutes before scooping. Scoop with a hot, dry scoop to produce beautiful, marbled rounds.

Salted Maple-Butter Pecan Frozen Yogurt

2 tablespoons chia seeds (see Yo!)

3 cups plain whole-milk yogurt (not Greek)

1 tablespoon unsalted butter

1 tablespoon plus 1½ teaspoons dark brown sugar

¼ teaspoon ground cinnamon

½ teaspoon kosher salt

¾ cup pecans, finely chopped

½ cup very cold maple syrup

MAKES 1 QUART

When you want a frozen yogurt that's sweet, salty, buttery, nutty, creamy, and tangy all at the same time, this is your flavor. Chia seeds and pecans add crunch, and maple syrup and brown sugar create a layered, complex sweetness. The salt is for contrast and a modern dash of sophistication.

SOFTEN THE CHIA. In a large bowl, whisk the chia seeds into the yogurt until fully coated and dispersed. Cover and refrigerate for 12 to 24 hours.

CARAMELIZE THE NUTS. In a small, nonstick skillet, melt the butter over medium-low heat. When it foams, add the brown sugar, cinnamon, salt, and pecans and cook, stirring constantly, until the nuts are coated and toasty, 2 to 4 minutes. Transfer to a plate and let cool completely.

MIX AND FREEZE. Whisk the maple syrup into the yogurt mixture. Freeze the mixture in an ice cream maker according to the manufacturer's instructions until thickened considerably but not completely, about 15 minutes. Add the pecans and scrape in any sugary bits left on the plate. Continue churning until the yogurt is thick and

scoopable, 5 to 10 minutes longer. You may eat it now, soft-serve style, but I recommend transferring it to a metal loaf pan to further chill and develop deeper flavor. Press a sheet of parchment directly on the surface of the frozen yogurt, then cover tightly with aluminum foil. Freeze for several hours.

SERVE. Let the yogurt stand at room temperature until scoopable, at least 20 minutes, before scooping with a hot, dry scoop.

Honey-Mascarpone Frozen Yogurt

2½ cups plain whole-milk yogurt

½ cup (4 ounces) mascarpone

Scant ⅓ cup sugar

⅓ cup honey

2 tablespoons extra-virgin olive oil

1 tablespoon pure vanilla extract

Scraped seeds from ½ plump vanilla bean

Finely grated zest of 1 lemon

MAKES 1 QUART

This ultrarich, creamy frozen yogurt has a clean, honeyed sweetness that pairs beautifully with fruit tarts or pies, or a simple bowl of fresh fruit. For an unusual twist, drizzle small scoops with extra-virgin olive oil and scatter with toasted walnuts before serving.

MIX AND FREEZE. In a large bowl, whisk together all the ingredients until almost smooth. (Small clumps of mascarpone may remain.) Freeze the mixture in an ice cream maker according to the manufacturer's instructions until thick and scoopable. You may eat it now, soft-serve style, but I recommend transferring it to a metal loaf pan to further chill and develop deeper flavor. Press a sheet of parchment directly on the surface of the frozen yogurt, then cover tightly with aluminum foil. Freeze for several hours.

SERVE. Let the yogurt stand at room temperature until scoopable, at least 20 minutes, before scooping with a hot, dry scoop.

Yo!

If the lemon zest clumps and adheres to the paddle during churning, just fold it in by hand after churning.

Mascarpone is a spoonable Italian cream cheese. Look for it in markets with a well-stocked cheese aisle. (It's sold in tubs.)

Saffron-Pistachio (Kulfi) Frozen Yogurt

½ cup heavy cream

Scant ¾ teaspoon saffron threads (do not use more)

1½ cups raw unsalted pistachios

⅔ cup sugar

Pinch of ground cardamom

2 cups plain whole-milk Greek yogurt

Yo!

During churning, the saffron threads may clump around the paddle. When transferring to the storage container, scrape in all the clumpy threads and stir to distribute.

MAKES 1 QUART

Kulfi, a popular dessert in India, is heady with spices, ground nuts, and dairy sweetened with generous amounts of sugar. Toscanini's Ice Cream in Cambridge, Massachusetts, serves a *kulfi* ice cream that's out of this world. My version is dense, with an almost macaroony chew from a big heap of pistachios.

MAKE THE SAFFRON CREAM. In a small saucepan, heat the cream just until bubbles dot the edges of the pan. Stir in the saffron, remove from the heat, and let steep for 15 minutes.

MAKE THE PISTACHIO SUGAR. In a food processor, grind the pistachios, sugar, and cardamom until fine and powdery, about 30 seconds.

MIX AND CHILL. In a large bowl, whisk together the saffron cream (scrape in all the saffron threads), pistachio sugar, and yogurt until completely incorporated. Cover and refrigerate for at least 2 hours.

FREEZE. Freeze the mixture in an ice cream maker according to the manufacturer's directions until thick and scoopable. You may eat it now, soft-serve style, but I recommend transferring it to a metal loaf pan to further chill and develop deeper flavor. Press a sheet of parchment directly on the surface of the frozen yogurt, then cover tightly with aluminum foil. Freeze for several hours.

SERVE. Let the yogurt stand at room temperature until scoopable, at least 20 minutes, before scooping with a hot, dry scoop.

A Natural Versatility

MONGOLIAN YOGURT CULTURE

In Mongolia, milk is sacred. When guests visit a home, the host greets them with a bowl of milk wrapped in a blue silk scarf as an offering of respect. One of the land's most revered staples, milk is also prized for its unparalleled versatility. "We make thirty-seven different dairy products from milk," said Ganmaa Davaasambuu, PhD., a researcher at the Harvard School of Public Health in the Department of Nutrition. And not just milk from cows, sheep, and goats, but from horses, yaks, and camels, too.

Davaasambuu doesn't consume much American dairy here in the United States. Our tendency to pasteurize and homogenize our milk gives dairy products a different flavor from those she grew up with in Mongolia. "The flavor there is totally natural," she said of the milk and yogurt of her youth. "It's very appealing."

Given Mongolians' reverence for dairy, it's not surprising that yogurt is popular. "In the countryside, everyone makes their own yogurt. You just warm up milk, bring it to a boil, add a small amount of yogurt, let it stand overnight in a warm place, and it's ready. Children eat yogurt every night before sleeping, especially in nomad families," Davaasambuu said. (One third of the population are nomads.) Yogurt is also transformed into other preparations, notably curds, "a hard, solid mass, kind of like a cake," that allows for long keeping.

To make the curds, yogurt is hung and strained. The resulting solids are pressed between heavy stones or wooden boards and then cut into different shapes. "We leave it on the roof of the yurt to dry in the sun and the wind," Davaasambuu explained. "You can take it with you when you go out with the livestock. Some kids eat it with sugar, but otherwise it's a combination of sour and sweet."

Mongolians also brew alcohol from yogurt (or kefir, as yeast is often added). The process goes like this: Accumulated yogurt goes into a wok, which sits over a fire. On top, a second wok filled with cold water sits in a wooden frame with a hole that leads to a funnel. When a fire is lit, the yogurt in the bottom wok boils and evaporation forces liquid up through the funnel into a collection vessel, where it condenses. "Evaporation makes alcohol through this contraption," Davaasambuu explained. She said the resulting beverage is potent, about 10 percent alcohol, but subsequent pots are less strong. This milk vodka or yogurt vodka, called *isgelen*, is a favorite of Mongol men, but everyone drinks it, especially during celebrations, festivals, or when entertaining guests.

Yogurt is added to Mongolian *bantan*, a soup simmered with beef broth, onions, and flour dumplings. It may be boiled, and the solid mass, known as *aarts*, is collected and added to soup or fried meals. "Some kids mix it with sugar, freeze it, and eat it like ice cream," said Davaasambuu.

Make

Make

If you've ever made your own applesauce, jam, ice cream, or bread, you know the special satisfaction you get when making a from-scratch version of a store-bought staple. Sure, it's quicker and easier to buy these items, but you'll miss out on the pleasure that comes from immersing yourself in their start-to-finish creation. By making your own yogurt, you can choose your milk, desired level of fat, and degree of tartness. You'll also be able to make yogurt in much larger quantities than are available in containers at the supermarket. Plus, you'll enjoy substantial cost savings and lessen your environmental impact by avoiding all those single-use cups.

The recipes that follow teach you how to make yogurt in several forms: the loose, traditional kind that falls easily from a spoon; the strained, Greek-style version that has overtaken dairy cases; and the thick, creamy, slightly salty labneh enjoyed throughout the Middle East.

Keep in mind that fermentation is as much an art as a science. Therefore, in the recipes that follow, I've offered several options to allow you some freedom in choosing your preferred equipment and technique. It's likely that you'll enjoy success straight out of the gate, but if you run into any difficulty, consult Troubleshooting and Frequently Asked Questions (page 332).

The Recipes

Homemade Yogurt

SUGGESTED EQUIPMENT

» A large, heavy stainless-steel pot or an enameled cast-iron Dutch oven with a lid

» Measuring cup and spoons

» A clip-on candy thermometer or an instant-read thermometer

» A medium bowl or a glass measuring cup

» A ladle and a whisk

» A long-handled metal spoon or silicone spatula

» A towel

» A large, lidded container to store the finished yogurt (or a wide-mouth funnel and a few glass jars)

Please note: Equipment pulled fresh from a hot dishwasher is the most sanitary, though you can decide for yourself whether this extra insurance is important to you. (Sanitize the thermometer by sticking the bottom half of the probe in a mug of just-boiled water.)

YIELD: ½ GALLON MILK WILL YIELD ABOUT 7 CUPS YOGURT; 1 GALLON MILK WILL YIELD ABOUT 14 CUPS YOGURT

Despite the length of the instructions that follow, making yogurt isn't hard. People have been doing it for thousands of years. I've included an equipment list to make the process foolproof for newcomers. Keep in mind that this is a simple, four-step process:

1. HEAT THE MILK TO 180°F.

2. COOL THE MILK TO 115°F.

3. INOCULATE WITH THE STARTER CULTURE.

4. INCUBATE FOR SEVERAL HOURS, UNTIL THICK.

About The Ingredients

Start by using ½ gallon of milk and 2 tablespoons yogurt (the starter). Once you get the hang of the method and if you find yourself craving a larger batch, scale up to 1 gallon of milk and ¼ cup starter.

You may make yogurt from reduced-fat milk following this method, though I prefer using whole milk as I find the results far superior. (See Let's Talk About Fat, page 36.) My second choice is 2% milk.

INGREDIENTS

½ gallon or 1 gallon milk, preferably whole and organic (not ultrapasteurized)

2 tablespoons or ¼ cup plain store-bought yogurt with live, active cultures, at room temperature

STEP 1: HEAT THE MILK TO 180°F. Rub an ice cube along the entire inside of the pot or Dutch oven. (The ice helps prevent the milk from adhering to the pot, easing cleanup.) Pour in the milk. Affix the candy thermometer (if using) to the side of the pot (otherwise, test the temperatures with an instant-read thermometer) and turn the heat to medium-high. Slowly bring the milk up to 180°F, without stirring. When you reach 180°F, turn the heat way down and maintain the milk at 180°F (or a few degrees higher) for 5 full minutes. This "hold" creates naturally thicker yogurt without the need for milk powders or thickeners. Remove the pot from the heat. Use the ladle to lift off any skin that formed.

STEP 2: COOL THE MILK TO 115°F. Allow the milk to cool down to 115°F, stirring gently to release steam. To accelerate cooling, fill the sink partway with lots of ice and some cold water, then set your pot carefully in the sink. Stir occasionally and check the thermometer frequently; if the milk dips more than a few degrees below 115°F, you'll have to rewarm it.

STEP 3: INOCULATE WITH THE STARTER CULTURE. When your milk has reached 115°F, place the plain yogurt (the starter) in the medium bowl or glass measuring cup, using 2 tablespoons yogurt for ½ gallon milk or ¼ cup yogurt for a gallon of milk. Ladle in roughly 1 cup of the warm milk and whisk to combine. (This is called tempering.) Scrape the tempered yogurt back into the pot. Remove the thermometer and cover the pot.

(continued)

STEP 4: INCUBATE FOR SEVERAL HOURS, UNTIL THICK. The inoculated milk must be kept warm (ideally between 100 and 112°F) throughout incubation, though slightly cooler temperatures should work. You have several options for where to incubate:

Use your oven. Keep the oven's heat off but flip on the oven light. Place the covered pot in the oven and drape the top with a kitchen towel. (Don't let the towel touch the light.) If your climate is especially cold, wrap the pot in a thicker towel. I always stick a post-it note on my oven door so I know there's yogurt in there and don't accidentally turn the oven on. Resist the temptation to open the oven during incubation. Depending on your climate and the oven's insulation, the modest heat generated by the light is, in most cases, sufficient to incubate your yogurt in 6 to 12 hours, but it may take a bit longer. The longer you incubate the yogurt, the tarter it will be.

Find a warm spot in your home. If you've got a warm spot in the kitchen or elsewhere in your home—near (but not directly on top of) a heating vent, or by a sunny and draft-free window—you can wrap your lidded pot with a thick towel and incubate it there. Depending on the warmth of your spot and the ambient temperature of your home, your yogurt should be ready in 6 to 12 hours, but it may take a bit longer.

Use a heating pad. See page 327 for a full explanation of this method.

How do I know when my yogurt is ready? Regardless of incubation method, your yogurt is ready when it's thick and looks like yogurt. It's really that simple. It should be set and wobble only slightly when you jiggle the pot. When you slip a clean spoon into the yogurt and push some gently aside, some watery whey will fill in the wake. This is perfectly normal, as is a layer of cloudy whey that may (in some cases) float on top. Don't taste your yogurt yet. Yogurt will thicken further and, in my opinion, develop optimal flavor only after chilling.

TO FINISH (FOR ALL METHODS). Remove ¼ cup of the yogurt to use as the starter for your next batch. Refrigerate this starter, covered and dated, for up to 1 week, or freeze for up to 3 months. (Thaw in the refrigerator before using.)

If the top layer of whey bothers you, ladle it into a jar or tip it into the sink. (See page 331 for what to do with whey.)

Transfer the remaining yogurt to a large container, or ladle into quart-size glass jars with the aid of a wide-mouth funnel. *Cover and refrigerate for at least 6 hours*, or overnight, before eating or using in recipes. Most homemade yogurt will be a bit lumpy. To smooth it out, simply whisk gently before eating. Store, covered, in the refrigerator. For optimal texture and flavor, consume within 7 to 10 days.

VARIATION

You may make goat yogurt following the exact same recipe, using pasteurized goat's milk and commercial goat yogurt as your starter in the same proportions given here for cow's milk (1 tablespoon starter per quart of milk). Keep in mind that even after full fermentation, goat yogurt will never be as thick as cow's milk yogurt. It generally remains pourable, with a viscous texture and without the distinct curds you'll find in homemade cow's milk yogurt. I love using homemade goat yogurt in smoothies and in the Goat Cheese Cheesecake on page 259.

Yogurt-Making Tips

» Incubating yogurt at home in stainless steel is a good choice, since it retains heat and is nonreactive. Most "vat-set" commercial yogurt is also incubated in stainless steel.

» Yogurt is a product of anaerobic fermentation, meaning it ferments in the absence of oxygen. After making yogurt, keep it covered to preserve the longevity of its live bacterial cultures.

» Yogurt becomes more acidic and sourer over time. Your week-old homemade yogurt will be noticeably tangier than the yogurt you made fresh yesterday.

» To make Greek yogurt, see page 324.

» For Troubleshooting and Frequently Asked Questions, see page 332.

Homemade Greek (Strained) Yogurt

SUGGESTED EQUIPMENT

» A large, deep bowl

» A large mesh strainer, preferably with hooks that will rest on the bowl's lip, or a colander

» Cheesecloth, a nut milk bag (a mesh bag generally used for making almond milk; see Sources), or a few long layers of paper towels

INGREDIENTS

Cold plain (not Greek) yogurt (homemade or store-bought), as much as you'd like to strain

Straining yogurt releases its whey, leaving behind thick, creamy, Greek-style yogurt with a tangy, milky flavor. The longer the yogurt strains, the thicker and "drier" it will be, so experiment with different straining times until you achieve your favorite consistency. I like to start with a full recipe (14 cups) of Homemade Yogurt (page 320) and chill it fully. I then strain about half of it for a few hours and leave the other half as is. This means I always have both traditional and Greek yogurt on hand for eating and using in recipes.

When yogurt is strained to make Greek yogurt, much of the lactose ends up in the whey. Keep this in mind if you're lactose intolerant.

Remember, whey has many of the same properties as yogurt, so you may experiment with it in any recipe that calls for yogurt. Because it's so much thinner, though, and lacks the same viscosity, use a bit less and expect the final texture to be a bit different.

Line the strainer or colander with 2 or 3 layers of damp cheesecloth, allowing a few inches to hang over the sides. (Alternatively, use the nut milk bag or a few layers of overlapping paper towels.) Set the strainer over the bowl. Spoon in as much yogurt as you'd like to strain. Fold any overhang over the yogurt to cover (or pull the nut milk bag's drawstring tight). Refrigerate.

(continued)

Homemade Greek Yogurt (continued)

The first time you strain yogurt, I recommend checking it every few hours to gauge its consistency, stopping the straining process when you have a thickness, texture, and mouthfeel you like. This can take anywhere from 3 to 15 hours. Transfer the yogurt and whey to separate, clean lidded jars, and refrigerate (labeled with the date). Greek yogurt will remain fresh for 7 to 10 days, but it does begin to lose its optimal texture and continue to release whey over time.

Incubating Using the Heating Pad Method

A high-quality heating pad is a great incubating option, as it generates consistent, reliable warmth. Maintaining a gentle, even temperature is also what electric yogurt machines do, but a heating pad allows you to incubate in your own pot. (Many yogurt machines are made of plastic, and they cost more than a good heating pad.)

When shopping for a heating pad, read the box carefully. Look for an extra-large heating pad that does not shut off automatically, or one whose auto-shutoff mechanism can be disabled with the flip of a switch. Your pad should also have a low setting that runs at or below 110 to 112°F. (You may want to call the manufacturer to inquire before making your purchase.) I use a Sunbeam XpressHeat XL heating pad on the lowest setting (number 1), which runs at 110°F. If you already have a heating pad, try it out, doing a test run with 1 quart of milk and 1 tablespoon yogurt starter to gauge its suitability for yogurt making.

To incubate yogurt using a heating pad. After following steps 1, 2, and 3 on page 321, place your lidded pot on the heating pad and pull the pad up one side. Wrap the towel around the pot and pad. (If your pad runs a little hot, use a bit of towel as a buffer between the bottom of the pot and the pad.) Turn the pad on to its lowest setting and disable the auto shutoff (if applicable). Using this method, yogurt generally incubates in 5 to 8 hours. Over time, you'll find the sweet spot that produces a flavor you like best. (For me, 7 hours is ideal.) This method may produce more whey on top; if you like, simply tip it off into a jar (or the sink) before chilling your yogurt.

Labneh

4 cups plain whole-milk or low-fat yogurt

¾ teaspoon kosher salt

Yo!

If you're straining yogurt with any frequency, consider investing in a $10 fine-mesh nut milk bag with a drawstring. It's less messy and cumbersome than using cheesecloth. (See Sources.)

MAKES 1¾ TO 2 CUPS LABNEH

Here are two methods for turning yogurt into the thick, creamy, spreadable Mediterranean and Middle Eastern "yogurt cheese" called labneh. If you think of Greek-style yogurt as strained yogurt, think of labneh as ultrastrained yogurt. Labneh is strained either under weight (or compression) or by hanging. I provide both methods below. While labneh is traditionally strained at room temperature, I'm more comfortable straining it refrigerated.

METHOD 1. Set a colander in a large, deep bowl. Line it generously with cheesecloth (with plenty of overhang), a nut milk bag, or two large crisscrossed paper towels that cover all the holes in the colander and hang generously over the sides. Mix the yogurt with the salt and scrape it into the colander. Cover gently with the overhang (or pull the bag's drawstring closed). To compress, set a pot lid slightly smaller than the colander's diameter on top of the cloth-covered yogurt. Cast iron is ideal because it's naturally heavy, but you can use a stainless-steel lid with a few cans on top. Cover the top of this apparatus with plastic wrap.

METHOD 2. You may also create a hanging apparatus. (This is far easier with a nut milk bag than with cheesecloth and impossible with paper towels.) After filling the bag with the salted yogurt, tie the drawstring to the center of a wooden spoon's handle, so that the top of the bag is close to the handle. Balance the spoon over a deep bowl or jug. The yogurt-filled bag must hang clear of the bottom by several inches so the whey has someplace to accumulate.

(continued)

Yo!

If your labneh is lumpy, whisk in a touch of cold water to smooth it out.

FOR BOTH METHODS. Refrigerate for 36 to 48 hours, until 1¼ to 1½ cups whey have drained away and you're left with thick, spreadable yogurt cheese. When your labneh is ready, transfer it to a covered container and refrigerate until needed. Labneh will keep for 10 days to 2 weeks. For longer storage, see Labneh Spheres Preserved in Olive Oil (page 100).

On Whey

When straining yogurt, don't throw out the whey! It will stay fresh for a good 2 weeks or so in the refrigerator, and you can use it to add a boost of flavor and nutrition to a variety of dishes:

» Use it in place of traditional yogurt (not Greek) in baked goods such as breads, flatbreads, pancakes, waffles, and biscuits. (For starters, try it in the Tenderest Cardamom Pancakes on page 80.)

» Add it to smoothies, lassis, and yogurt sodas like Pomegranate Doogh (page 138).

» Use it as a poaching medium for leeks and halibut, as suggested by Chef Viet Pham, co-owner of the Utah restaurant Forage.

» Keep in mind that whey is acidic like yogurt, so you can use it in baking recipes to activate baking soda and in marinades to help tenderize meats.

Troubleshooting and Frequently Asked Questions

Q: I'm making yogurt and my milk accidentally boiled over. Do I have to throw out the batch?

A: Absolutely not. Even milk that has been brought higher than the 180°F target temperature can make wonderful yogurt. It'll be nice and thick, and your yield may be a bit less, but go ahead and cool it down and incubate it. (Clean up the stove as soon as you can.)

Q: What if I've incubated my yogurt for much longer than indicated—say, for 20 hours—and it hasn't thickened at all?

A: It's possible your starter was too old (and the bacteria were therefore no longer active), or that your milk was too hot when you inoculated it, or that the yogurt pot was too cool for proper fermentation. Don't give up! Yogurt making involves a bit of trial and error. If at first you don't succeed, work with 1 quart of milk and 1 tablespoon of yogurt starter before scaling back up.

Q: What if my yogurt is lumpy?

A: This is perfectly normal. Your yogurt's texture will continue to change in the refrigerator, so don't try to smooth out lumps until it's cold and you're ready to eat each serving. Smoothing it out is easy: Just dole out the yogurt you want to eat into a bowl, then whisk gently for 10 to 20 seconds. The lumps will vanish, turning what may initially look like cottage cheese into the smooth, creamy yogurt you crave. If your yogurt is gritty or ropy, however, that's a different story and is generally a sign that you're incubating at too high a temperature.

Q: My yogurt is too sour! What should I do?

A: Next time, incubate it for less time. Yogurt gets sourer the longer it ferments.

Q: My yogurt isn't sour enough!

A: Incubate it a little longer, until you get a flavor profile you enjoy.

Q: I love straining yogurt, but what am I supposed to do with all the whey? Throw it out?

A: There's no need to discard it. I offer suggestions for using whey on page 331. I keep my whey in a covered jar in the fridge for up to 2 weeks. By then, I've usually made more Greek yogurt and simply replace the old whey with the new.

Q: I overstrained my yogurt, and now it's too thick.

A: Whisk in a little extra whey, or use additional water or milk if using the yogurt in recipes. Or make labneh (page 329).

Q: What's the shelf life of fresh yogurt?

A: Remember, yogurt is a food traditionally prized for its long shelf life. Refrigerated, homemade yogurt should last 7 to 10 days, if not longer. Over time, it will "weep" (release more whey) and slowly lose its optimal texture. I generally eat mine within 1 week.

Q: Can yogurt spoil?

A: It's possible, yes. Environmental contaminants like yeasts and molds can occasionally grow in yogurt, producing off smells, off flavors, and visible signs of decay. If your yogurt appears, smells, or tastes spoiled, throw it away. You're likely to recognize signs of spoilage when you encounter it. Do not use spoiled yogurt to incubate a fresh batch.

(continued)

Q: Is it actually safe to incubate yogurt overnight? I would never let any other food stay out overnight in warm conditions.

A: The time indicators hold true whether you incubate your yogurt during the day or overnight. So long as you check your yogurt for doneness within the 6- to 12-hour window, it doesn't matter when you incubate it. My suggestion is to make yogurt for the first time during the day. If you like the results after a 12-hour incubation, go ahead and leave it overnight the next time you make it.

Q: A recipe calls for Greek yogurt, but I only have non-Greek at home. What should I do?

A: Strain your yogurt (see page 324) to release some whey, then proceed with the recipe.

Q: A recipe calls for traditional-style (not Greek) yogurt and I only have Greek. What should I do?

A: Whisk in a little extra whey, water, or whatever liquid is featured in your recipe to loosen.

Q: If I inoculate my milk with a starter culture that has specific bacterial strains, how can I be sure that these strains will "win" rather than some ambient "bad" bacterial strains floating around in the environment or in the milk?

A: By bringing the milk up to 180°F, you wipe out any bacteria that may be present in it, creating a new, sanitized medium in which the "good" bacteria can grow. Pankaj Uttarwar, Quality Assurance and Resource and Development Director at Straus Family Creamery, says that harmful bacteria have minimal chances to grow in a highly acidic medium like yogurt. If you're still nervous, go ahead and sanitize your utensils in the dishwasher before using them in yogurt making.

Q: *I live in an extremely cold climate and my house is drafty. Am I really going to be able to make my own yogurt?*

A: Yes! Bear in mind the number-one rule: Do what it takes to keep the yogurt pot warm. In the winter, my friend April Paffrath in Cambridge, Massachusetts, closes the doors to her kitchen and turns on both her kitchen light and oven light for several hours before incubating her yogurt. She also wraps her yogurt pot in a towel. If her yogurt works, and yogurt making works in harsh climates in places like Mongolia, you should be fine. (Using a heating pad may up your chances of success.)

Q: *What does pH in yogurt mean?*

A: pH refers to the acid content and is used as an indicator of whether fermentation is complete. When yogurt's pH drops to a target range, it becomes inhospitable to harmful (pathogenic) bacteria, making it safe to eat. The low pH also explains why yogurt is naturally tart: It's the lactic acid that makes it taste pleasantly sour. (Some brands "pull" their yogurt at a higher pH within that target; their yogurt will taste milder and sweeter. Other brands pull their yogurt at a lower pH, creating a tarter profile.)

Q: *Do I have to refrigerate my yogurt?*

A: Yes. Refrigeration improves yogurt's shelf life. If you want your yogurt to last more than a day or two and to firm up to the texture you're familiar with, store it in the refrigerator. In some parts of the world—India, for example—fresh yogurt is consumed warm and may not be refrigerated, but it's also consumed quickly, with new batches made on an almost daily basis.

Selected Bibliography

Algar, Ayla. *Classical Turkish Cooking; Traditional Turkish Food for the American Kitchen*. New York: HarperCollins, 1991.

Chandan, Ramesh C., and Arun Kilara, eds. *Manufacturing Yogurt and Fermented Milks*. 2nd ed. Chichester, UK: John Wiley & Sons, 2013.

Chernila, Alana. *The Homemade Pantry: 101 Foods You Can Stop Buying and Start Making*. New York: Clarkson Potter, 2012.

Durand, Faith. *Bakeless Sweets: Pudding, Panna Cotta, Fluff, Icebox Cake and More No-Bake Desserts*. New York: Stewart, Tabori & Chang, 2013.

Hirshberg, Meg Cadoux. *Stonyfield Farm Yogurt Cookbook*. Charlotte, VT: EatingWell Books, 1994.

Husseini, Suzanne. *Modern Flavors of Arabia: Recipes and Memories from My Middle Eastern Kitchen*. Toronto: Random House, 2012.

Katz, Sandor Ellix. *The Art of Fermentation: An In-Depth Exploration of Essential Concepts and Processes from Around the World*. White River Junction, VT: Chelsea Green Publishing, 2012.

Kiros, Tessa. *Food from Many Greek Kitchens*. Kansas City, MO: Andrews McMeel, 2011.

Krahling, Heidi Insalata. *Insalata's Mediterranean Table*. San Anselmo, CA: Laura Parker Studio, 2009.

Kremezi, Aglaia. *The Foods of the Greek Islands: Cooking and Culture at the Crossroads of the Mediterranean*. Boston: Houghton Mifflin Harcourt, 2000.

Lewin, Alex. *Real Food Fermentation: Preserving Whole Fresh Food with Live Cultures in Your Home Kitchen*. Minneapolis: Quarry Books, 2012.

Lustig, Robert H. *Fat Chance: Beating the Odds Against Sugar, Processed Food, Obesity, and Disease.* New York: Hudson Street Press, 2012.

Mendelson, Anne. *Milk*: *The Surprising Story of Milk Through the Ages.* New York: Knopf, 2008.

Pollan, Michael. *Cooked: A Natural History of Transformation.* New York: Penguin, 2013.

———. *Food Rules: An Eater's Manual.* New York: Penguin, 2009.

Salloum, Habeeb, and James Peters. *From the Lands of Figs and Olives: Over 300 Delicious and Unusual Recipes from the Middle East and North Africa.* New York: Interlink Books, 1995.

Shafia, Louisa. *The New Persian Kitchen.* Berkeley: Ten Speed Press, 2013.

Smetinoff, Olga. *The Yogurt Cookbook.* New York: Frederick Fell, Inc., 1966.

Uvezian, Sonia. *The Book of Yogurt: An International Collection of Recipes.* New York: HarperCollins, 1978.

Whyte, Karen Cross. *The Complete Yogurt Cookbook.* San Francisco: Troubador Press, 1970.

Yildiz, Fatih, ed. *Development and Manufacture of Yogurt and Other Functional Dairy Products.* Boca Raton: CRC Press, 2010.

Sources for Specialty Ingredients and Yogurt-Related Products

World Spice Merchants (Worldspice.com)
An extensive array of spices

Cultures for Health (Culturesforhealth.com)
Unusual starter cultures (for both dairy and nondairy yogurts), cotton and muslin nut milk bags for straining yogurt, and tips and information about all kinds of cultured products and processes, including yogurt

Indian Markets
chickpea flour (sometimes labeled besan or gram flour)
black mustard seeds
red chile powder

Kalustyan's (Kalustyans.com)
An extensive array of exotic spices as well as lavash, flatbreads, Medjool dates, freekeh, and preserved lemons

Middle Eastern Markets
flatbreads
labneh
lavash
Medjool dates
orange blossom water
pistachios
pomegranate molasses
preserved lemons
quince
rose petals (dried)
saffron
sumac
tahini
za'atar

Natural Foods Stores
chia seeds
chickpea flour
coconut oil
flaxseed
hemp seeds
Bulk bins also have reasonably priced nuts,
pepitas (pumpkin seeds), and dried fruits.

*Sandor Katz's website Wild
Fermentation
(Wildfermentation.com)*
An enormously rich resource for anyone
interested in the art and science of all things
fermented

Whole Foods and Trader Joe's
Lavash, flatbreads, freekeh, and dates

End Notes

1 www.foodtimeline.org/foodfaq2.html#yogurt

2 *Microbiology and Technology of Fermented Foods* by Robert W. Hutkins (p. 107) notes that "cultured dairy products have evolved on every continent" and that yogurt in particular was mentioned "in Hindu sacred texts and mythology."

3 *Development and Manufacture of Yogurt and Other Functional Dairy Products*, Fatih Yildiz, ed.

4 May 13, 2013, phone interview with Michael Neuwirth, director of public relations at Dannon.

5 "Modern Culture: Yogurt's Unstoppable Rise," by Beth Kowitt, http://features.blogs.fortune.cnn.com/2012/07/17/yogurt-united-states/

6 "Yogurt's domination goes beyond the dairy aisle." *Dairy Foods*, April 2013.

7 Yogurt and Yogurt Drinks: US: August 2013 report provided directly to me by Mintel.

8 "Just Add Sugar: How an immigrant from Turkey turned Greek yogurt into an American snack food," by Rebecca Mead, *New Yorker*, November 4, 2013

9 www.nasdaq.com/press-release/chobani-to-ring-the-nasdaq-stock-market-closing-bell-20140107-00732

10 www.forbes.com/sites/marketshare/2013/04/13/the-yogurt-wars/ and www.nytimes.com/2012/07/09/business/pepsico-with-muller-by-quaker-yogurt-aims-at-a-surging-market.html

11 foodproductdesign.com/news/2013/09/frozen-yogurt-sales-grow-74-to-486-million-in-201.aspx

12 www.huffingtonpost.com/2013/05/30/cups-froyo-hooters-of-frozen-yogurt_n_3361397.html

13 postfoods.com/our-brands/honey-bunches-of-oats/greek-honey-crunch/

14 www.yappytreatscart.com/

15 happyfamilybrands.com/product_lines/happy-yogis/

16 A study reported in the October 8, 2012, edition of the journal *Gastroenterology* found that a four-week intake of fermented milk products with probiotics "affected activity of brain regions that control

central processing of emotion and sensation." At www.gastrojournal.org/article/S0016-5085(13)00292-8/abstract

[17] Michael Pollan has written about the microbiome both in his 2013 book *Cooked: A Natural History of Transformation* (Penguin) and in an article in the May 19, 2013, *New York Times Magazine* called "Some of My Best Friends Are Germs," available at www.nytimes.com/2013/05/19/magazine/say-hello-to-the-100-trillion-bacteria-that-make-up-your-microbiome.html

[18] www.accessdata.fda.gov/scripts/cdrh/cfdocs/cfcfr/CFRSearch.cfm?fr=131.200

[19] Food Dyes: A Rainbow of Risks. Center for Science in the Public Interest, 2010. Available at cspinet.org/new/pdf/food-dyes-rainbow-of-risks.pdf

[20] Yoplait's pink lids were introduced in the late 1990s. Consumers were encouraged to collect and return lids, and in exchange, Yoplait would donate funds toward breast cancer research. The initiative came under fire at times, however, for promoting "pinkwashing." In 2009 watchdog Breast Cancer Action successfully campaigned to have Yoplait remove rBGH (recombinant Bovine Growth Hormone) from its yogurt, citing the hormone's implication in the development of certain tumors. Online here: bcaction.org/2009/02/09/breast-cancer-action-victorious-in-yoplait-"pinkwashing"-campaign

[21] "The New Yogurt Culture" by Denise Shoukas. *Specialty Food Magazine*, May/June 2013, at www.specialtyfood.com/news-trends/featured-articles/article/new-yogurt-culture/

[22] "Lactose Intolerance: Information for Healthcare Providers." National Institute of Child Health and Human Development, National Institutes of Health, online at www.nichd.nih.gov/publications/pubs/Documents/NICHD_MM_Lactose_FS_rev.pdf

[23] maplehillcreamery.com/products.html

[24] "Defusing the Health Care Time Bomb" by Robert H. Lustig in the *San Francisco Chronicle*, January 4, 2013.

[25] "The Trek to a Yogurt Less Sweet," *New York Times*, May 10, 2013, at www.nytimes.com/2013/05/11/business/dannon-cuts-sugar-carefully-in-childrens-yogurt.html

Acknowledgments

Were it not for post-its, this book would not exist. In late 2012, my wonderful agent, Jenni Ferrari-Adler of Union Literary agency, told me she had an idea for my next book. She'd written it on a post-it a few weeks prior, and every week when she turned the page on her calendar, she moved the post-it as well. She said that was how she knew the idea was worth bringing to my attention. The post-it had just two words on it: "Yogurt. Cheryl?" Deepest thanks to Jenni for tossing this idea in my direction.

Thanks, too, to Rux Martin and her stellar team at Houghton Mifflin Harcourt, including associate editor Stephanie Fletcher, who gave the manuscript such patient and careful attention and whose eye for detail lent increased clarity to my words and recipes. Learning that I would be working with Rux was like learning I'd be directed by Martin Scorsese, only better. My utmost appreciation to Ellen Silverman, whose stunning talent behind the lens imbued each photograph in this collection with such beauty. Sincere thanks to food stylist Christine Albano, prop stylist Marina Malchin, copyeditor Jessica Sherman, typist Jacinta Monniere, designer Rita Sowins, production editor Jacqueline Beach, and indexer Cathy Dorsey.

I would be nowhere without Team Yogurt, a group of dear friends and cooking enthusiasts who so generously gave their time, energy, and attention to the careful testing of this book's many recipes. To Julie Angelica, Betsy Block, Jacqui Cohen, Kate Fichter, Cynthia Graber, Lena Joseph, Elisa Koff-Ginsborg, Margie Kriebel, Beth Lee, Clare Leschin-Hoar, Michael Lesniak, Don Lesser, Liz Linehan, Kathleen Lingo, Melissa Loerch, Denise Madruga, Amee Meghani, Nancy Owens, April Paffrath, Melissa Pasanen, Kathy Pindzola, Wendy Schleicher, Elaine Schultz, Barbara Shiers, Jennifer Simons, Lola Tenorio, the late great Aleta Watson, and Dana Wootton, thank you truly.

To Stacy Dobner, Jason Goldstein, Lisa Hoffman, Melissa Shafer, and Heather Walker, thank you for going above and beyond, again and again (and again).

To Diana Pisciotta, thank you for intrepid testing and also for connecting me with Commonwealth Dairy.

To Julia Schiff, thank you for recipe testing and joyful, head-clearing meals out with the lovely Alison Brunner.

To Judy Hood, who tested more of the recipes in this book than anyone else, thank you. You deserve a cheering squad and fireworks display.

To Denise Marchessault, thanks for your warm smile, Canadian calm, and always kind words; Jill O'Connor, for your cheerful baking troubleshooting; and Tara Coles, for sharing medical and health expertise.

To Andrea Mello, thanks for lending me the metal insert to your ice cream machine so I'd have two. I'm sorry I said I'd return it in one month and kept it for two years.

To Mark Sternman, Joel Sternman, and Barbara Shiers, thanks for your proofreading skills and enduring love and support. To Clifton, Ian, and Beth Rule, thanks for being the best in-laws anywhere, always.

To Alana Chernila, in whose wonderful book *The Homemade Pantry* the "ice the pot" tip appears and who has therefore saved me (and you) from a lifetime's worth of scorched yogurt pots, thank you. Alana learned this tip from Ricki Carroll, so by the laws of the transitive property, I'd like to thank Ricki, too.

To Elaine Schultz, my close friend and neighbor with whom I walk every day, I'm so grateful for your friendship and always helpful advice.

(continued)

To Emma Christensen, Coco Morante, Sheri Codiana (who also tested recipes), Michelle Tam, and Danielle Tsi, thanks for your weekly company, good cheer, and excellent home-made snacks at our Wednesday writing salons.

To Tara Mataraza Desmond, fellow author and close confidante, thanks for your empathy, hilarity, and frequent texts.

To Amanda Niehaus, thanks for plunking academic and scientific articles into Dropbox from your perch in Australia so I could access them with a single click. To Wes Helms, thanks for sending me so much great information from Canada on yogurt-related business stats. And thanks to Viet Pham, for taking the time to talk with me about whey.

To my hosts in Greece: Aglaia Kremezi, Ela Allamani, Costas Moraitis, and Nehama Weininger, thanks for your tremendous hospitality, and thanks to my sister Julie Sternman, who accompanied me on the adventure of a lifetime.

To Helen Lentze, Pankaj Uttarwar, Albert Straus, Michael Neuwirth, and Ben Johnson, thank you for the insiders' view into the workings of your respective companies. I'm so grateful.

To Sumaya Abdurrezak, Maureen Abood, Donia Bijan, Hande Bozdogan, Ganmaa Davaasambuu, Humaira Ghilzai, Mebrat Ibrahim, Chittu Nagarajan, Nayaki Nayyar, Shefaly Ravula, Avigdor Rothem, Louisa Shafia, Svetlana Watkins, and Aisha Piracha-Zakariya, thanks for sharing your insight into how yogurt is used in your respective cultures. This book is far, far richer for your contributions.

Finally, to Colin, Andrew, and Alex: I do love yogurt, but I love you three more. You're the best probiotics anywhere, hands down.

Index

A

Abood, Maureen, 125
Abu-Rabie, Balkees, 196–97
Afghan yogurt culture and flavors,
    168–69
    beef noodle soup with yogurt (aush),
        166
Algar, Ayla, 254
Allamani, Ela, 150, 182
allspice-plum compote, 54–55
almond(s):
    artichoke soup with chives, 152–53
    cream, chicken curry with, 205–7
    lemon loaf cake, iced, 248–50
    triple, raisin stir-in, 64
    ultimate granola, 92–94
amaretti:
    lemon–poppy seed mousse with
        raspberries and, 285–86
    triple almond–raisin stir-in, 64
apple:
    grape sauce, rosy, 58–59
    green, scones with cider glaze, 90–91
    harvest waffles, 86–88
    sausage, and spinach pot pie, 214–15
apricot halves, burnt sugar, 53
artichoke-almond soup with chives,
    152–53
asparagus-pea soup, springtime, with
    crispy pancetta, 147–49
aush (Afghan beef noodle soup with
    yogurt), 166
avocado(s):
    lime crema, 212
    mini, with yogurt, salmon (or trout)
        roe, and dill, 181
    ranch dressing, 108
    tomato, and cucumber salad, 68

B

bacon:
    cauliflower soup with saffron yogurt,
        157–59
    romaine hearts with tomato,
        Gorgonzola drizzle and, 174
baked goods, 246–80
    blueberry-topped pavlovas, 275–76
    cherry galettes with yogurt-ricotta
        cream, 269–71
    green apple scones with cider glaze,
        90–91
    Parmesan and sun-dried tomato
        quick bread, 280
    raisin–poppy seed flatbreads with
        cardamom-honey butter, 277–78
    see also cakes; tarts
banana:
    cherry smoothie, 129
    deep purple smoothie, 131
Barber, David and Dan, 66
barberry gremolata, 198–201
beef:
    curry, regal creamy (shahi korma),
        222–23
    noodle soup with yogurt, Afghan
        (aush), 166
    skirt steak, dry-rubbed, with
        caramelized onion yogurt, 218–19
    -stuffed Swiss chard rolls with yogurt
        sauce, 220–21
beet raita with cumin and mustard
    seeds, 112–13
beverages, 128–38, 281
    cherry-banana smoothie, 129
    deep purple smoothie, 131
    ice-cold cocoa breeze, 133
    Mongolian, with alcohol brewed
        from yogurt, 316–17
    my green smoothie, 131

    pomegranate doogh (yogurt soda),
        138
    Turkish, 281
    see also lassis
Bice, Jennifer, 30–32
Bijan, Donia, 136–37
black bean–chorizo tacos with avocado-
    lime crema, 212
blackberry-lavender or blackberry-Pinot
    frozen yogurt, 308–9
blueberry(ies):
    deep purple smoothie, 131
    roasted, compote, 46
    -topped pavlovas, 275–76
Blue Hill Farm, 66
Bozdogan, Hande, 281
bread(s):
    Parmesan and sun-dried tomato
        quick, 280
    salad, tomato, with yogurt, Eritrean
        spicy (fata), 190–91
    see also flatbreads
breakfast, 74–97
    cardamom pancakes, tenderest, 80
    challah French toast, overnight, 89
    granola, ultimate, 92–94
    green apple scones with cider glaze,
        90–91
    harvest waffles, 86–88
    omelet, flat, with yogurt, hot sauce,
        and herbs, 75
    omelet, folded, for one with lox,
        shallot, and yogurt, 77–78
    September (sweet-and-sour
        flatbread), 95–97
    yogurt crepes with assorted fillings,
        82–83
brownie tart, labneh-dimpled, 272
brunch:
    shiitake frittata with labneh, kale,

345

and shallots, 185–87
see also breakfast
Brussels sprout leaves, glossy,
    homespun split pea soup with,
    164–65
burnt sugar–apricot halves, 53
butter:
    cardamom-honey, 277
    pecan–maple frozen yogurt, salted,
        312–13
butternut squash soup with toasted
    seeds, 160–61

C

cakes, 248–65
    almond-lemon loaf, iced, 248–50
    frosted mocha cupcakes (a small
        batch), 251–53
    goat cheese cheesecake, 259–61
    mixed fruit and yogurt sheet, for a
        crowd, 256–58
    orange phyllo, syrup-drenched,
        262–65
    walnut, with rum-soaked currants,
        254–55
caramel panna cottas, salted, 296
cardamom:
    honey butter, 277
    pancakes, tenderest, 80
carrot(s):
    cumin soup with cumin seed oil,
        154–56
    fennel, and pear slaw, 71
    roasted vegetables with spiced
        yogurt, pistachio, and lemon,
        238–39
cauliflower:
    bacon soup with saffron yogurt,
        157–59
    roasted, with tahini yogurt and
        pomegranate, 236–37
celeriac, in roasted vegetables with
    spiced yogurt, pistachio, and
    lemon, 238–39
chaas (savory lassi), 135
challah French toast, overnight, 89

chamomile-poached quince, 60–61
cheddar, chive, and cornmeal pancakes,
    little, 177
cheese, yogurt, *see* labneh
cheesecake, goat cheese, 259–61
cherry:
    banana smoothie, 129
    galettes with yogurt-ricotta cream,
        269–71
    raspberry stir-in, 50
chicken:
    cast-iron, with barberry (or
        cranberry) gremolata over freekeh,
        198–201
    coriander-lime grilled, 204
    curry with almond cream, 205–7
    twice-cooked yogurt-marinated,
        202–3
chickpea(s):
    Afghan beef noodle soup with yogurt
        (*aush*), 166
    quinoa bowl with harissa yogurt,
        194–95
chilled treats, 284–301
    candied kumquat spoon sweets, 290
    fig spoon sweets in red wine syrup,
        291–92
    lemon–poppy seed mousse with
        raspberries and amaretti, 285–86
    milk chocolate yogurt pots with
        salted peanut crush, 295
    salted caramel panna cottas, 296
    stripy fruit gelées, 289
    tiramisu, 298–99
    whipped cream, yogurt, 301
Chobani, 19
chocolate:
    frosted mocha cupcakes (a small
        batch), 251–53
    labneh-dimpled brownie tart, 272
    milk, yogurt pots with salted peanut
        crush, 295
chorizo–black bean tacos with avocado-
    lime crema, 212
cilantro shrimp with tomatillo-tomato
    salsa, 226–28

cinnamon-toast croutons, fresh oranges
    with, 63
clove-orange lassi, 137
cocoa breeze, ice-cold, 133
coconut:
    plum tart in a date-nut crust,
        267–68
    ultimate granola, 92–94
coffee:
    frosted mocha cupcakes (a small
        batch), 251–53
    tiramisu, 298–99
    yogurt, 67
Commonwealth Dairy, 22–23
compotes:
    blueberry, roasted, 46
    cranberry-pomegranate, 56
    kumquat-date, 51
    plum-allspice, 54–55
    strawberry-rhubarb, 45
coriander-lime grilled chicken, 204
cornmeal, cheddar, and chive pancakes,
    little, 177
cow's milk yogurt, 30, 32
cranberry:
    gremolata, 198–201
    pomegranate compote, 56
crepes, yogurt, with assorted fillings,
    82–83
crostini, mushroom, with yogurt,
    lemon, and thyme, 178–79
croutons, cinnamon-toast, fresh oranges
    with, 63
cucumber(s):
    cold yogurt soup with herbs, rose
        petals and, 144–46
    my green smoothie, 131
    tomato, and avocado salad, 68
    tzatziki, Stella's, 109
cumin (seeds):
    beet raita with mustard seeds and,
        112–13
    carrot soup with cumin seed oil,
        154–56
    savory lassi (*chaas*), 135

onion:
  caramelized, yogurt, 218–19
  red, blood orange, and kalamata
    dip, 106
orange(s):
  blood, kalamata, and red onion dip,
    106
  clove lassi, 137
  fresh, with cinnamon-toast croutons,
    63
  phyllo cake, syrup-drenched, 262–65
  stripy fruit gelées, 289
organic dairy, 36
origins and history of yogurt, 14–16

P
Pakistani yogurt culture and flavors,
    229
  golden curry with shrimp and peas,
    224–25
  regal creamy beef curry (*shahi korma*),
    222–23
pancakes:
  cardamom, tenderest, 80
  cheddar, chive, and cornmeal, little,
    177
panna cottas, salted caramel, 296
Parmesan:
  potato-leek tart with thyme and,
    188–89
  and sun-dried tomato quick bread,
    280
pasta marinara, creamy, 192
pavlovas, blueberry-topped, 275–76
pea(s):
  asparagus soup, springtime, with
    crispy pancetta, 147–49
  golden curry with shrimp and,
    224–25
  split, soup, homespun, with glossy
    Brussels sprout leaves, 164–65
peanut crush, salted, milk chocolate
    yogurt pots with, 295
pear:
  fennel, and carrot slaw, 71
  scones with black tea glaze, 91

peppers, labneh-stuffed, with feta and
    pistachio, 182–84
Persian yogurt culture and flavors,
    136–37
  cold yogurt soup with cucumber,
    herbs, and rose petals, 144–46
  pomegranate doogh (yogurt soda),
    138
pesto, pistachio, labneh with tomatoes,
    tapenade and, 118–20
phyllo cake, orange, syrup-drenched,
    262–65
pineapple:
  lassi, 132
  my green smoothie, 131
Pinot-blackberry frozen yogurt, 308–9
Piracha-Zakariya, Aisha, 224, 229
pistachio:
  labneh-stuffed peppers with feta and,
    182–84
  pesto, labneh with tomatoes,
    tapenade and, 118–20
  roasted vegetables with spiced
    yogurt, lemon and, 238–39
  saffron (*kulfi*) frozen yogurt, 315
pita wedges, toasted, 120
Pittas, George, 151, 216
plum:
  allspice compote, 54–55
  tart in a date-nut crust, 267–68
Polllan, Michael, 26
pomegranate:
  cranberry compote, 56
  deep purple smoothie, 131
  doogh (yogurt soda), 138
  raita, 114
  roasted cauliflower with tahini
    yogurt and, 236–37
  stripy fruit gelées, 289
poppy seed:
  lemon mousse with raspberries and
    amaretti, 285–86
  raisin flatbreads with cardamom-
    honey butter, 277–78

pork:
  chops, skillet, with quick mustard
    sauce, 213
  and veal meatballs, baked
    (*yiaourtlou*), 216–17
potato:
  leek tart with Parmesan and thyme,
    188–89
  mash, tangy, with scallions, 242
  pot pie, sausage, spinach, and apple
    pot, 214–15
  pots, milk chocolate yogurt, with salted
    peanut crush, 295
probiotics, 24–27, 121
pumpkin, in harvest waffles, 86–88

Q
quince, chamomile-poached, 60–61
quinoa-chickpea bowl with harissa
    yogurt, 194–95

R
raisin–poppy seed flatbreads with
    cardamom-honey butter, 277–78
raitas, 115
  beet, with cumin and mustard seeds,
    112–13
  pomegranate, 114
ranch dressing, avocado, 108
raspberry(ies):
  cherry stir-in, 50
  lemon–poppy seed mousse with
    amaretti and, 285–86
Ravula, Shefaly, 112, 115
red wine syrup, fig spoon sweets in,
    291–92
Redwood Hill Farm, 30
rhubarb-strawberry compote, 45
ricotta-yogurt cream, cherry galettes
    with, 269–71
romaine hearts with bacon, tomato, and
    Gorgonzola drizzle, 174
rose petals, cold yogurt soup with
    cucumber, herbs and, 144–46
Rothem, Einat and Avigdor, 233, 240